best, and the helicopter was an important safety factor other shorter circuits should have copied by now. I loved racing there, better even than Monza, but after my friend Parlotti was killed there [on the Morbidelli, in 1972] I say, enough, what is important is life itself, not just to enjoy yourself. Because we get so much pleasure from racing in the Isle of Man, it was difficult to see the dangers and respond to them. But after many years you see so many riders die in the TT and you wonder why it's necessary to race there. OK—the satisfaction is very good, the atmosphere is fantastic, but why go on racing there when each year there's another friend who leaves you forever because of that wonderful, terrible circuit—killed for what? Pleasure? OK, so we go to another circuit, and maybe we have less pleasure but we keep more friends, because it's safer. But that doesn't stop me from saying the Isle of Man is the greatest racing circuit in the world; it's just that, kilometre for kilometre, it is also the most dangerous.'

So what circuit in the modern idiom does Ago regard as his favourite? 'Well, OK, I am Italian, so I like very much Monza—but Monza *come c'era*, as it was, the good Monza—not like today which is a bit sad. I love the Monza of my youth, when I lived very close to the circuit and I have a very good souvenir of the *Autodromo*. When I hear the name "Monza", something makes my blood start to run faster; just driving slowly in a car round Lesmo or Curvone or Parabolica fills me with a special fascination, a sense of tradition mixed with deep nostalgia. If I just stand beside the track I can hear the echo of the machines we raced there nearly 20 years ago—the deep roar of my MVs, the shriek of the Hondas—it all comes back to me each time I hear the simple name "Monza".

'In my day, the atmosphere there was incredible. For the Gran Premio there were always 80–100,000 spectators, and for three days it seemed to be the centre of the world. My proudest moment in all my life was when I won my first world title at Monza in 1966. Afterwards it seemed that every single fan came to the MV truck to celebrate my title. All of Italy was with me in those days, because I am the first Italian for many years to win the blue riband of motorcycle racing, the 500 world title.'

Agostini began racing in 1961 at the age of 19 on a 175 cc Morini. His first event was the Trento–Bondone hillclimb, leading to Italian Junior titles in both circuit racing and mountain events. In 1963 he joined the works Morini team and began riding in GPs as number two to Provini, whom he supplanted for [illegible] year, winn[illegible] [illegible]50 class. Th[illegible] join the all-conque[illegible] 1965, thus beginning o[illegible] and long-lasting partnerships i[illegible] motorcycle sport. What was it like [illegible] for the mercurial Count Domenico Agusta[illegible] [illegible]il, in 1965 riding for MV Agusta was like driving for Ferrari now: when I signed the contract, my hand was shaking, it was such a great honour to me. Every Italian kid dreamt of riding for MV, and here it was coming true for me, Agostini. I could hardly believe it. But I remember before then, Count Agusta called me to see him, but I waited three, nearly four hours from five in the afternoon to almost nine at night to talk with him. When he comes out of his office, his first words to me are: "Well, what do *you* want?" I say, I am Agostini, and I want to ride for MV Agusta, but he says: "My bikes are too fast for you!" I wasn't sure how to take this, so I make a joke and say maybe I can learn to ride them. So he says: "Well, try slowly please, and be careful!", and then we all laugh. He was a very determined man, but he like to joke a lot, too. Many people find him very difficult, but never me. He demanded a lot from you, but he also knew how to give, which made it possible to forgive him almost anything. I never forgot he was the boss, that in the end he had the final decision because they were his bikes and his team, so we get on together very well.'

Did riding for Count Agusta teach Ago things about team management which were beneficial later in his motorcycle career when he became boss of his own team, Marlboro-Yamaha Team Agostini? 'I race for nearly 20 years,' says Ago, 'in bikes then cars too, and now I know most of what it is possible to know about racing from both sides. I know what the rider needs and I know too what the boss wants! That's why running a team isn't so difficult for me as it could be for someone else, plus I enjoy what I'm doing, which makes it even easier.'

Back to Monza, then. What was his favourite bike that he raced there? 'For sure, the three-cylinder MV Agusta; it was lighter and much nicer to ride than the four, which was big and heavy and much more tiring. Because the engine was wider, we had to put it higher in the chassis to give the ground clearance required, which compromised the handling: the bike like to control you instead of the other way round, which is no good—just like *una bella ragazza*, a pretty girl. You must be in charge, not her! Before 1969 when they change the rules, we have seven speeds, but afterwards we make a few little changes to the power and with only six speeds the three is still perfect. From 6000 rpm you have some power, but at 8000 it is really strong, up to a maximum of 12,000 rpm—exactly the same as our V4 Yamaha 500 today with reed valves!'

So how did Ago ride Monza with the 500 MV triple, beginning with the Curva Grande, or 'Curvone' (Big Curve), a flat-out right after the finish line which was the scene of both 1973 accidents which led to Monza's near-demise? 'Really, those accidents were the result of the pressure by the car drivers, led by Jackie Stewart, to line all the circuits they raced on with armco. But he make a mistake—armco is maybe more dangerous than what is before: look at all the car drivers like Rindt [at Monza], Cevert, Rodriguez and Siffert who are killed because of armco! If you crash at Curvone you crash at 250 km/h, very fast—but with the armco there is no room for the bike to escape. Maybe with runoff area like they have now it might not have happened, but I think sand is the best, like they have at Donington. I tested there a lot

with my cars, and maybe for the machine the sand isn't so good, but it's better for your life!'

Monza's response to high cornering speeds has been to reduce them by installing three universally unpopular chicanes at crucial points to slow competitors down. Sadly, they cannot be bypassed as the one at Woodcote on the Silverstone car circuit was when bikes were allowed to run there. Does Ago approve of Monza's 'chicanitis'? 'With all the chicanes, it's not any more the real Monza. They made a big mistake putting so many artificial corners in which are so tight. It would have been much better to spend a little more time and money to make a big, sweeping second-gear S-bend instead of a narrow chicane which makes every-body slow down too much and use bottom gear. A chicane is nothing—everybody takes it at more or

Graeme Crosby (Suzuki) leads Barry Sheene (Yamaha) up the hill into the Variante Ascari, the chicane which now replaces the old Vialone curve, in the 1981 Italian GP at Monza. Croz finished second behind winner Kenny Roberts, with Sheene third

TRACK SECRETS OF CHAMPION ROAD RACERS

TRACK SECRETS OF CHAMPION ROAD RACERS

Alan Cathcart

Published in 1987 by Osprey Publishing Limited
27A Floral Street, London WC2E 9DP
Member company of the George Philip Group

British Library Cataloguing in Publication Data

Cathcart, Alan
   Track secrets of champion road racers.
   1. Motorcycle racing
   I. Title
   796.7'5   GV1060
ISBN 0-85045-774-2

Editor Tony Thacker

Filmset by Tameside Filmsetting Limited,
Ashton-under-Lyne, Lancashire
Printed in Hong Kong

Contents

Acknowledgements

My sincere thanks go above all to the 14 great riders of yesterday and today who so kindly gave me their time in order to set down a small part of their expertise on paper. Without them, this book literally could not have been written, and I am most grateful to them, one and all, for having collaborated with me on it. I would also like to thank Paul Butler for his help in setting Kenny Roberts' thoughts on Laguna Seca down on tape, as well as Peter Hillaby, race organizer at Scarborough in addition to his duties as a leading ACU official, for his assistance in uncovering the early history of the Yorkshire circuit. Thanks are also due to Mike Nicks, former editor of *Classic Racer*, in which some of these chapters first appeared, for having given encouragement when I first proposed the idea of a series of 'track secrets' to him, and for publishing some of them.

I am also grateful for their assistance in presenting the book as you see it to the several photographers whose work, mostly of an archive nature, is used to illustrate the chapters: space precludes me from mentioning them all, but thanks to Nick Nicholls, Mick Woollett, Don Morley, Kel Edge and the late Ken Jones especially, as well as the several others who allowed me to use their photos. Thanks also to my friends Claudio Boet and Javier Herrero of *Motociclismo* in Spain for allowing me to raid their extensive and well-ordered photo files in search of material covering all the circuits in this book. I also owe a debt of thanks for their extreme patience to my two editors at Osprey, Tim Parker and his successor Tony Thacker, who between them managed to extract the manuscript from me not more than the odd year or two late! Their encouragement and understanding has been invaluable, and is much appreciated. So too was the forbearance of my 'model mum-in-law', Betty Todd, who once again allowed me to litter her home in Perth, Western Australia, with the paraphernalia of book-writing so that I was able to finally get the project under way while staying with her. Yes, I promise to get a quieter typewriter next time!

For apparent reasons, I don't think it would have been easy or even possible for someone who had not raced motorcycles himself, on however humble a basis compared to the great riders whose stories lie in these pages, to have written this book. My continued gratitude for all her support and forbearance while I rush round the circuits of the world on two wheels is, as always, due to my wife Stella, who to her great credit has never tried to persuade me to live my life in any other way. Thanks again, darling.

Alan Cathcart
Perth, Western Australia 1986

Introduction

I first had the idea for the series of magazine articles which led to this book some years ago, when I read a programme introduction by John Blanchard for a Vintage race meeting at Brands Hatch. In it, he described how he used to ride the circuit in his time as one of the famous (or notorious!) 'Brands scratchers'—one of the leading short-circuit British riders of the late 1960s.

John's article contained several little tips and pieces of advice that were as valid to me then, as a latter-day Brands racer, as they had been in his heyday. I digested the contents, thought about them a lot, and decided to put some of them into practice the next time I raced at the Kentish circuit a fortnight later. Not only did I succeed in cutting over a second from my sub-one-minute lap time as a result, but I won two races that day, one through obtaining an unusually good start as a direct result of following the Blanchard blueprint. From then on, I realized that here was one of the most interesting and exciting, as well as useful, untold stories of motorcycle sport, if only the great riders of the present as well as the past could be persuaded to impart some of their skilful knowledge about how

The author exits Daytona Speedway's Turn 4 en route to victory in the Lightweight BoTT race during Cycle Week 1984, aboard the 580 cc Ogier-Laverda

to race at a given circuit to me. Happily, I'm glad to say that none of the men I approached needed any persuading to do so, and I can only add that selecting the list of riders and circuits to be covered was in some ways the most difficult task I set myself in compiling the 14 different chapters, on a wide variety of circuits in several different countries, that comprise this book.

Inevitably, there have to be some omissions, and I'm only too well aware, for example, that there is no Irish circuit covered in the book, in spite of that country's wealth of tracks and great riders, nor is there a circuit secret told from the point of view of a sidecar driver. I can only offer my apologies, and say

that if, as I hope, this book is favourably received, I have already drawn up my 'hit list' for a follow-up volume! At the same time, I do feel that the various chapters cover a wide range of eras, countries and types of circuit, all of which make up the fabric of motorcycle racing history. As far as I know, this is the first time such a book has been attempted which covers either two- or four-wheeled sport and the tracks on which they are held; I hope that the reader, whether past or present practitioner of road racing or enthusiastic spectator alike, will find the track secrets of some of the most famous names in motorcycle history as compelling to read, as I did in writing them down.

Giacomo Agostini—Maestro of Monza

Put the three words 'Italy', 'motorcycles' and 'racing' together and you automatically think of a fourth: Monza. Though sadly today a shadow of its former self, the story of the Autodrome set in the spacious confines of the Royal Park of Monza, ten miles to the north-east of Milan, is the story of Italy's passionate love affair with motorcycle sport. In true Hollywood style it has drama, tragedy, thrills and spills, and of course villains and heroes too: who better to play the latter than the Maestro of Monza—dashing, handsome Giacomo Agostini, the Morini, MV and Yamaha star whose phenomenal success at the home of Italian motor sport is unmatched by any other rider—or driver?

Strange as it might seem at first, there was no permanent racing circuit in Italy when the announcement was made in the spring of 1922 that an autodrome would be built in the Regio Parco di Monza, previously famous only as the venue of the assassination of King Umberto I in 1900. Brooklands had been built in Britain in 1907, Indianapolis in the USA in 1909, but the only Italian competition held on two or four wheels in a country then still struggling its way into the 20th century were long-distance events on public roads, such as the gruelling Milano–Napoli marathon, or the 'Italian TT', the Circuito del Lario round the shores of Lake Como.

The construction of the Autodromo di Monza, accomplished in a remarkable 110 days from scratch with the aid of 3500 workmen, gave Italian motor sport a permanent home which it still, partially at least, occupies. Though a try-out car race was held in August 1922, the first major event was the first-ever Italian motorcycle GP, then as now dubbed the Gran Premio delle Nazione (or Grand Prix of all the Nations). On the morning of Friday 8 September 1922, a field of 23 riders, nearly all mounted on Indian or Harley-Davidson V-twins, christened the new track in the first (and last) Italian GP for 1000 cc machines. Winner of that inaugural event was Harley ace Amedeo Ruggieri, who

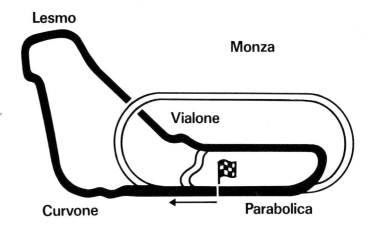

Agostini with Phil Read. 'Always he tries to stir things up against me a little . . .'

9

Start of the 1961 Italian 125 cc GP, won by no. 8, Degner's MZ. Sharing the front row with him from left to right are: Taveri, Redman and Phillis' works Honda twins, Brehme's MZ and Tanaka's Honda

averaged 62.83 mph for the 40 laps of the 10 km circuit, which combined both a road section out into the park and a speedbowl with 38-degree bankings permitting hitherto unheard-of speeds. The two sections of the circuit shared the pit straight, which was divided in half by pyramid-shaped cones. This meant that the huge crowd of spectators, many of them seated in the spacious grandstands (which unfortunately had to be rebuilt in later years after the depredations of the local rabbit colony whose burrows undermined the foundations!), saw the bikes passing by in front of them twice each lap, doubtless adding to the confusion as well as the spectacle.

The first lap record was established by the Austrian rider Winkler on a Harley at 74.53 mph, a figure easily beaten by Gillard's works sohc eight-valve Peugeot twin in winning the 1923 500 cc GP in front of 80,000 spectators, some way ahead of British expatriate Eduardo Self's Norton. The Frenchman's average speed of 74.85 mph alone beat the previous lap record comfortably, and thereafter speeds rose rapidly as Monza and the Gran Premio delle Nazione became an integral part of the European classic scene. The great Tazio Nuvolari was inevitably an early star of the Autodrome on both two and four wheels, winning the 350 cc bike GP four years in a row, twice leading home all the 500s (races were for many years run concurrently) and once doing so after having to be lifted on and off his dohc Bianchi for

the simple reason that he was wearing a body-cast after severely injuring himself in a car-testing crash shortly beforehand.

A series of fatal car accidents on the 4.5 km banked oval meant that from 1933 onwards it was no longer used for car racing, though it continued to form a part of the 10 km bike circuit until it was demolished just before the war, by which time it had also proved invaluable for high-speed testing and record breaking, just like Brooklands. Like its British counterpart, Monza was defaced by the military during the war, a final tank parade after the surrender adding insult to injury by tearing up the track surface, and in ravaged post-war Italy it was not until 1948 that work could begin on its reconstruction. But unlike in the case of Brook-lands, the Italian passion for motor sport defeated all bureaucratic objections and the Monza track reopened with a 6.3 km course effectively following the road section of the old Autodrome combined track. This was shortened to 5.75 km in 1955 by the construction of a new banked oval, which proved, however, to be too bumpy for latter-day motorcycle racing and in time for cars too.

Nevertheless, the new road course was a very fast one, with wide, sweeping bends that made it one of the quickest circuits in the GP calendar. In 1950

Above *A different view of a Monza start, as the riders
get away at the start of the 1970 500 cc Gran Premio
delle Nazione. Pasolini's Benelli (no. 2) leads
Agostini's MV three (no. 1), but not for long.
Bergamonti's MV (no. 3) finished second, while
Gallina's Paton (no. 16) and Perrone's Kawasaki (no.
12) look set on a collision course*

Right *The Monza* tifosi *have their own style of
communication*

Geoff Duke averaged more than 100 mph for the
first time to win the 500 Italian GP on his Manx
Norton, while in 1967 Agostini became the first and
only man ever to average more than 200 km/h in
winning a Monza GP, on his three-cylinder 500 MV
Agusta. In 1971 he set up the all-time lap record,
again on the MV triple, of 127.13 mph, though
team-mate Pagani won the race after Ago's bike
failed. The following year a series of chicanes were
introduced, primarily in response to the urgings of
the car world, who sadly also insisted on lining the
whole circuit with armco. This was responsible for
the most tragic two-wheeled accidents to occur at

Above *Ago on the 350 MV four: jousting with the armco*

Below *Marsovsky's Linto at home on Monza's fast straights and sweeping curves*

the Monza Autodrome, when Renzo Pasolini's Aermacchi two-stroke seized at the first corner of the 1973 350 cc GP, casting him off before bouncing back into the middle of the track off the armco, sending down the advancing pack of riders like skittles. Pasolini and reigning world champion Jarno Saarinen were killed outright, and in response to the inadequacies of the track in motorcycle terms and to the pathetically slow reaction by the circuit's safety services to the accident, a government inquiry was initiated into Monza's suitability for motorcycle racing. Hardly had this been constituted than three more riders were killed seven weeks later in an Italian national event at the same corner in a grotesque replay of the GP tragedy. Monza's fate was sealed.

Or so it was thought. Extensive alterations to the circuit, offering increased runoff and other safety improvements fuelled by the profits from the car GP which continued to take place at Monza, saw the circuit again declared adequate for motorcycle racing, even in the new, more safety-conscious era of the 1980s, and in 1981 the Autodrome again hosted the Gran Premio delle Nazione, but with new, tighter chicanes that dropped lap speeds. Though sanitized, the 'Magic Track' (as the Italians name it) still has the same unique atmosphere each time it hosts a motorcycle GP, even if this is less frequent today now that it has to share the honour with Mugello, Misano and Imola—though the introduction of a second Italian GP, under the label of the San Marino city-state, has alleviated this pressure nicely.

However, those who visited it in the old days, before the chicanes were introduced, remember Monza as an ultra-high-speed test of skill and nerve, where groups of slipstreaming riders swapped positions back and forth until the last-lap dash for the flag determined the winner—generally the one whose machine had that couple of hundred revs in hand for the final desperate burst to the line.

Born in Brescia but for most of his racing life domiciled in Bergamo, not 30 miles from the gates of Monza Park, Giacomo Agostini was—and still is—an idol to the *tifosi*, the mad-keen Italian fans whose roar of approval as his red and silver MV Agusta fire-engine burst into view down the pit straight at the end of the first lap of a GP used to send the blood curdling—especially if you were not Italian, and were secretly hoping Mike Hailwood might win on the Honda! But then the *tifosi* loved and respected Mike the Bike, too; it was just that he was neither Italian nor on an MV any more. . . .

Agostini (background) and Hailwood stop together to refuel during their classic duel in the 1967 Senior TT in the Isle of Man. 'We never see each other till the fuel stop, when we are in the pits together for a little while'

Hugh Anderson screams his 14-speed 50 cc Suzuki twin round Lesmo en route to fourth place in the 1966 Italian GP, in which Anscheidt's similar bike averaged over 95 mph to win

With 13 Italian GP victories to his credit, nine of them at Monza, as well as innumerable wins in national championship events, the Autodrome must be the favourite circuit of the only man to have ever won 15 world titles on two wheels—is it? A surprise was in store! 'Well, that depends,' says Ago thoughtfully. 'If it's just from the point of view of riding motorcycles, then my favourite circuit is the Isle of Man—it has everything. You go uphill, downhill, over bridges, under trees, through villages, round first-gear hairpins and 200 km/h corners: for me, it's the best. You must climb a high mountain, then come down to near the beach, and in between the sun might shine or the rain might fall. Nothing else in motorcycle racing can compare to this. For me, it is the purest form of racing: if a

rider is fast on the Isle of Man, he is fast everywhere. From a technical point of view, to win a TT race there must be the highest achievement of a rider's career. If you win there, you are ready to win anywhere, because it's the most demanding and most technical circuit in the world.'

This is remarkable praise, coming from the man who more than anyone else was responsible for the Continental boycott of the Island which led inevitably to the TT's loss of GP world championship status. 'OK, that's true—but I am talking only about riding, without any other considerations at all. I tried not to admit it even to myself in those days, because when you are young you don't think of danger, you just want to ride the bikes. But if you have any concern for security, any thoughts of danger, you must forget the Isle of Man, and not race there any more because there's no protection if you crash, no space for you to slide away in most corners. It's impossible to protect such a long circuit adequately, though the people there always try their

less the same speed, and a good rider can't get any advantage because there's only one way to do it. In a fast corner at a circuit like Monza, if you are good and another rider is not so good, you can take half a second from him, but in a chicane you never gain any time. It interrupts the rhythm of your riding, and I believe chicanes cause more accidents than they prevent, because so many riders must squeeze themselves into a narrow line, all in single file.

'In the old days at Monza, you see groups of riders with ten, maybe 12 machines slipstreaming each other all the way round the track. It is very exciting for the spectators, and for us too, because we know that all will be decided on the last lap. But now the chicanes break the groups up too much, and many of the races get strung out into a procession—look how exciting races were at Silverstone, where there were no chicanes and only one slightly slow corner. Chicanes encourage lazy riding, too: you see a lot of people touching and hitting each other's bikes in them, because they think it doesn't matter, whereas in a fast corner they take more care and ride properly.'

So a black mark in Ago's book for the trio of Monza chicanes now defacing the circuit— primarily, be it said, for car purposes. The first of these lies just before the Curvone (and did not stop Ronnie Peterson being killed there in his Lotus in 1978). Before it was installed, how did Ago take this demanding corner? 'On a flying lap past the tribunes I would go over the finish line in top gear, gradually cross over to the left and just snick it back one gear to fifth, still with the power hard on but just easing the throttle slightly as I laid it into the bend. On the MVs we could change the internal gearbox ratios, and so for Monza I would space the gears equally, with maybe a long second gear for the Parabolica—otherwise we only used the top four gears once the race had begun. I'd line myself up very carefully on the left for Curvone, brake just a little, then come down that one gear and stay right under the screen as I clipped the apex on the right and drifted out again. I think this is the most difficult corner at Monza, because if you ease the throttle just a little bit in the middle, for sure that's half a second gone. Curvone is the corner you can win the race on: for example, on the 350 MV, not all the time, but many times I try to take it at the maximum—flat out in top gear. On the way in I just peep over the screen for a moment, then again on the way out to check my line against the grass on the exit. It was a big test of the handling, which was mostly very good on the MVs when I rode them.

Jon Ekerold (Bimota) leads the Green Meanies of Toni Mang and Kork Ballington into Lesmo in the 1981 350 cc Italian GP. He won

'After Curvone I would get top gear again on the 500 as I drifted out to the left on the exit, staying over on that side of the road as it climbs gently round to the left on the Curva della Roggia, which is not really a corner at all, more a slightly bent straight. The next true bend is Lesmo, which in fact is not one corner but two, which we called Lesmo Uno and Lesmo Due (one and two), both right-handers with a short but definite straight in between, so that they are taken as two distinct corners. I would brake very hard and late for Lesmo Uno down the left-hand side, coming down two gears and maybe three, and using all the road going in and out. In the wet, you must be very careful at Lesmo because of damp patches under the trees on the inside, but even in the dry it can be very slippery too, because the sap drips off the trees on to the track and makes it greasy; many people think they fall off on oil there, when it's really Mother Nature they should blame!

'If I use fourth gear at Lesmo, I hold it till the middle of Lesmo Due, which is a more open corner, not so tight, though the trees prevent you seeing out of it till quite late. Then I get fifth halfway through and sixth once I'm straight and dropping down the slight dip afterwards, under the north banking of the old speed circuit. If on the other hand I used third gear for Lesmo Uno, it would be just for the first part, which would give me more control and steady the bike up. Then I'd get fourth in the middle of the short straight between the two corners, and the next two gears as before.'

As the road runs slightly downhill after Lesmo, it curves to the left, though the so-called Curva del

Serraglio is insignificant on a bike. But just ahead lies the Curva del Vialone, probably the fastest corner in GP racing until the third of the Monza chicanes, the Variante Ascari, was installed in the middle of it in 1972; the other, added later, slows traffic down just before the pair of Lesmo bends. How did Ago take this ultra-fast left-hander? 'This is an important corner, because you have the Rettilineo Centrale [the Central Straight, which bisects the old banked circuit] after, along which you must maximize your velocity. I stay right under the screen, keep the throttle hard open in top gear, and lay the bike a long way over so as to keep my speed up. You must not let the bike drift too much out in the exit, otherwise you will scrub off speed and lose many hundred revolutions which it will be impossible to regain. How fast did I take the corner? I suppose about 240–250 km/h on the 500 MV, because the slight downhill drop from Lesmo Due allows you to build up speed quite quickly, though the approach to Vialone is uphill!'

Corners of over 150 mph are a rare commodity anywhere, but after that nail-biter the riders were soon faced with an even more challenging corner, the Parabolica, often nicknamed the 'Curvetta', or Little Curve. The longest corner on the Monza circuit, it is a 180-degree bend, but not a constant-radius one. Ago: 'Parabolica is a difficult corner, because the first part is quite tight before it opens out, so you must slow down more on the way in than if it was the same angle all the way round, but not lose too much speed which will compromise your exit. This corner was another reason I preferred the MV three over the four, because since we developed the bike at Monza, which has so many right-hand corners, we put two pipes on the left and one on the right, which permitted me to lean it further over, especially at Parabolica. I suppose this is the one corner at the Autodromo that I would take in a controlled rear-wheel drift, balancing the power of the engine against the adhesion of the rear wheel, cranked over all the way, accelerating gradually harder, harder, harder as the road opens out again, while you feel all the time the rear tyre sliding and gripping under you. The spectators can't see it, but you're aware of the bike drifting about all the time. Many riders fall off at Parabolica, including my friend Mike Hailwood one time [1968] when he race the 500 Benelli four against me in the Gran Premio. By then the Benelli is very good: they do a lot of work on it at Monza and I expect I will have to fight hard to win. Sure enough, we are together at the start, but on the third lap Mike crashes at the

Parabolica, which made me very unhappy, even though next lap he waves to me to say he is OK. I was looking forward to racing with such a great man on two magnificent Italian four-cylinder bikes, but it was not to be.'

Which gear did Ago take the Parabolica in? 'Normally in second, but this corner gave me many problems with the gearchange, because I change gear with my right foot, one up for first, and so it was hard for me even to change up being cranked over so far on the bike. So for Parabolica I would have preferred a very long second gear, which would give me more control because I could take the engine to peak revs in the first part, then change up to third as the track opened out. But because I had problems to change gear, I usually selected a lower third-gear ratio, and held it all the way round the corner, changing up into top gear just before the finish line.'

Being such a high-speed blast, was slipstreaming important at Monza? 'Oh, yes, especially on the smaller bikes but on the MVs too, against the Honda and Benelli fours which were just as fast as my bikes, but maybe didn't handle so well. Particularly for the last lap it's important at Monza to take advantage of the slipstream, so if you're in a group of riders coming out of the Curvetta for the final time, you must get the power on as early as possible so as not to lose contact with the ones in front, then time your moment correctly to pull out and pass them just before the line. Too late, and you won't win; too soon, and someone will repass you, perhaps one who's been slipstreaming *you* all the time! The smartest rider will usually win in this sort of situation, someone like Taveri who can think it all out.'

Did Ago feel pressure to do well at Monza, either from the rabid *tifosi*, or the equally demanding Italian press, or the mercurial Count Agusta, or perhaps all three? 'Nobody put me under pressure as such, but I know I am Italian, I ride an MV Agusta, and this is *our* race, so we must do well. The *tifosi* were a problem, but I understand them: all season maybe they wait to see me at Monza, especially to win on the MV machines, and they are very enthusiastic for our success. But sometimes this responsibility is too heavy for me, and once I get very angry with the crowd. I am leaving Monza after the race and the people put me on their shoulders and come and pat me on the back to congratulate me. . . . They feel good, they are happy because I have won, the MV has beaten the Japanese bikes— but they don't realize I am Agostini, I am only a man,

First lap of the 1970 350 cc Italian GP at the Parabolica, and Agostini is already poised to swoop on Pasolini's Benelli four aboard the MV three. Bartusch's 300 cc MZ (no. 34) finished fourth

not made of steel. Everybody was hitting me and made me very angry; when I get home I look in the mirror and see I am, how you say—black and blue?'

Was that his worst experience at Monza? 'No, because after all, we still win! Of course, we go testing with MV many times at Monza, and I'm sure it gave us a big advantage, but also a big responsibility, just like Honda at Suzuka. I know Monza very well everywhere, and so it push you; in your heart you feel "I must do well, this is my home"—you want to win so badly, you concentrate hard like you never do before. To win any Gran Premio is important, but to win at Monza is a duty, to our public, to all of Italy, who expect it of us. So when in 1971 both my bikes break down, after I make the absolute lap record on the 500, too, it was terrible. It was very rare for the MVs to do this, but even though my team-mate Pagani won the 500 on the second bike, we were desolate. For such a thing to happen at Monza, on our home circuit just a few

kilometres from the MV workshop and my home, in front of the *tifosi*—it was a disaster. To win at Monza is the most important thing for all of us. We had very long faces that day.' Did Count Agusta fly off the handle into one of his legendary rages? 'No, it was worse. He just walked towards his car, turned round and said: "Tomorrow morning I want to see *everybody* in my office at 8.30!", then he left—and I knew everybody meant me, too. Even though I had just gained another double world championship, I didn't sleep very well that night!'

What was the best moment at Monza, though? 'In 1966, when I won my first world title: for me, it's the most important. All my life, I wait for this moment, I dream of being the champion, and it is at Monza that it comes true. The day after I am at home and I think about it and say to myself, it's impossible, I am world champion—can this be true? I don't believe it—but it *is* true! I am the champion many times after that, but never am I so happy as for that first title.' Was that day Ago's most satisfying in his long racing career, spanning so many world titles as both rider and team manager? 'Yes, but there were two races that gave me particular pleasure to win. One was my first-ever GP victory on the 350 MV at the Nürburgring in 1965, in my first season with Agusta. In those days I don't know Jim Redman or Luigi Taveri or Hugh Anderson—even Mike I don't know very well, though he is always fantastic to me when we start to race together that year for MV. It's the first time I meet all these big champions, because riding for Morini we race with just a small van and a tent and stay in *pensione*.

'So when I arrive to the hotel in Adenau in the evening, it is full of Honda staff and Honda riders, all sitting at a big table for dinner at the centre of the racing world. I sit down alone at the table for one, eating by myself because my mechanics are still at the circuit. I hear the Honda people talking about me, but I don't understand English so good yet, so I think they are talking bad about me, which makes me angry. I think to myself, OK, I show you tomorrow—and I win the race in front of Honda, in front of Redman, on the Nürburgring as well, only the second time I ever race there. Afterwards when I go back to the hotel, everybody is looking at me with another face. I am very happy because I win my first GP, but also because I show Honda that I am Agostini, I am Italian and we too know how to win races!'

What was the other race? 'The Daytona 200 in 1974—my first race ever on a two-stroke, first time on a Yamaha after leaving MV, and the first time on a banked circuit—but still I beat Kenny Roberts and Gene Romero and Gary Nixon and all the American champions. After when I win, Kenny is not so happy: General Motors give me a new car, and they say, Agostini is winner of Daytona and 13-times world champion. I think Kenny is a little jealous and he says: "Agostini is not world champion, I am, because the world is America and I am the American champion!" He says it for a joke, but I know he is not so happy! Afterwards, we become very good friends, and we both enjoy very much that we race together when he rides for my team on Yamahas, because he is very professional and very fast. But now we are rivals again, as team managers, but still friends!'

Was it difficult swapping the four-stroke MV for the two-stroke Yamaha, a move which stunned the racing world at the end of the 1973 season? 'The riding is not difficult, only the decision is a big problem, because I don't want to hurt the MV team;

they are my family, that I grew up with in racing and have many happy years with. But I think about my future, and I realize that the two-stroke is lighter, easier and has more power, while the four-stroke is already at its maximum, so I decide to change. Also I am not so happy with Phil Read being in the MV team. He tries always to stir things up against me a little, even though I have my bikes and mechanics and he has his. I don't feel any more I am number one—so I go to Yamaha and soon I know I am right, because even Honda could not make the four-stroke any longer competitive.'

Was Kenny Roberts Ago's most respected rival over the years? 'Kenny is a friend now, and a great rider, but even he cannot compare with Mike Hailwood, who was a friend even when I raced against him. Mike was a real gentleman; he was very fast, but he respected other riders—he didn't try to win by putting out the other riders from his way, like some others do. He was very honest, but very fast—the best I ever raced against.

'I shall never forget my fiercest race with Mike—yet we hardly saw each other for more than two hours, while we were locked in such a bitter duel. It was the 1967 Senior TT: he was on the 500 Honda four, I on the MV three. I am leading sometimes on the Mountain by ten seconds, but by five only at Ballaugh Bridge, then he is in front again, then me. But we never see each other till the fuel stop, when we are in the pits together for a little while before we resume our lonely paths, still—how you say?—neck and neck? On the fifth lap we are still together on the clock and I think, OK, I win now—but then I stop on the Mountain with a broken chain. I cry all night, I am so disappointed because to me the Isle of Man is the most important race for a rider to win, and to beat Mike Hailwood is not easy. This is why I think the Isle of Man is so fantastic: you race against your rival whom you may never even see, but also against yourself, the time and the Lady of Luck. This is the purest form of racing, but always so hard. I remember when I finish in the TT, my shoulder is sore and bruised, because I touch the wall with it sometimes. And also Mike: I watch him and he does the same—we finish with chalk on our elbows, our shoulders, even the knees. I think we both give 100 per cent: compared to the Isle of Man, Monza is an *autostrada*!'

Hugh Anderson and Assen:
good boy made local

Madijk
Ossebroeken
De Vennep
Stekkenwal
Stroomdrift
De Strubben
De Bult
Mandeveen
Duikersloot
Bedeldijk
Assen
Ramshoek
Meeuwenmeer

Though the Belgian and Italian classics narrowly beat it for the honour of the oldest Continental Grand Prix, the Dutch TT is generally considered to be the most prestigious road race in the international motorcycle calendar and, after its counterpart on the Isle of Man, the most historic. There are several reasons, not least the huge crowd of around 160,000 people which regularly braves the temperamental Dutch midsummer weather to watch a full programme of racing which has traditionally embraced every single GP solo class, as well as, since 1955, sidecars and latterly the World TT Formula 1 championship as well.

However, the Dutch TT's importance lies mainly in its traditions. Like the Isle of Man Tourist Trophy, from which it takes its name, it has been run on the same course, or parts thereof, since its very inception, but in contrast to the Isle of Man has successfully adapted its public roads heritage to meet the demands of present-day safety and other considerations. In spite of the construction of the rival Zandvoort permanent circuit in the 1950s, GP motorcycle racing in Holland enjoys the same historic home now that it has always done: Assen.

Situated on the flat North Holland landscape not far from the German border, Assen is the capital of the Drenthe region, an area of narrow tree-lined brick roads and peaceful meadows which is one of the oldest parts of Holland. Back in the mid-1920s, many of these country roads were still dirt tracks, a fact which did not deter the good burghers of Assen

Anderson weighs up carburation and gearing decisions on the Suzuki: 'I used to go into a trance for almost an hour or more before a race'

Start of the 1971 350 cc Dutch TT. Agostini's MV won, as usual

from organizing the first-ever motorcycle road race to be held in Holland, on 14 May 1925, over a 28.4 km circuit between the villages of Rolde, Borger and Schoonloo. A mixed-class event attracting 35 starters saw Piet van Wijngaarden from Rotterdam take overall honours on his 500 Norton, a feat he repeated the following year over a shortened version of the track, roughly triangular in shape and measuring 16.5 km, between the hamlets of De Haar, Hooghalen and Laaghalerveen.

This remained in use until 1954, in which year Geoff Duke set the all-time record for the old, longer and faster circuit, which apart from gradual improvements in the road surface was essentially unchanged since the mid-1920s, by lapping at 105.47 mph on his 500 Gilera four. Construction of a new main road, as well as safety considerations, resulted in the use of a new circuit using part of the western half of the old one, but mainly comprising a completely different series of country roads running through a wooded area to the south of Assen.

The new circuit measured 7.675 km and was much twistier and more 'technical' than the old course it replaced, as evidenced by Duke's opening 500 cc lap record in 1955, again on the Gilera, of 81.42 mph (shared with team-mate Reg Armstrong). Much wider than the old circuit, the new one was able to host a sidecar Dutch TT for the first time, won by Faust/Remmert on their BMW, though Cyril Smith/Stan Dibben set up the new lap record on their Norton-Watsonian at 74.33 mph. Giacomo Agostini on the works YZR500 Yamaha was the first to break the three-minute barrier for the revised Circuit van Drenthe, as the track is correctly known, in 1974, and in spite of the introduction of a well-designed chicane in 1976 to slow down riders just before the pits, Freddie Spencer broke the 'ton' barrier in 1982 with a lap of 100.81 mph on his NS500 Honda triple. By 1984, when the track adopted its present format, the sidecar lap record was up to 94.10 mph, courtesy of Biland/Waltisperg and their LCR-Yamaha. In that year, construction of a new motorway bisecting the circuit forced it to be reduced in length to 6.134 km, with the construction of a new, but still demanding, link road from just after the pits to Madijk. However, like the Spa–Francorchamps circuit, the modernization of Assen has not destroyed its unique and demanding character, and thanks in no small part to the efficient organization led by 'Mr TT' Jaap Timmer, the Dutch TT is one of the most popular races in the GP calendar for both competitors and spectators alike.

Spaniard Angel Nieto is the undisputed 'Ace of Assen', with no less than 15 Dutch TT victories to his credit. However, one star of the Continental

Cavalry charge at the start of the 500 cc race in 1971, as the leaders thunder through the fast right/left flick after the pits. Pagani's Linto (no. 16) retired, but Simmonds' Kawasaki (no. 2) finished third behind Agostini, whose helmet can just be seen behind Pagani's head

Circus for whom Assen was more than just another stop on the racing trail, though he has just a single win in the Dutch classic to his name in the 1963 125 cc GP, is Kiwi Hugh Anderson, works Suzuki rider and four-times world champion in the 50/125 cc 'tiddler' classes in 1963, 1964 and 1965. Not only did he meet and marry his wife Janni there, but thereafter Anderson was based in Assen throughout his time with Suzuki, as well as for a couple more years after he retired from road racing, when he campaigned Husqvarna, CZ and the first factory-supplied Suzuki motocrossers in the gruelling European and GP off-road world. Though the family would return to New Zealand for the European winters, Assen was their home during the racing season—not so much a case of a local boy made good, as a good boy made local!

'After we were married and settled down in Assen, I was really touched how quickly I was accepted as a local, especially after I learnt to speak Dutch,' says Hugh. 'I'd wake up on the morning of the race each year and find a crowd of people outside the house waving New Zealand flags and cheering me on. It was quite a thrill especially to win

Kenny Roberts and Barry Sheene chase Takazumi Katayama after the pits at Assen during their 1977 race duel

a GP there in 1963 for that reason, even if I did have rather too many beers that night to celebrate it!'

Does that mean Assen was his favourite circuit during the time he raced in Europe and the GPs? 'Nearly, but not quite; my favourites were the Sachsenring or Solitude, fast tracks where you could use the Suzuki's speed but which weren't flat-out blinds like Spa or Monza—they bored me, and I was never really all that keen on fast corners anyway. But the two German tracks had a whole series of fast, swooping curves that it was just possible to take flat out—but only if you knew what you were doing. Rhythm was all-important, and that's what appealed to me. If Assen had been a bit faster, or alternatively if I'd been riding a Honda all

those years, then it definitely would have been the tops as far as I'm concerned, because it has to be one of the most challenging circuits in the world, second only to the Isle of Man or Ulster in terms of the technical skill required. I preferred circuits with a series of S-bends where one corner led into another, which doesn't happen at Assen, where instead you mostly have a series of major corners, each of which has to be taken individually. This makes it much more of a four-stroke circuit, where the fact that you have to be on and off the throttle so much really told against the two-strokes, especially in the 1960s when powerbands were so narrow and the bikes seized so easily. The Hondas had a definite advantage there with their much wider rev bands, and of course the engine braking too. But the reason I liked Assen so much, apart from living there, was that though the Suzukis were tricky to get the best out of at it, it's a real rider's circuit, very technical and requiring great precision because it's so narrow and there's basically only one very tight racing line all the way round. You had to be inch-perfect everywhere, which suited my very controlled style of riding. I never thought of myself as more than a good rider, not the best like Mike—but I also believe success in racing demands 20 per cent ability and 80 per cent effort and concentration: I gave it that.'

Hugh Anderson began riding bikes back on the family farm in New Zealand's North Island when he was very young. From an early age he dreamed of racing in Europe, brought up as he was on a steady diet of British bike magazines. 'The Dutch TT was one of the events I always hoped to ride in, along with the Island and Ulster,' he recalls. 'I used to read Fergus Anderson's columns about the Continental Circus avidly, and Assen was always one of the meetings that seemed to have most charisma.' His racing career began at the age of 15 on the grass tracks of his native country, but by the time Hugh was 24 he had made enough of a name for himself Down Under to come to Europe with a brace of Manx Nortons, achieving almost immediate success as one of the band of hard-riding colonials

who dominated the privateer ranks in those days. In due course, this led to help from the AMC factory where he worked during the off-season, then to a works ride with Suzuki from the 1962 Isle of Man TT onwards. Yet at the same time as he was racing the fast but fragile two-strokes from Japan, Hugh initially also rode for Tom Arter on the semi-works AJS and Matchless machines; it is hard to imagine a greater contrast, even if the performance of the 125 Suzuki and the 500 Matchless G50 single were almost identical!

Riding those early Japanese two-strokes must have been quite a challenge, especially at a demanding technical circuit like Assen? 'That's a fact. People who race two-strokes today have absolutely no idea how fortunate they are. If you guess wrong on jetting, for instance, it'll probably still run unless you're way off, but it just won't go as fast as it could. In our day, getting the carburation right was absolutely crucial, because if you got it

Jacques Cornu displays balletic technique after gunning the throttle of his 350 Yamaha too hard exiting Bedeldijk in 1982

wrong you could well end up hurting yourself. I used to go into a trance almost for an hour or more before a race, reliving the best two or three laps of practice in my mind, remembering what the weather had been like, how high the ambient temperature had been on a given lap, looking at the notes to see how the bike had been set up—all to decide whether to maybe drop the float level $\frac{1}{32}$ in. or not.

'I was always specially hot on carburation, even in my early days in New Zealand; I'd play around for hours on end, getting it right to the last degree. There were three main jet sizes you could use on the Suzukis, once you'd narrowed it down in practice, each of which also required a different grade of

Hugh Anderson leads Phil Read on Suzuki and Yamaha 125 twins respectively in the 1965 Dutch TT. Anderson finished third, in a race won by Read's team-mate, Canadian Mike Duff

plug—one wouldn't work without the other. With one jet installed, you'd oil a plug, with another you'd seize, and the third would get you to the finish. The engines were so temperamental that it took someone who could almost feel what the engine was about to do to get them home, let alone win races on them. For example, in 1963–64 many Suzuki riders broke down on the fifth or sixth lap of a circuit like Assen because, as I think I was the only one to discover, the bikes would gradually lean out—I never found out why. So I used to choke my bike for the next four or five laps, and by then it would have richened up again. I'd finish the race and often win it, because in general the bikes were so fast—but oh, so fickle as well.'

Presumably it was vital to get the gearing right, as well? 'Yes, it was almost as vital as carburation, though it wouldn't kill you if you got it wrong. I'd be up at six on the morning of a race to check the wind direction, and I'd walk the circuit, even a long one

Giacomo Agostini (MV three) leads Mike Hailwood (Honda four) during their epic battle in the 1967 500 cc Dutch TT. Mike won

like Assen, to see how it would affect me at each corner, so I could decide on the gearing. The Japanese would give you a graph showing the powerband and peak revs for each engine, but I found that if you took it to the limit they said you could, it'd always do the big-ends. If you came back just 100 revs it'd be OK, and the reason was that on the test-bed they could hold the engine at constant revs, but on the track you might be skipping about, especially on such a light bike as the 50, which by 1965 weighed only 128 lb; the 125 wasn't a lot more (170 lb), yet it had a top speed of over 135 mph. Getting the back wheel off the ground for a fraction of a second at the wrong moment would be enough to over-rev them. It was also very easy when changing up to slightly over-rev the bike by being a bit too clumsy with the clutch, and that again would do a big-end.

'Tighter, twistier circuits like Assen were a real challenge on the Suzukis, not because of the handling which was pretty good after 1963, but because of the engine characteristics. People today have no idea how narrow those early two-strokes' powerbands were: 800 rpm was a luxury, 500 rpm the average. You couldn't drive off in bottom gear like on a modern stroker just by revving it to 5000 rpm and slipping the clutch. You couldn't even open it flat. You had to hold it at two-thirds throttle, then gradually feed in the clutch. I used the clutch constantly in a race, not only out of corners but slipping it as I changed up through the gears like an automatic drive. Because of the narrow powerband, you'd be changing gear all the time to

keep it on the boil, and it was important to count to keep track of where you were in the gearbox, because there were so many gears—ten on the 125 and 14 on the 50! I always changed up without shutting off, not only to avoid losing revs but because also if you did, it would seize. Later on we had a cut-out button to help us, but before then I used to snick the clutch just a fraction to get the next gear home and keep it in the power. Then you'd wait for the 400 revs you'd just lost to build up, and do it all over again.'

Presumably coming down through the box was just as much of a problem—especially at a circuit like Assen where there were two bottom-gear corners after fast straights on the classic 7.675 km circuit on which Hugh raced? 'Definitely. The fastest part was the straight past the pits, especially since in my day there wasn't the chicane before the start line that there is now. On a flying lap you'd take the right/left kink just past the pits with a little farm on the right [actually the hamlet of De Haar] flat out in top on all bikes, after which the road curves slightly till there's a straight run down to the right-hand hairpin at the end, called Bedeldijk. Coming down from such high speed, this called for considerable judgement, but I was always a very hard braker—I think I was the only one to get the front wheel of the 50 cc Suzuki locked up and jumping in the air under braking! I always used braking markers wherever I rode, for that reason, and particularly so at Assen where there are so many corners where it's important to get your braking just right—fortunately on a road circuit there's never any shortage of suitable points: a tree here, a gate there, and so on.

'Changing down through the box at the end of the straight on the Suzukis would be very difficult

New Zealander Kim Newcombe lays his flat-four 500 König into Stekkenwal on his way to second place in the 1973 Dutch TT, a position which put him in second place in the world championship. Tragically, he was killed later that year at Silverstone

especially, simply because there were so many gears and you had to go all the way down to bottom so quickly and without losing track of where you were. Also, it was difficult to get the throttle synchronized to each change. Other riders used to blip the throttle between changes, even on two-strokes, but I was one of the first to go straight down through the box like riders do today on them. This saved a lot of time, meant I could brake later, but made counting the gears even more important! In the end, I found it beneficial to half lock the back wheel with the rear brake, which took a bit of strain off the transmission and engine—with so many gears squeezed into a small space, they were very narrow and you didn't like to abuse them if you could help it. So I tried to be very methodical about changing down, but one big problem with having so many gears and needing to change so quickly

was that the muscle in your leg at the base of the shin started to seize up because you were doing it so fast!'

Was Bedeldijk a conventional corner from the point of view of line? 'Yes, but it was also a favourite place for passing up the inside under braking, and Luigi [Taveri] especially was good at using the four-stroke engine braking of the Hondas to best advantage here, so you had to keep your eyes open to stop people creeping up the inside. Assen was always very grippy, even in the wet, so you could brake hard and crank it well over, even on a bottom-gear corner on the skinny tyres we ran on, and get the power on early. I'd go down the left-hand side of the road, looking out of the corner of my eye for anyone coming up the inside, aim to get down to bottom gear by the time I finished my braking just as I was about to peel off, then into the corner and start slipping the clutch for the drive out almost at once.'

On such small-capacity bikes, was it still important not to get too much power on too soon, for fear the back wheel might step out? 'Certainly, though being a good deal bigger and stronger than the average tiddler rider I was one of the few people again who could save the 50 or 125 cc Suzukis once they started sliding—in fact, I twice collapsed a rear wheel on the 50 while wrestling it back into line after the back end stepped out. On the 50 especially, the skinny little Dunlop triangulars would be pumped up to 37–38 psi to stop them rolling on the rims, which was far too hard and meant, of course, that you couldn't drift the bikes at all. Dunlops insisted on blowing them up this hard, but what I used to do after they'd done so was to go round the back of the tent and let them down to a point about 30 psi or so, where they just started to roll on the rims but wouldn't come off. Then you could use this as an early-warning device which you ignored at your peril!'

At 5 ft 9 in. and 11 stone, Hugh Anderson was considerably bigger all round than his rivals on the small-capacity bikes—yet from contemporary photos he appears to have tucked himself away just as well as one of the star midgets he raced against. Was his stature a problem? 'Not till each of the riders was weighed at the 1965 Japanese GP after the new FIM regulations came into force,' smiles Hugh. 'Suzuki never bothered to weigh or measure me before then, and I managed to keep it from ever being a point of discussion, but at Suzuka they were absolutely staggered to find out my weight. People like Jim Redman, who weighed the same or even less than me, were thought to be too big for 50 cc racing, yet because I've always been slight of build and supple in the joints, I managed to tuck myself away on the bikes as well as any of the others. But by then weight had begun to be a factor in racing, which is the reason Suzuki were so concerned about mine that they immediately started talking to Anscheidt about the following season.'

After Bedeldijk, the twisty part of the circuit starts, lined by trees and skirted by deep ditches: did this aspect concern Hugh from a safety standpoint? 'No, that sort of thing never bothered me and it still doesn't; so long as the corners are properly protected with bales or sandbags, I can't see the difference between a row of armco, like most modern circuits are lined with, or a row of trees, except one's a bit more scenic than the other. Having said that, I was never aware of my surroundings while I was racing, nor of the crowd, even at a meeting like Assen where there are so many spectators. I'd be riding in a vacuum: concentration was the key to success as far as I was concerned, and all that mattered was that ribbon of tarmac and the people I shared it with.

'I'd get over the right-hand side of the road after Bedeldijk, changing up through the gears and accelerating round the gentle left curve leading to Stroomdrift, another sharp right. It's impossible to say what gear I'd take any particular corner in on the Suzukis—so much depended on the wind, the atmosphere and thus the gearing and jetting—but on the four-speed AMC singles I'd take the left in third, then come back one gear as I came down the left side of the road, braking for Stroomdrift. As I accelerated out of there, I'd get over to the right again for the fast left-hander at De Vennep, which is the start of the fast section that follows and is crucial to a good lap time. I'd take it in third on the 7R, but try not to let it run too far out to the right on the exit, otherwise it would spoil the line for the fast right kink after that, where I'd just get top.

'After that there's a short straight to the most difficult corner on this section, a right-hander called Madijk. I'm not likely to forget this one, since it's thanks to it that I met my wife, Janni! The first time I rode at Assen was in 1961, my second year in Europe, and the race after I'd had my first ride on a Suzuki, in the 250 Isle of Man TT. The Japanese weren't going to Assen, but I was making enough of an impression that AMC loaned me a works engine for the 7R. What with one thing and

Phil Read at speed behind the Assen pits on the 500 MV four—an ideal bike for the twisty Dutch circuit

another, I didn't arrive at Assen till 5 am on the second morning of practice, still needing to install the new engine in my bike before I could get out there. When I did so, I found the works motor was a good bit quicker than my own one, and I was able to keep up with the faster privateers even though it was my first time there, which enabled me to pick up the lines from them. Unfortunately, I ended up doing a bit of socializing the night before the race, which was the sort of thing you took for granted in those carefree days—though with characters around like Paddy Driver, Peter Pawson, John Hempleman, Ralph Rensen and the like, you had little choice! Anyway, I ended up starting the 350 race having had no sleep for three nights, and found myself in a typical privateers' dice for fourth place behind Hocking on the MV, McIntyre's Bianchi and the Jawa twin of Stastny. There were eight or nine of us at first, but after a few laps it was down to just myself, Phil Read on the Manx Norton he'd just

won the Junior TT on, and Brambilla on the second Bianchi twin who was all over the shop in the corners but would come tearing past us in a straight line.

'Phil and I were evenly matched, but after he'd put me on the grass for the second time I realized he was doing it deliberately, so I sent him up the slip road at Stekkenwal, which left just me and Brambilla. The Bianchi was faster than the Ajay single, but then his brakes must have started fading and he went up the slip road at Bedeldijk on his own, which left me in fourth place and first single, which would have been a great finish for my first ride at Assen. Unfortunately, I got carried away trying to make sure Brambilla didn't catch me up, and tried to take Madijk hard against the stop in third, and failed. I grounded the megaphone, which sent me off on to the grass on the outside where I had no choice but to lay it down at high speed, just because I'd lost concentration, probably being so tired. I must have stuck my foot out as I did so, because when I woke up in Assen hospital I had a dislocated and cracked hip, a fractured skull and a broken collarbone. I could see five of everything for a long time and ended up staying in hospital for a month, during which I got friendly with Janni, who

Ernst Degner (no. 1) and Hugh Anderson (no. 2) dominating the 1963 50 cc Dutch TT on their works Suzukis. They finished the race in that order, but Hugh won the world championship. Here they play to the gallery at De Strubben

was a nurse on my ward. We started writing to each other after that, and I used to visit Assen whenever I could, which wasn't often enough for her—I got the sack a couple of times before I saw sense and we got married the following year!'

So Madijk was quite an important corner in the Anderson book: how would he take it with a full night's sleep behind him? 'You had to be careful of the dip in the road on the way in, which is probably what sent me on to the grass that time. But it was vital to get through it as fast as you could, because you could practically straight-line the next series of fast S-bends in top, just clipping the apexes from one side to another. On the 7R I'd just roll the throttle slightly in third, dab the brakes and then accelerate hard through once I'd passed the dip. After that you had to be careful on the last left kink so as not to drift too far over to the right, which would put you wrong for the next tight right, Ossebroeken.

'This was a long right-hander that was slightly banked, so I'd go into it a bit faster than I might otherwise, down the left-hand side of the road, braking hard but scrubbing off the last few mph against the positive camber of the corner. That way I'd be achieving my exit speed early on in the corner, keeping the momentum up to get a nice early drive out of the turn, maybe in second gear if I was going well on the 350, but certainly bottom on a four-speed 500. The next bit was very important: you could pretty much straight-line it under the bridge, up to a sharp right-hander taken in second gear after briefly getting third, which you'd go into braking hard—I'd certainly expect to be drifting the bike here. But you couldn't run too far out on the exit, because then you had to heave it back to the right for the long, banked horseshoe turn called De Strubben, which is a long, long left, very tight, taken in bottom gear in front of a packed amphitheatre of spectators—it was where you might go to watch other classes race or practise if you had time yourself.'

De Strubben is a favourite place for the photographers, not least for the generally harmless spills that often occur here when a rider opens the throttle too soon and too hard on the exit. 'That's right,' says Hugh, 'you have to avoid letting the back end get too light on the way out, in which case it'll step out when you switch the power on. I'd keep to the inside all the way round, then gradually open the throttle as I could see the exit appearing—quite a tricky corner. After that you run behind the pits, accelerating hard all the way up into top gear, but

perhaps easing it a touch on the 500 single through the fast right/left flick a third of the way along—the line is very narrow here, and it's one of the places Phil put me on the grass in that 350 race. Mind you, even that was nothing to the time my own team-mate, Katayama, came under me at the next corner, the fast left-hander called Veenslang leading down to the bottom-gear hairpin at Stekkenwal.

'This was in 1965, when I came off in practice on the 50 after a pilot jet came unscrewed and stuck in the rotary valve. I grazed myself up a bit, so they gave me an anti-tetanus injection which I turned out to be violently allergic to. I was delirious most of that night (apparently I whistled myself to sleep!), then went out to the circuit for race day and promptly fell asleep again. They woke me up for the 50 cc race, which I came second in, then I came back and dropped off for another snooze almost at once, with the 125 race still to come. Again they woke me up for it, but this time I wasn't really on the ball, and I had a bad start when the thing flooded. Read would have won on the Yamaha but he packed up, so Mike Duff got it because he started so much better than me. But I set a new lap record working my way up to second, in spite of the fact I was still half-asleep—shows how well you can ride when you're completely relaxed. There was no way I was going to catch Mike, so I eased up near the end, only to have Katayama on another Suzuki come right under me on the fast left, partly on the grass, partly on the track and in a hell of a state. We never had any team orders at Suzuki—it was every man for himself, which saved a lot of the problems Yamaha ran into later on with Read and Ivy, so I reckoned if he wanted second place that bad he'd better have it. But though I only ever won one Dutch TT, I set up lap records in both 50 and 125 classes, and if it hadn't been for various things like machine problems and so on, I'd certainly have won more often there. But that's racing.'

That fast left is a real tester at the best of times: would Hugh hope to take it hard on in top gear? 'Yes, but it took some working up to each year as the bikes gradually got faster, but then you had to get hard on the brakes while crossing over to the left-hand side of the road and coming down the gears to bottom for the right-hand hairpin at Stekkenwal. This was another favourite outbraking point, though not too many people ever sat it out successfully there with me—it was one of my best corners. But then the most technical part of the circuit follows, which I never really started to get right till one day I saw an aerial photo of Assen

The all-action style of Ralph Bryans on the 250 Honda six at Assen in 1967. He finished third

and realized that a couple of the corners were much longer in reality than they appeared from a map or on the track. I immediately noticed the basic errors I'd been committing, and the next time I went out I took two whole seconds off my lap time, with the same gearing—they were that important.'

Such as? 'Well, for example, as you accelerate away from the hairpin there's a little wiggle which you can straight-line before De Bult, which is a long left—but I didn't realize how long till I saw that photo. I was peeling off too early, whereas the ideal is to hold yourself on the right till the last moment, coming down to second from third on the 7R, then really lay it over and hug the apex till you can see the road opening up again. Then there's a short squirt down to Mandeveen, which is the same thing, only a right-hander. The next corner, Duikersloot, is also a right and very close but not so near that you can make a single apex out of the two, though it does open out a good deal on the exit so you could really crack through it hard on in second, ready to face what I thought was one of the most testing corners in European GP racing, Meeuwenmeer, followed soon after by another strong contender, Ramshoek.

'The problem with Meeuwenmeer is that it's perfectly flat, the road is quite narrow, and you can't see the grass verges easily on either side at all, yet it's a very fast right-hander that you must take accelerating hard on in top gear on the 7R, maybe back one or two on the Suzukis and in third on a 500. Because it's so flat, you can't pick up the line, yet you must be inch-perfect to get the fastest exit which is vital to your lap time, yet not back off in the middle of the corner for fear you might drift out on to the grass. Assen's been pretty safe over the years, but sadly this is the corner that Peter Ferbrache was killed at, so it's not one to be treated lightly.'

Ramshoek, the left-hander after this, is almost equally tricky, especially now that there's a chicane soon after which Hugh did not have to contend with in his day. Many good riders have bitten the dust, or to be more accurate the grass, here, since this part of the circuit is open, though the presence of several drainage dikes, such as the one Neil Webster's sidecar ended up in while in the lead of the 1985 GP, is a bit of a damper—literally! 'I almost got there ahead of him,' recalls Hugh. 'Bill Ivy passed me here on the V4 Yamaha 125 in 1966 by using the grass on the inside to come underneath me, then running wide on to it again coming out. He almost took me with him—to this day I don't know how he got away with it, and didn't even put a foot down either. I was so impressed with this I let him go, but afterwards he had the nerve to complain I'd carved *him* up—I could tell then that with him and Phil in the same team there were going to be fireworks before very long, and I was right!'

Was Ramshoek a third-gear corner on the British singles? 'Yes, on both 350 and 500, though it took some nerve doing it on the big bike because the spectator banking was built out a fair bit and you couldn't see all the way round the corner—it was a bit blind. After that you'd get top again quite soon, and would hold it on the stop all the way through the right sweeper leading on to the main straight, with the finish line just after it. It was important to do this right, since it determined how quickly you'd reach peak revs down the straight.'

Who were the riders Hugh Anderson most respected amongst his many rivals in those heydays of 50 and 125 cc racing? 'No doubt about it—Luigi was fantastic, though if everything wasn't going 100 per cent he'd turn into a percentage rider and

aim for a good finish: nothing wrong with that, though, especially if you're chasing a championship. You just mustn't let it become a state of mind. Phil Read was too big for 125s, plus he wasn't really sufficiently committed to mastering the intricacies of the smaller bikes, especially the importance of being in the right gear at the right time and the critical aspects of carburation. Jim Redman could do all that, but in spite of being a bit smaller than me he was generally thought to be too big for 125s and impossible for a 50; I tried very hard not to be seen standing up next to him, and I certainly never raised the subject in conversation, even as a joke! It was difficult enough winning races and titles in those days without having to contend with the likes of him on a 50 as well as a 125.'

John Surtees and team-mate Gary Hocking take time out alongside the 500 MV during the 1960 Dutch TT

John Cooper and Mallory Park

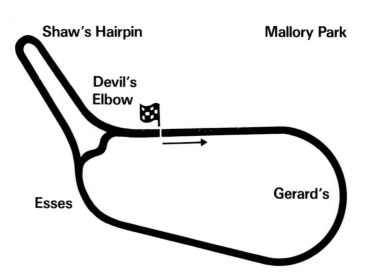

Shaw's Hairpin　　　　**Mallory Park**

Devil's Elbow

Esses

Gerard's

'Moon-eyes'—Coop to his friends

If Derek Minter was the King of Brands, tall, bespectacled John Cooper was most certainly the Master of Mallory. In a competition career spanning 20 years, old 'Moon-eyes' became a firm favourite of the avid crowd that peopled the 1.35-mile Leicestershire track throughout its heyday in the 1960s and early 1970s. As a home-town rider from nearby Derby, Cooper's string of Mallory victories made him a local hero, even though it was matched by equal success on other tracks throughout Britain. Yet somehow Coop became identified inexorably with Mallory in the mind of the racegoing public, an idea fuelled by his trio of victories in the circuit's most prestigious event, the annual Race of the Year in September, which he won in 1965 and again in 1970 and 1971; the last two wins helped secure him the coveted title of MCN Man of the Year two years on the trot.

Like its Kentish companion in the MCD stable for 25 years, Mallory began life as a grass-track venue situated just outside the little hamlet named Kirkby Mallory (near Hinckley) from which it took its original name. Landowner Clive Wormleighton had the one-mile grass oval paved in 1955–56, with a 0.35-mile extension up to the edge of the stable block which lay at the head of the driveway leading up from the village; ever since the circuit's inception, it has been an idiosyncratic if frustrating fact of Mallory life that the only way into or out of the paddock is along the racetrack itself, making the 'Mallory queue' an inevitable feature of competing there.

The inaugural Kirkby Mallory road-race meeting was held on 13 May 1956, in front of a packed crowd of 20,000 people. Organized by the Leicester Query club, it featured no less than 248 riders competing in 29 races which took $7\frac{1}{2}$ hours to run

off, thus setting the henceforth traditional Mallory pace of several short, sharp races run in quick-fire succession. Winner of the first (200 cc) race was Fron Purslow on his Tiger Cub, but while he did not take part in that inaugural meeting, the winner of the same class a week later at the nearby Osmaston Manor circuit was one John Cooper on a 197 cc Francis-Barnett. The twain would shortly meet.

Coop had started competing in trials and scrambles at the age of 16 in 1954 on a 197 James, graduating to racing on the same bike at Osmaston by the simple expedient of making his own air scoop for the front brake and fitting some second-hand racing tyres he had scrounged from someone. Much to his surprise he won his first race on the bike; hooked, he came back for more. 'To be honest, I found road racing much easier than off-road riding,' he admits, 'so I got deeper into it and ended up riding for the Lomas family on their specials. Then I went into the army for two years' National Service.'

As an officers' mess cook Cooper had to work weekends, so did not resume racing until after his demob in 1958. After a spell with a Tiger Cub engine slotted into his James Captain's frame, he moved upwards and onwards via a 350 Goldie special with a Manx chassis to a brace of Manx Nortons supplied by local sponsor Don Warren. In 1961 he broke into the big-time by winning the 350 final at the Scarborough international, and there-after became rapidly accepted as one of the cream of British short-circuit stars, becoming British 350 champion in 1964 and double 350/500 title-holder in 1966. Even so, it was termed a giant-killing act when he scored his first major win at Mallory in the

A star-studded field gets away at the start of the 1958 Race of the Year at Mallory. From right to left, the front row comprises Surtees' MV, then the Manx Nortons of McIntyre, Hailwood, Bob Anderson, Minter and King. Towards the back is no. 32, the Matchless G50 prototype of John Holder, still racing today in historic events almost three decades later

1965 Race of the Year, defeating a star-studded field on a pouring track which included Mike Hailwood on the 500 MV and Phil Read on the works Yamaha. Plain-spoken, forthright and un-complicated, Cooper seemed for some time to be on the edge of a works ride with one of the Japanese teams, but nothing transpired and after Minter's retirement he became the unchallenged prince of the privateers. The distinctive red helmet with the twin moon-eyes ('I used to have a Jiminy Cricket, but it didn't show up very well when I painted the helmet red, so I cut the eyes out of fablon one day and they just caught on') was invariably found at the head of the pack, matched to the upright, knees-out, leaning-off modern riding style commonly adopted today but which Cooper, together with Anderson and Smart, undoubtedly pioneered—as he did the wearing of coloured leathers. 'I don't know why I started riding sitting off the bike,' he admits. 'I just thought to myself one day that I'd try it that way and it seemed to work; I felt more comfortable and started lapping quicker, so I stuck to it.

'The leathers were something else, though. I had a chum called Nigel Boocock who rode speedway for Coventry—they called him 'Boy Blue' because he wore blue leathers, and he was always egging me on to get something similar. "Go on, Coop," he'd say, "drag yourself into the 20th century!" So I got a yellow pair, and suddenly there was everyone looking at me saying to themselves: "Who's this odd bloke, then?"—but it got me noticed and talked about, and that was the name of the game, especially in 1967. I always tried to make a conscious effort to turn myself and the bikes out smartly, unlike some of the others—I never much cared for the black leathers and grease-type image of motorcycling.'

A bad fall at Cadwell in 1969 threatened to end John's career, but at the age of 32 he bounced back to success with the famous self-built Yamsel, a 350 air-cooled TR2 Yamaha engine in the ex-works Seeley 7R frame. On it he won a string of races in 1970 and beat the world's best to win the Race of the Year again that year at Mallory. Yet 1971 was even better, with 15 major wins and several lap records all over the country on the Yamsel, as well as an unprecedented string of success in the space

Kork Ballington's Kawasaki and Keith Huewen's Suzuki dispute the entrance to Gerard's in a 1981 500 cc race, with the Mallory lake in the background

of four weeks that autumn aboard the booming works BSA triple. Yet he nearly never got to ride the bike.

'I remember in 1970 watching the BSA/Triumph triples at the meetings I was racing at and thinking what lovely bikes they were. Trouble was, the riders seemed to be always either blowing them up or falling off. Then BSA asked me to ride in the inaugural Transatlantic series in 1971; because it was a one-off and everyone was mounted on triples I was sort of left to get on with it, but I thought the bike was terrific—bags of torque, easy to ride: I loved it. So I asked Doug Hele if there was any chance of another ride on it, but he said no, they were full up. Well, I was determined to pursue it, especially since after the first round at Brands when I was getting used to the bike I didn't finish out of the first three in the Transatlantic. So I went to see Peter Deverall, who was the Marketing Director at BSAs, and told him if he would see I was given a bike for the Race of the Year, I'd guarantee to win it for them! Bloody cheek, really, but it worked, though Doug Hele was most unimpressed. They built a bike up for me out of spares—it was a racing engine but it didn't have any of the trick stuff like a

squish head or suchlike that the others had. Anyway, I went to Mallory to try it and after four laps I was breaking the lap record every lap in spite of being miles undergeared—I was getting top before the start line. Doug couldn't understand it, because it was the same gearing that the others used but they were all screaming the engine, instead of using all that lovely torque it had.'

As history now records, Cooper won the 1971 Race of the Year after a titanic scrap with Agostini's MV Agusta that is still talked about today, then went on to beat the Italian ace even more convincingly at Brands two weeks later. Later in October he was sent off to California for his first race in America in the Ontario 200, now a fully-fledged member of the BSA works team in what was to prove their last official appearance. After a nail-biting finish to the second leg, when the BSA pit lost count of the number of laps run, Cooper started the last lap 200 yards behind Carruthers' Yamaha, screaming the engine to over 10,000 rpm on the banking to win by less than the diameter of his worn-out front tyre. Coop thus won the richest road race ever run at that time and became the first non-American to win a US national road race, pocketing the then colossal sum of $15,500 into the bargain.

Winner of the Man of the Year for the second time in a row after his 1971 feats, Cooper campaigned the same BSA but as a privateer in 1972, with almost equal success in the UK. However, even he could not match the flying Jarno Saarinen in the Race of the Year at Mallory, though he admits he

Above *Cal Rayborn on a Harley-Davidson and Ray Pickrell on a Triumph three at the entry to Gerard's in one of the 1971 Transatlantic Match Races*

Below *Phil Read heading for a slight case of concussion on the exit from Gerard's in 1959*

should have beaten Paul Smart's ill-handling Kawasaki for the runner-up slot; instead, he was third. An ill-advised but lucrative move to the works John Player Norton team for the 1973 season

*First lap of the 1973 Race of the Year, and Percy Tait
leads the pack through the Esses on his Triumph
three, with Peter Williams' John Player Norton and
Phil Read's MV Agusta close behind. Croxford opts
for the outside line as usual!*

found him plodding along the Daytona banking in
March flat out at 132 mph on his particular
slowcoach vertical twin, while DuHamel's Kawasaki was timed at 185 mph. 'We had a big barney
when I got back,' says John, 'and Croxford ended
up riding the bike from then on, so I wheeled out the
good old BSA again. Unfortunately, I was trying so
hard to beat Dave at the King of Brands meeting I
fell off going down to Bottom Bend and hit one of
the new armco barriers they'd put up for car racing: I
smashed my leg up quite badly, and decided then
and there to call it a day. I haven't raced a
motorcycle since 28 May 1973.'

In spite of his 6 ft stature and chunky build,
Cooper was equally at home on the 250/350
Japanese two-strokes as on the bigger singles and
triples; he was one of the first privateers to achieve
sustained success on the Yamahas in Britain.
John's views on why he did so are illuminating:

'Other people had constant trouble with their
strokers, but I never had much machine trouble
throughout my career because I used to gear all my
bikes high to use the bottom part of the powerband
and avoid over-revving the engines. Lower the rpm
and use the engine's torque, and you get fantastic
reliability. I used to gear two teeth higher on the
BSA than Smart or Pickrell or Tait and still be
quicker than them, because I wasn't screaming the
engine to 8500 rpm in every gear and along the
straights. I used to change up early as a matter of
course, and so long as I kept in the powerband I'd
be saving wear and tear on the engine as well as
going quicker, because I was taking advantage of
the torque curve rather than the power curve. The
only time I ever deliberately over-revved a bike was
at Ontario that last lap to catch Kel. When I beat Ago
at Mallory I was using 500 rpm less than the BSA's
top whack.'

On to the scene of that famous victory now,
which by the time John Cooper first rode there in
1959 had been acquired by MCD and changed its
name to Mallory Park. 'I remember Mike Hailwood
had his Mondial there in the 250 race, and I had my
Tiger Cub-engined James: no contest! The circuit's
hardly changed much since then, apart from getting

bumpier and nastier, although actually I think there's a lot to be said for bumpy circuits, because you can't go so fast round the corners, so it becomes safer.'

How did John ride the tricky 1.35-mile track (there was also a one-mile 'Indy' circuit cutting out the loop to the hairpin, but this was rarely used for motorcycle racing)? 'On a flying lap on a bike like the 500 Manx or Seeley G50 I'd come down one gear on a five-speed box for Gerard's [named after Bob Gerard, a Leicester garage owner who raced in the car GPs as a privateer for many years in a Cooper-Bristol] and brake very hard—on the BSA I'd be doing around 130 mph on the straight, and around 122–125 mph on the 500 singles.' That straight past the pits is called the Kirkby Straight,

after the village; was it any faster than the other 'back' straight on the other side of the two lakes which form the Mallory infield and which is known as the Stebbe Straight? 'No, they were both almost the same for top speed, though a lot depended on how well you came out of Gerard's. Fourth gear was just right for me because of the way I liked to use the bike's torque, whereas third which a lot of people used was too low: you'd be coming out of the bend with the engine screaming and then you'd hit the bumps on the way out and—bang, the back

Cooper winning the 1965 Race of the Year on his Manx Norton, defeating Hailwood's works MV. 'I used to pray for rain, because then it equalled things up'

wheel would step out. Keeping it in a higher gear made everything more controllable, as well as being easier on the engine.'

Gerard's is one of the great corners in British short-circuit racing, as well as probably the longest; surely line is all-important here to keep up maximum speed through the bend? 'True,' replies John, 'but only to give yourself as much room as possible. I used to go in really wide to begin with, peeling off very late and cutting in close to the grass on the apex: you'd be cranked over for what seemed like an age before straightening up. There was a strip of tarmac in the middle of the corner you had to get inside of, and on the way out there were ripples and another patch that was a bit bumpy. I used to stay inside this bit too, but if you had to pass someone on the outside it was OK, if a bit choppy. You'd know you were on song if you just clipped the grass on the left coming out, before straightening up for the back straight!'

Down to the Esses, scene of the famous Cooper slide in the 1971 Race of the Year immortalized on film. Was this where the Mallory expert made up time? 'Yes, I suppose it was,' says John, 'if only because a lot of people tried to straighten the corners out, whereas the right thing to do is almost to accentuate the curves so you end up correctly placed for the exit. It was important not to waste time on the back straight, so you'd stay right over to the left coming out of Gerard's unless you had to pass someone. If I went into Gerard's at around 4500 rpm in fourth on a G50 with peak revs of, say, 7000, I'd reckon to just snick it into top nicely at around 6800 as I was about to put it upright, then flat on the tank down the straight before sitting up for the Esses, braking hard and coming down two gears. I'd peel off really late, which was the secret to a nice corner, clip the grass on the way in then crank hard over to the left so I effectively ended up running round the kerb on the way out. If you peeled off too soon for the first part you'd be in an offside position for the second half, because you'd be drifting a bit close to the tree on the right of the exit and might even have to shut off slightly: that would ruin your drive up the hill to the hairpin. So I'd stay over to the left as much as possible, but get the power on nice and early to keep my momentum going up the hill—I'd get fourth just as I started climbing it, while still cranked hard over to the left. I'd drift out about three-quarters of the way across the road to the right, which would set me up nicely to straight-line the approach to Shaw's Corner, which most people like me just call the hairpin.'

There are two distinct schools of thought about the best way to take Mallory's infamous hairpin, with its total lack of runoff, slightly banked surface and superb viewing for spectators: high, wide and handsome, or cut and thrust up the inside. 'Nonsense!' says Coop emphatically. 'Nowadays they all come up the inside on the wrong side of the road, brake almost to a standstill, make a sharp right turn, then wheelie out, and it's *miles* an hour slower! When Mike Hailwood came back in 1978 on the Ducati I watched him going round the hairpin, and he was the only bloke to do it properly. If you go up the inside you'll find yourself boxed in and into a situation you can't get out of—it's an offside trap. I used to ride right up the left going into Shaw's, brake hard in a straight line, coming down from fourth to bottom gear, then just as I peeled off get the clutch out again and try to drive it round on the pilot jet. If you drifted right out to the left and used all the road on the way out you could sometimes get away without slipping the clutch at all, but even so I'd only have to use it momentarily, unlike the blokes who came charging up the inside, braked almost to a dead halt, then had to clutch it like mad to get going again.

'I remember once I took Nigel Boocock with me to Mallory, and I said to him: "Go and watch at the hairpin, Booey, and you'll see Dave Croxford bite the dust!" Well, off he went and sure enough there was Dave and me leading the 500 race together: I'd pass him down the straight or round Gerard's, and he'd come charging up the inside at Shaw's and outbrake me—or so he thought, because in fact I was shutting off early. On the last lap I went right up the wrong side of the road, slammed the brakes on at the last moment—and when I turned round to look behind me on the way out, there was Dave sitting on his backside in the road! Booey couldn't believe it—but I knew Dave always used to time his braking by other riders and that was fatal. I always used different marks—a straw bale here, a tree there, and it was the only way.'

So the important thing at the hairpin was to keep your rolling speed up? John nods: 'Absolutely. Even if someone did manage to draw level with you by cutting inside, you could outaccelerate them on the way out because you'd kept your speed up. And anyway you'd have the inside line for Devil's Elbow, and if you used all the road there, there was no way anyone could pass you. I'd change up fairly quickly through the gears coming out, then get hard over to the right, peeling off just as I came level with the Devil's Elbow board. I'd get fourth just there, then crank hard over to the left just clipping the grass before drifting over to the right as I came down the hill to the start line, just missing the armco barrier by the pits. Being downhill it meant that the revs picked up quite quickly, so I'd usually get top by the start line, but always changing up early, remember.'

Devil's Elbow has the reputation of being one of the most dangerous corners on a British circuit: how did Cooper feel about it? 'I never really thought of anywhere at Mallory being particularly dangerous, but then you don't while you're racing, do you? Nowadays I can see that there's no runoff at the hairpin, or at the Elbow, and there probably should be. Fritz Scheidegger got killed at Shaw's when the brakes failed on his BMW outfit and John Robinson was badly hurt, and Paul Smart and Tony Jefferies were both badly injured there, though Tony was run over by someone, which wasn't really the circuit's fault. I've fallen off at every corner at Mallory and never got badly hurt, so I suppose I was lucky.

'Mind you, I thought my number was up once, the first time I rode Ray Petty's "back-to-front" Norton. I had a broken collarbone, and the bike kicked back on me at the start so I was last away—

probably couldn't shove hard enough. Anyway, by the time I got to Devil's Elbow on the first lap Bill Ivy had fallen off and there were bikes everywhere. I hit Bill's machine and flew right over the top of the bars: I only just missed the steel barrier, and needless to say landed squarely on my injured shoulder which promptly broke the collarbone again! But I did realize afterwards I was lucky to get away with that one—still didn't stop me riding just as hard at the next meeting, though.'

Presumably the 1971 Race of the Year was John's finest hour at the Leicestershire circuit? 'Well, everyone remembers that race with Ago, but in a way I was just as satisfied the first time I beat the MV fair and square, which was in the 1965 Race of the Year. It had been raining, and though Mike led at the start he found the 500 MV four a bit of a handful in the wet. Later on, a dry line developed, but by the time he and Read on the works Yamaha

Ron Haslam leads the pack out of the Hairpin on his 1128 cc Honda in the Superbike race at the Race of the Year meeting in 1981. Keith Huewen's Suzuki paws the air in pursuit, with Sheene's Yamaha close behind

Ago lays the MV into Devil's Elbow in his thrilling 1971 battle with Cooper in the 1971 Race of the Year. 'Come on, Coop, you can do it!'

could start using the power of their bikes I had too big a lead on the old Norton for them to catch me. I used to pray for rain, because then it equalled things up, and it certainly did that day.

'But yes, the dice with Ago is something I'll never forget, either. I was sure before the race I could do it, but I knew it was going to be very difficult. So did Ago, because he objected when they tried to change the start to a clutch one from the push-start in the regs. So I had to push-start the Beeza, and if I hadn't been a fairly big bloke and the bike a bit detuned, I don't really think I could have done it. I just pushed for miles then jumped right up in the air and almost broke the seat when I landed on it, but it fired. I was so surprised, I thought to myself: "God, it went!" I could hardly believe it when I found myself tucked in behind Ago going down the back straight the first lap, because I'd been resigned to having to work my way up through the field. Barry Sheene was trying to keep up with us on his 500 Suzuki, but then he fell off at Gerard's and it was just Ago and me; I saw Barry afterwards and he said the footrest grounded, but as I said to him: "They do when you fall off, kiddo, they do!" He just overcooked it trying to keep up with us.

'On the tenth lap Ago shut off early for the Esses and I outbraked him to take the lead. It was fantastic—I could actually hear the crowd shout above the roar of the engines. It was like a football match, with all the programmes waving and people jumping up and down and cheering. I wasn't usually aware of the crowd during a race, but this time I was and they gave me a great boost. I thought: "Come on, Coop, you can do it!" Then he passed me back, and I suppose everyone thought he was just biding his time, especially when I almost fell off coming out of the Esses one lap: I got really crossed up—it was completely sideways, but fortunately I was in a high gear having just changed up early as usual, and I managed to control it. If I'd been in a lower gear and revving, I'd have been spat off for sure.

'Anyway, I soon caught him up again and then got in front near the end. It was obviously going to be a last-lap nail-biter, because there was never more than 20 yards in it throughout the whole race. There was an oil patch at the hairpin, and I was doing my usual wall-of-death act round the outside, while Ago was going up the inside. On the last lap I was really nervous: I was in front, but my knees were trembling, and I could hear his engine wailing all the time, just behind. I thought: "What shall I do? I know, I'll start off up the left as usual, then cut over sooner while I'm still braking, because that's where he'll want to go." Sure enough, Ago tried everything on earth to outbrake me up the inside that last time at the hairpin, but I just hung on and beat him over the line by a length.

'Though I probably got more ultimate satisfaction out of winning Ontario, I can't deny that Race of the Year win brought me a tremendous feeling of justification: I'd said I could win the race if BSAs gave me a bike, and I had. But there was more to it than that. I'd been kept out of the GP works teams in the 1960s by all the yes-men who were hired instead of the likes of Degens and me—people who had minds of their own and weren't afraid to say their piece. Each team had one strong rider who didn't want too much competition from within the team, and was influential enough with the team manager to have a say in the selection of any new riders; with Suzuki it was Hugh Anderson, Yamaha had Phil Read of course, though he made a bit of a boob letting in Bill Ivy, and Honda had Redman. I actually got as far as being given a bike by Honda GB which Jim then took off to Silverstone for a test session and promptly blew up, so I never got my ride. Beating Ago on the 500 MV when they were both at the height of their success was proof I shouldn't have been passed over, as far as I was concerned—I know I had a 750 and his was only a 500, but the MV had a better power-to-weight ratio

and was a purpose-built cammy GP bike, whereas the BSA was basically a souped-up road engine, so they cancelled each other out round Mallory. I think both bikes were a bit difficult to steer at the maximum, and we were both on the limit the whole race: he had a bad slide at Gerard's one lap to match mine at the Esses—there just wasn't a cameraman there to record it, that's all!'

Was Mallory John's favourite circuit after all? 'I suppose so, but in the end I wound up liking them all. My old mechanic used to say to me: "If you're going to do any good at motorbike racing, you've not got to dislike anywhere"—and it's true. That's why I think I ended up having the success I did for so long: I just loved racing motorcycles, and though I certainly got taken advantage of by promoters who cottoned on to that and paid me less start money than the rest because they knew I'd come anyway, I don't care. I had a grand time in the sport, didn't get hurt badly, had a lot of good wins and got set up nicely in business by that win at Ontario. I did all right—and now I can still go to all the big meetings as a spectator and enjoy myself.'

The leaders cross the line in the 1974 Race of the Year: Agostini, Read, Sheene and Roberts—four of the greatest riders in the history of road racing

Dave Degens at Montjuich Park

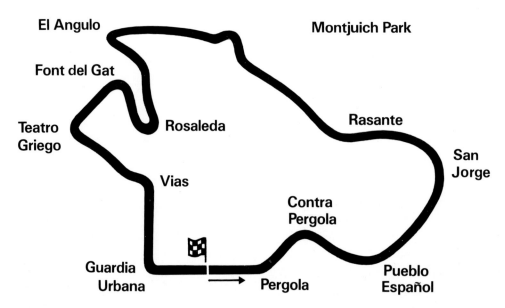

El Angulo · Montjuich Park · Font del Gat · Teatro Griego · Rosaleda · Rasante · San Jorge · Vias · Contra Pergola · Guardia Urbana · Pergola · Pueblo Español

Of all the world's great road-racing circuits, Montjuich Park is unique. Located in the very heart of the Catalan capital of Barcelona, the Spanish track is the latter-day motorcycle equivalent of the Monaco car circuit, a hilly, demanding course between buildings, kerbs, shrubbery and lamp-standards, run on streets in everyday use as a vital part of the road system of one of Europe's most important cities. True, it does not have Monaco's harbour, or the run along the Mediterranean Sea, but instead there are the famous Montjuich fountains, which play uninterruptedly throughout even the most hard-fought long-distance race, and provide an impromptu swimming pool for overheated riders and mechanics at a moment's notice.

However, unlike Monaco, Montjuich has played host down the years to both car and bike Grands Prix, as well as to what all but the French would claim to be the most arduous and demanding long-distance motorcycle race in the world: the 24 Horas. First run in 1955, the event has been held annually ever since then, usually on the first weekend in July when the Spanish summer is at its height. As a test

of the endurance of men and machine it has little equal, and the very nature of the tight and winding circuit means that a combination of qualities, rather than sheer speed, is required to win. As evidence of this is the number of times the little Spanish Bultaco and Montesa two-strokes have humbled machines of four times their engine size, or the incredible total of 12 victories registered to date by Ducati twins and singles, latterly against the might of the Japanese multis.

The 3.79 km track is laid out in the grounds of the Parque de Montjuic (note the Catalan spelling: the 'h' is only added in Spanish), which occupies the slopes of one of Barcelona's many hills, with a sheer bluff on the other side overlooking the dockyards and sea. The Park was the venue of the 1929 World's Fair, and many of the exhibition's buildings have been retained, to provide a historic and colourful setting for the circuit as it slaloms between them; many of the corners are named after these edifices. The idea of holding motor sport events on the exhibition's access roads was first mooted in 1932, and the inaugural Gran Premio de Barcelona was held the following year on exactly the same

circuit that is in use today, apart from a couple of chicanes which were added in 1982. No road widening, runoff areas, catch fences or smoothing out of corners—the Montjuich track is that rare thing: a circuit that is identical now in almost every way to the first time it was used 50 years ago.

That first meeting attracted a good entry from all over Europe, including one Fergus Anderson with a brace of Excelsiors and a 500 Imperia. 'Fair-goose' was out of luck that year, but the massive crowd of 50,000 lining the pavements around the circuit left no doubt as to its popularity. Barcelona, traditionally the most motorcycle-minded city in Spain (and post-war the home of Montesa, Ossa, Bultaco and Derbi) would henceforth not be without a racetrack of its own. Three more Barcelona GPs were held before the outbreak of the Spanish Civil War in 1936 tore the country apart and put an end

Left *Dave Degens—rider turned constructor*

Below *Degens utilizing all his skills to stay aboard an early Triton special at a soaking Crystal Palace in 1966*

to any form of motorcycle sport for many years. Honours were divided between the Anglo-Portuguese rider Alejandro Black, who with Rudge and Norton machinery was arguably Iberia's finest racer of the vintage era, and the great Stanley Woods, who scored a 250/500 double on works Guzzis in 1934, had to give best to Black the following year, but returned to win the 500 race on a Velocette in 1936 as the country hovered on the brink of war. Some idea of the track's excellent condition, as well as of Stanley's amazing abilities, can be gauged by the record lap of 2 min 11 sec (104.170 km/h) he set up that day, which remained unbeaten well into the 1950s.

After the trauma of the Civil War, racing eventually began again in Spain, with Montjuich one of the key tracks in the *Carreras de Otoño*, an autumn series of street races held in several Spanish cities which, like the Spring Italian Adriatic series which they complemented, were contested by many of the leading GP riders. The first Spanish GP world championship event was held at Montjuich in 1951, with Tommy Wood one of the winners on his 250 Guzzi, and though the races were suspended for a time between 1955 and 1961, they began again and became an integral round of the world championship. Sadly, though, Montjuich no longer plays host to the Spanish GP thanks to the dislike of the majority of today's GP riders for tracks lined with walls and kerbs and other unyielding objects; after alternating for a time with the purpose-built Jarama track on a dusty plain just north of Madrid, Montjuich held its last GP in 1976, when Kork Ballington broke the 130 km/h race-record barrier there for the first and only time on his TZ350 Yamaha. Though still continuing to host Spanish national events, Montjuich's key race now became the 24 Horas, but sadly this too lost its world endurance championship status in the 1980s. Like the Isle of Man TT, though, the Barcelona 24 Horas

Charge! Start of the 1978 Barcelona 24 Horas, with Christian Leon's works Honda RCB already in the lead

Benjamin Grau, seven-times winner of the 24 Horas, sweeps through Contra Pergola on the 860 Ducati prototype which took him to victory in 1973, paired with Salvador Canellas

is greater than the world championships and continues in its own right as an event, attracting big grids of 50-odd bikes and up to 80,000 spectators.

British riders were for many years the backbone of the 24 Horas, and none more so than Peter Darvill, who won it twice on a BMW in 1959 and 1961, as well as finishing in the top ten on several other occasions, and short-circuit star Dave Degens. Degens rode in the race five times between 1964 and 1970, finishing on the leaderboard every time (though he was controversially disqualified from sixth place on a semi-works BMW in 1964), and won the race twice on Dresda machines of his own construction in 1965 and 1970. Such a consistent and successful record speaks for itself, but at the time it sat ill at ease with many enthusiasts' perception of him as a Brands Hatch scratcher who either fell off or won. How did he ever get involved in endurance racing in the first place?

'I started racing in 1959 after being wound up to do it by the blokes I used to ride with at the local café,' recalls Dave. 'I fell off in my first race challenging for the lead, but I won the next one at Thruxton, and after that I started racing pro-fessionally all over Britain, riding for some of the great-name sponsors like Geoff Monty, Syd Lawton, Steve Lancefield and Paul Dunstall. I even managed to keep racing during my two years'

National Service—I was one of the last lot to get clobbered—so by the time 1964 came around I was well established as one of the leading British riders on short circuits.

'I didn't even know endurance racing existed, and I'd certainly never heard of the Montjuich 24 Hours, but at the same time BMW had been doing really well in such events and entered a couple of bikes for all the races through their British concessionaires at the time, MLG. I got a phone call from them the week before the Barcelona race in 1964 asking if I'd like to ride in it with Ginger Payne—apparently someone else had dropped out, and I'd given him such a hard time at Brands the week before he reckoned I'd be a good bloke to ride with! So I said sure, why not—you really got paid something then for a ride like that, so I flew out to Barcelona not quite sure what to expect, and teamed up with Ginger.

'Having been dropped in at the deep end I found I got the hang of it all quite quickly, and even began to like it. The bikes were semi-works jobs—bit like Honda today: you know, same as you can buy across the counter but all the parts have been

J. M. Busquets, the Peter Pan of Montjuich Park, takes his 250 Montesa through Pueblo Español in the 1964 Spanish GP ahead of another competitor

blueprinted and there's a team of factory mechanics who just happen to be taking their holidays in Barcelona that week! The bikes were 600 cc models—the R60S, I think—and not only were they easily the biggest bikes in the race, they were also bloody hard work round a twisty track like Montjuich for 24 hours. They didn't have much ground clearance, so we wore away one side which wasn't helped by my slipping off at one of the hairpins—the one and only time I ever fell off in an endurance race, which I'm quite proud of considering how often everyone else did—and we had a lot of trouble with the dynamos: the lights kept packing up and we had to replace them at least twice. Even so, we would have been sixth at the finish, except I ran out of petrol halfway round the last lap. That would have been all right, because the last part of the lap is all downhill, so I coasted home only to find the finishing straight totally blocked with thousands of Spaniards making *fiesta*. There was no way I could push the bike through them, but they disqualified us for not completing the last lap in the minimum time, which seemed very unfair.

'Mind you, to tell the truth I didn't really care. I'd enjoyed myself and discovered not only that I liked endurance racing, but also that I was quite good at it. I've always had very good eyesight and that helped at night, especially with all the lighting problems we had that year—they do have street lights around most of the track, but in those days they were the 60-watt bulb variety and rather dim. I was quite a bit faster than Ginger at night as a result and ended up doing three-hour stints after dark, getting off for half an hour to stretch my legs and spend a penny before getting on again. I never ever used to go to bed during a 24-hour race—wouldn't have slept if I had. I did have my hair cut at Montjuich one year, though! There was a barber across the track doing a roaring trade, so I thought, why not nip over for a short back and sides while Ian Goddard was on the bike—it was the year we won, 1970. The locals thought it was a good laugh, and I got a good haircut for less than half what it would have cost me at home!

'That was just typical of the Barcelona atmosphere: it's not like at Le Mans where you have this artificial sort of village that goes full blast through the night. At Montjuich you're racing for 24 hours in the middle of a huge city, and life goes on all around you. I loved the Latin atmosphere, and straight away then I decided I'd come back the next year with my own bike and would try to win. All the time I wasn't riding I'd be wandering up and down the pits looking at the other teams, trying to work out what they were doing wrong so as not to make the same mistakes myself, and trying to pick up tips from the smart ones. I remember seeing old Geoff Dodkin, for example, who was going through primary chains like they were going out of fashion—his poor old Velocette was just eating them: all the hairpins, I suppose. All the time I was going round on the BMW I was sitting there thinking, and in the end I dreamed up a bike I was sure I could win the race on. So when I got home I set about building it.'

Shortly before then, Degens had taken over a firm named Dresda Autos in Putney, a scooter shop whose name was formed from the initials of the partners, whom he had met when racing a Rumi scooter at Crystal Palace. He had built his first Triton special in 1961, using a Manx Norton frame that Geoff Monty had given him to construct one of the first hybrids of the type which later became so famous. Now Dresda gave him the opportunity to do so on a semi-series production basis.

'I'd built a lot of Tritons by then,' recalls Dave, 'and actually went on to construct over 800 in all, but at that time I hadn't built one specifically for racing, though most of the customer bikes were fast enough to be raced very successfully. But I did

know all the little tricks to make one work that amateur special builders and quite a few so-called pros hadn't a clue about, so that was obviously going to be the basis of my Barcelona bike. I ended up using a 1962 pre-unit 650 Triumph engine with a 1965 nine-stud head and barrels and a duplex primary chain (having learnt my lesson from Geoff!), fitted in a wideline Manx Featherbed chassis. We used standard valves with racing springs, Bonneville 3134 racing cams and followers, twin $1\frac{3}{16}$ in. Amal Monoblocs with the inlet ports opened up to match, and did quite a bit of lightening work inside the engine. I'd noticed a lot of the non-Spanish bikes had had pre-ignition problems, because of the petrol I suppose, so I dropped the compression to 8:1 and had no worries.

'I knew a bloke in Lucas who built me a special twin-spark magneto, and also a 12-volt one-off AC generator; then we made two covers at the back behind the number plates and dropped a 6-volt

Jean-Claude Chemarin cranks the works RCB Honda into El Angulo in the 1979 24 Horas, en route to victory at record speed

battery in each. That way if we had dynamo trouble like on the Bee-Em the engine would still keep running OK on the mag, and next time we came in to refuel we could just change batteries with the quick-fit connectors without losing time. Nowadays that's all taken for granted in endurance racing, but I was definitely the first person to dream it up. We also got some sponsorship from Cibie in the form of a really cracking headlamp—it was so good you could tell in the pits when we were rounding the last corner before the start because our lights were so much brighter than anyone else's!

'I decided to ask Rex Butcher to ride with me, and he had an Oldani 4LS front brake in his Manx which we fitted to the Triton. With his Manx rear it meant

Dave Simmonds' Kawasaki (no. 9) leads a group of riders into Rosaleda, also known as the Museo Etnológico, during the 1969 500 cc Spanish GP. He retired, but Gyula Marsovsky's Linto (no. 11) went on to finish fourth, while Angelo Bergamonti on a Paton (no. 30) was second to Ago's inevitable MV, already past the camera

we had a spare set of wheels, but we never needed them: the Avon tyres we used lasted the distance— why, oh, why did they stop making them? They were the best racing tyres ever made, far grippier than Dunlops and just as long-lasting.'

Degens' father had calculated that in order to win at record speed, the pair needed to lap at a given speed throughout the race, rather than join in the early-laps Grand Prix and risk overstressing the engine. Keeping to a conservative 6500 rpm instead of the engine's usual peak revs of 7200, the team took the lead in the 17th hour when the second works Montesa retired, and went on to win comfortably by three laps from the Spanish opposition; in fact, they lost a £300 bonus they would have earned for breaking the race distance record by coming in for a leisurely oil change and to clean and polish the bike, a fact which still chagrins Degens to this day: 'Most expensive service ever,' he grins.

The following year, having won the British 500-mile race at Castle Combe in 1965 and Brands

'Min' Grau guns his NCR Ducati 900 out of Teatro
Griego in the 1975 24 Horas, which he won once

again with Salvador Canellas. Dutch rider Rob
Noorlander (no. 20) has a production Ducati 900

The Grau/Canellas 860 Ducati leads Quique de Juan's second-placed 360 Bultaco through Vias in the 1973 24 Horas

Hatch in 1966 on Lawton & Wilson machinery, Degens rode for Syd Lawton at Montjuich on a works-backed Triumph Bonneville, finishing fourth, again partnered by Rex Butcher, after innumerable setbacks. The Bonnie was apparently a much heavier bike to ride than the Triton, a factor which told strongly against the team around the twisty track; Montesas dominated, finishing first and second by some way.

'Then I ran into trouble with the ACU and got my licence taken away for being a naughty boy,' recalls Dave whimsically, 'so I didn't ride at Barcelona again till 1969. By then I was doing much less short-circuit racing and really the 24 Hours was the main event of the year for me, but though I had a good co-rider in Ian Goddard, the bike [another 650 Dresda Triton] was too highly tuned and we had a lot of bother, including a couple of broken chains—one of them flew off and flayed my back. I'd forgotten my own lessons.'

So for 1970 it was back to the recipe of a softly tuned engine with reliability and tractability rather than outright speed the watchwords. The recipe proved successful, as Degens and Goddard won by

the huge margin of 11 laps on another Dresda Triton, taking the lead only in the 18th hour after sitting out the faster bikes which failed to last the distance.

'By then the supply of Norton frames had dried up,' says Dave, 'so I was making my own, which were much lighter but even stronger than the Featherbeds. I'd made a chassis for a 500 Daytona engine which I won the Scarborough Gold Cup on ahead of all the pukka racing bikes: it had the same wheelbase as an Aermacchi and was incredibly light-steering and easy to ride. So I put a 650 unit Triumph engine in it, but lightly tuned with only a single carb which curiously didn't seem to affect the top speed by more than 2 mph—the bike would do 130 mph—but made it much more tractable and easier on juice: we averaged 45 mpg for the 24 hours. I used 9:1 pistons, 3134 cams, polished the ports and ran 34 degrees ignition advance instead of 36 degrees, with a 32 mm carb; the bike weighed only 310 lb ready to go with a fairing and lights, and one of the 8LS front brakes that John Cerhan made for me, which was the business at Barcelona, with all the hairpins: it was only 20 per cent worn at the end. We used Castrol R in the four-speed box, and straight 50 oil in the engine because of the heat: it was 115 degrees in the shade that year!'

Though he was to return once more with the British Honda équipe, 1970 marked Dave Degens' finest hour in the Barcelona 24 Horas, and stamped him as one of the masters of Montjuich, together with Ducati's Spanish aces Benjamin Grau (seven times a winner of the race) and Salvador Canellas (three times the victor, each time with Grau). How did he approach the tight and demanding track?

'The thing I remember more than anything else was the atmosphere: a huge crowd of excitable Spaniards, this great circuit, and so much going on all around you. The pits were set up on the pavement on the short straight by the entrance to the Park [at the end of the Recinto Ferial, a wide avenue leading down to the Plaza España in the centre of Barcelona], and they were always cramped, so there were inevitable squabbles about pit space. You had to have at least two mechanics with you because strangely enough we didn't refuel at our own pit, but instead had to use a communal set of pumps at the entrance to pit lane. You had to drive in there as you were coming in, refuel, then ride to the pit to change riders. We always programmed our stops but sometimes there'd be a bit of a queue, in which case you needed a mechanic to "remind" the pump attendant that you were there, and stop the Spanish riders on their little buzz boxes holding you up. We used to watch to see which of the attendants was quickest, then we'd go to him if at all possible, but if not there was a first reserve, and so on. It seems hilarious now, but at the time it could all be a bit fraught, especially if you were leading and there was a Bultaco or Montesa only a lap adrift; there used to be a bit of trouble with the bloke's trigger finger then!

'We had a Le Mans start, so with the Dresdas we'd leave the bike balanced on a tin can with the ignition on and set up on compression so as not to be wasting battery juice. I was reasonably quick across the road, but even so I preferred to get away in midfield for psychological reasons; with a big bike I'd be able to pull through to the top ten or 15 by the end of the first couple of laps, and I reckoned that if the rest of the team saw that from the pits, it'd raise everyone's morale.

'Though the Triumph engines would go to 7200 revs we never took them over 6200 or so—6500 at the most—and they were so flexible it didn't matter if you came out of a corner a gear higher than you really ought. I found at Montjuich it was important to gear for the hairpins rather than the straight, so you could get a good pull out of a very slow corner—there are six in all on the circuit, which is a lot—in bottom and squirt it down to the next one in second without faltering.

'Anyway, the start was opposite a restaurant called La Pergola, which is the name of the first bend, a left-hander which starts the climb up the hill, followed immediately by a right called, appropriately, Contra Pergola. The road's really wide here, so I found the best bet was to stay more or less in the middle of the track, but watching out for the white road markings which could be very slippery. I did all that in second on the four-speed Dresdas, then notched third on the way in to the next corner which comes almost at once and is really one long, long bend to the left, climbing all the time. The first part is called Pueblo Español, after the sort of Spanish Disneyland on the inside, then the second bit's called San Jorge after a pub on the outside of the same name. Right here is where you start using all the road, clipping the kerbs from left to right and back again—the quick way round San Jorge was to practically buy yourself a drink from the bar before you peeled off to the left. I remember one year some local rider on a little Bultaco or something did practically that; he tried to stick his nose up my inside at the Pergola, but I had more power up the hill, so the next time he makes his presence felt is when he tries to ride round the outside of me by the pub. I held my line and went exactly where I'd intended to go all along, drifting right to the outside, and suddenly he wasn't there any more. Next lap I came round and they were trying to put the straw bales out where he'd slid off into them and his bike had caught fire. Hope he enjoyed his drink!'

The whole circuit was lined with straw bales, as well as some very solid walls and kerbs, not to mention the trees and shrubbery. Did that mean Dave thought it was dangerous? 'No, because I'd raced at places like Aberdare Park which were much narrower, not so well surfaced, and a lot more bumpy. I rode a big Honda at Montjuich in the 1970s and that was all right too, so I don't know what all the fuss was about later on: just the French being themselves, I suspect. The only thing that did bother me was the flies—Spanish flies at that!— which used to get everywhere, all over your goggles and leathers and face. That was the only real reason I fitted a fairing to the 1970 bike—it did give some protection, as well as ducting some cool air to the engine, which because it was so hot that year was important.

'Anyway, you'd be powering all the way round San Jorge, round the end bit which was called Rasante but which was really all the same corner, then up the first part of the only really decent straight of any length, which was called the Recta del Estadio. About halfway along was the highest point of the course, and after that you were descending, sometimes quite steeply, back to the start line.' The Estadio in question is on the right of the course here, a sort of Spanish White City built for the 1929 World's Fair and later used as the paddock for the bike and car GP circuses, while on the left at the end of the straight is the Palacete Albaniz, the King of Spain's official residence in Barcelona. The present monarch, King Juan Carlos, is a keen bike racing fan: must be convenient having a house right on the course. . . .

At the end of the straight is the sharpest hairpin on the circuit, called just that: El Angulo. Dave Degens used to make up a lot of time there: 'It was the one corner at Montjuich you could stick your

neck out at, because there was a slip road if you got into trouble. There was a bloke holding a piece of rope up across it and when he saw you coming he'd drop it for you—I always used to hope he didn't go to sleep at night! In the early laps especially I'd use my Brands training to the full and go whizzing up the inside there—it wasn't so much a question of picking one or two of the locals off as seven or eight at a time, particularly once we started lapping them while they were still bunched up. The bike would get both wheels off the ground twice towards the end of the straight at 130 mph on the Dresda [Victor Palomo flipped his Yamaha here in 1976 and was severely injured, leading to the introduction of a chicane just before the stadium], and the second one was my braking point: soon as I landed it was hard on the brakes, and move aside please, *señores*.'

Did Dave use markers much otherwise for his braking points? 'Yes, all the time—a tree here, a road sign or whatever there; one year I was using a girl in a bright pink dress at the end of the straight, and so it transpired was Rex. He told me so one time we were changing over, and I said so was I, but what happened if she moved? She did of course, and in the end I was braking so far down the hill it was frightening even me! Then she started walking round the circuit, so each time we swapped over we'd report on her progress, and I'd give her a wave when I went out—helped to relieve the boredom at the end, even if I never did get to find out if she spoke English!'

Tarquinio Provini takes the chequered flag to win the 1963 Spanish 250 cc GP on his Morini single and score a notable victory over the works Honda team led by Jim Redman

What gear did Dave take El Angulo in? 'Bottom, and I used to take it very close in, because the road drops quite steeply downhill afterwards, and it meant I could stay over to the left for the next right-hand curve which I'd take hard on in second. Anyway, it didn't do to drift too far over to the right, because there was an unprotected 15 ft drop into the Botanical Gardens if you ran out of road! I used to experiment in practice by going round each corner on the wrong line to see what I could get away with; you had to figure you'd have at least two or three avoidances during each 24-hour race, when someone fell in front of you or some loony Spaniard tried to show you he was the next Mike Hailwood, so I felt it was important to practise finding myself in the wrong gear, off line, leaning the wrong way—then if it happened to me in the race I'd know what to expect and how to deal with it. It also helped me if I spotted anything on the road and had to change direction: my excellent eyesight meant I was able to pick up spilt petrol—there was always a lot of that, especially on the approach to the hairpins, with all the overfull tanks and hasty refuelling—or suchlike on the tarmac and usually avoid running over it. Saved me more than once, that did.'

The right-hander after El Angulo is aptly named La Ciega—literally, the Blind Woman—and it is indeed completely blind. 'A lot of people used to knock it off there,' recalls Degens, 'especially as there was a corner of the King's palace that used to jut out into the road right on the exit, but if you knew where you were going it was no problem. A lot of riders did fall off there, though, probably through bottling out once they were committed to a line.' Then almost at once the next hairpin looms up, this time a right-hander called Rosaleda, with the Museo Etnologico on the inside: bottom gear again? 'Yes, and again a quick squirt in second down to the next left-hander only 100 yards or so away, with a restaurant on the outside; I used to see the people sitting out on the balcony watching the race and tucking into a nice three-course *table d'hôte*, and think how nice it would be if I could be up there with them sinking a couple of beers in all that heat—quite off-putting it was, almost like a mirage when you were racing!'

The restaurant is called the Font del Gat (Cat's Fountain), and so is the corner, a 120-degree left leading to another short straight before another not-so-long left named after the Teatro Griego (Greek Theatre) on the outside, with some unpleasant bumps in the braking area which could

A nail-biting moment after 22 hours in the 1973 24 Horas, as Bultaco mechanics work frantically to repair de Juan's second-placed 360 which has just been crashed. They succeeded

upset the bike badly. 'You had to be careful coming out of there too,' recalls Dave, 'because there was the Archaeological Museum on the left and a place where they used to hold the Flower Market on the right, with a high kerb and no room for error. Mind you, I used to use the kerbs as cushions to stop the back wheel sliding too far if it got out of line, but you had to be sure you were well cranked over before you played that game, else you'd finish up cracking the crankcase. But it was definitely a help.'

Next up is another blind right-hander called Vias. 'It took a while to get worked up to doing this one flat out in third,' says Dave, 'and a lot of people never did; there was this 30 ft high wall in front of you and absolutely nowhere to go but into it if you came off—which you shouldn't really do, since it wasn't that tight a corner, but lots of people psyched themselves up and you could make up quite a bit of time there just by not rolling the throttle. Then there was another short straight down through the most built-up part of the track, with public buildings and offices on either side, including the HQ of the Barcelona traffic police with whom I had a couple of more or less friendly encounters! At the end was a 90-degree left called Tráfico or Guardia Urbana (after them), with the lap scorers' stand and timekeepers on the outside. That was a normal short-circuit corner, then it was into the Recta de Tribunas, the finishing straight, and off for yet another lap; we covered 656 in all when we won in 1970, and about half an hour from the end I pulled in and gave the bike to Ian Goddard to finish the race with. He thought it was a great honour, but what he didn't know was that in 1965, when I won before, I'd been mobbed by the crowd and tossed around over their shoulders while they tried to grab the number off my back, and so on! They really are enthusiasts there, but after going through that once I decided it was his turn!'

Does Dave have happy memories of his forays to Montjuich? 'Very definitely, and not just because I won twice, though that helped of course. Looking back, it was all very enjoyable; about the only time I wondered what on earth I was doing out there was when we were ten laps in the lead towards the end in 1970, and it just got boring, quite apart from imagining things like misfires and rattles and so on that didn't exist. It was all very well organized too, apart from the odd excitable Latin official, and the main credit for that must go to Masset, who was the chief organizer when I raced there. He was scrupulously fair, even to foreign riders, as well as having a great sense of humour—he lent me his tie one year to go to the prizegiving with when I didn't have one, and then at Christmas another one arrives with a note saying it's for next year's do! It was a great race on a great track, and I'm glad they've managed to keep it going even today.'

Sadly, the future of Montjuich as a racetrack is in doubt, since after Barcelona's successful application to stage the 1992 Olympic Games, the Park has been earmarked as the site of the Olympic Stadium. Time will tell if the last of Europe's city-centre circuits will remain in use.

Endurance racing has the added excitement of racing in the dark when everything becomes an exhausting blur of light

Joe Dunphy and Crystal Palace

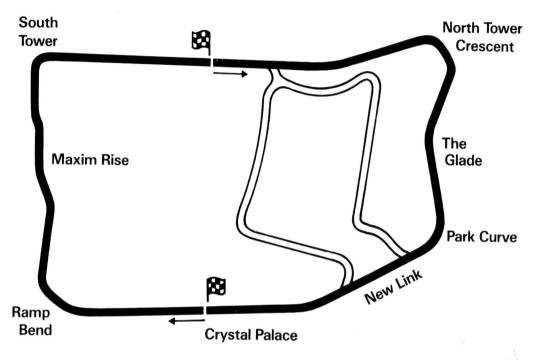

South Tower

North Tower Crescent

Maxim Rise

The Glade

Park Curve

New Link

Ramp Bend

Crystal Palace

Of all the several British circuits which have been lost to motorcycle racing enthusiasts down the years, few are as keenly missed as Crystal Palace, which hosted its last race meeting in 1972. The South London track was unique in British racing annals: a Continental-style parkland circuit, recalling Bremgarten or Montjuich, built in the 'Phoenix Suburb's' principal attraction, the site of the great wrought-iron and glass edifice which previously housed the Prince Consort's Industrial Exhibition of 1857 in Hyde Park (generally credited with introducing the Victorian era of mechanization) before being moved to an ornamental park on the side of Sydenham Hill. Sadly, the Crystal Palace itself succumbed to fire in 1936, replaced by the Eiffel-like BBC transmitter tower which today has become an equally well-known landmark and around which the racing circuit weaved, until it was closed in 1972 to make way for the access roads and car parks of the National Recreation Centre

which represents the home of British athletics and swimming competition today.

Though car racing often stole the limelight over the years, culminating in a round of the European Formula 2 championship being staged in 1971 and won by Mike Hailwood in a Surtees TS10, Crystal Palace was first and foremost a motorcycle circuit. Indeed, to begin with only bikes raced there, with the first meeting held as long ago as 21 May 1927, and dominated by Coventry-Eagle machines which won both solo and sidecar classes. However, this was path rather than road racing, with narrow dirt tracks lined by a huge crowd of 10,000 spectators and a heady average speed for the fastest lap at that inaugural meeting of 28.20 mph! Over the next decade local stars such as Gus Kuhn and Harold Daniell came to prominence at the Palace, whose ease of access by Tube, train or bus ensured large crowds for every meeting and a grand day out for Londoners from all over the capital in those pre-TV

*Joe Dunphy photographed by Ken Jones at Brands
Hatch in July 1962*

days before we were spoilt for choice of leisure pursuits.

Encouraged by the success of these meetings, and under pressure from the car brigade who were eager for another purpose-built racing circuit on which to compete besides Brooklands and Donington, the Crystal Palace trustees decided to construct a two-mile road circuit. Of 30 ft in width, this was inaugurated on 15 May 1937, with the first tarmac event known as the Coronation Grand Prix, in honour of the crowning of King George VI. This presaged three successful seasons of bike and car competition until World War 2 broke out in September 1939, but after the war the Palace was derelict and the track in a state of disrepair. Fortunately, the London County Council Parks Department took over the grounds in 1951 and decided immediately to restart racing, first however constructing a link between The Glade and the start and finish line, then located on the bottom straight, which cut out the inner loop (ironically the route of the original path course of the 1920s) and considerably speeded up lap times. The circuit now measured 1.39 miles, and remained unchanged (apart from resurfacing) until racing ceased in 1972.

The inaugural motorcycle meeting on the new circuit took place on 27 June 1953; given that this too was a Coronation year, that of the present Queen, the coincidence was too obvious to resist and the new Coronation Trophy was won by Bob Keeler on a Manx Norton in front of 10,000 shirtsleeved spectators on a sun-drenched afternoon. Though organization, then as later, was in the experienced hands of Bemsee, the starter appears to have suffered a touch of sunstroke, for in the first scheduled ten-lapper he flagged everyone off after just nine laps, and a few races later forgot to give the two surviving outfits out of the seven starters in the sidecar final the flag at all!

No practice was ever permitted outside of race meetings at Crystal Palace, yet curiously enough local riders always excelled there. John Surtees, from Forest Hill, dominated the South London track in the 1950s, frequently opting to race his single-cylinder Norton rather than the more powerful but cumbersome MV Agusta four: power was often an embarrassment on the tight and still twisty track which placed a premium on handling ability. From just under 60 mph before the war, the lap record went up to 71.49 mph for a 70 sec lap in Bob Keeler's hands at the inaugural post-war meeting, soon to be hoisted to 75.82 mph by Surtees in 1955

The Crystal Palace era lasted from 1927 until 1972 when local pressure caused the circuit to close

on his Manx, which incredibly enough equalled Reg Parnell's Ferrari lap record on four wheels.

Surtees' record of 31 Palace wins was never bettered, but in time his lap record was equalled and then beaten by another local man, Sydenham's Joe Dunphy, who became the first rider to break the 80 mph barrier in April 1963 when he lapped in 62.4 sec (80.19 mph). Eltham's John Blanchard and Wimbledon's Griff Jenkins came close to breaking this mark which, however, stood for over five years until Paul Smart, from as far away as

Maidstone, fractionally raised it but needed a 750 Curley Norton to do so. Smartie made his real mark in 1970 though, when he incredibly set a total of six race and lap records in one meeting, and in September 1971 he became the first man to break the minute barrier, lapping in 59.2 sec (84.53 mph) on his works Triumph triple, a figure equalled only in the very last race ever run at the Palace on 28 August 1972 by Dave Nixon on the Seeley-framed Boyer Trident, in a heroic battle with Kuhn Norton riders Dave Potter and Graham Sharpe for the honour of taking the last-ever chequered flag at the South London circuit.

If one man apart from Surtees and Smart established himself not only as a firm favourite of the Crystal Palace crowd but also as one of the circuit's true masters, it was Joe Dunphy. Though

The Palace, packed both on and off the grid for the Easter 1967 meeting

born of Irish parents, as the green shamrock on his white helmet used to denote, the quiet Dunphy was a true Londoner, born in Paddington, brought up in Victoria and later proprietor of a large car accessory and spares business in Sydenham, literally a stone's throw from the eastern edge of the Palace circuit. He was also, like so many others who started racing bikes in the 1950s and 1960s, one of the white-scarved café racers who cut his riding teeth on the public roads before taking to the tracks before (or in some cases after) losing the unequal battle with the guardians of the law and winding up without a licence.

'I had my first race at Brands Hatch in 1956 when I was 18,' recalls Joe. 'I was one of the Chelsea Bridge mob, and myself and Griff Jenkins, who's still a good mate of mine, used to go up the Bridge every night on our bikes. There was a little tea stall on the bridge itself that formed the meeting point, even though the tea and coffee they served were atrocious. That didn't matter much—all that

125s running through The Glade in August 1963. Mike Cook on a Ducati leads Basil Keys and R. A. Minster on Bultacos

counted were the bikes and how fast you could get about on them.

'I had a Triumph Tiger 110 which I used to start racing at Brands Hatch with. I'd been mad keen on the idea ever since I was a little 'un, and to show you how serious I was I stopped using it on the road and took the bus or rode on the back of someone else's bike till I could afford a van. But I fell off at Paddock Bend in my first race and that put me out for the rest of the year, while I scraped up enough money to fix the bike and have another go. I wasn't hurt, just my pride, but it was the first of 13 times in all that I fell off at Paddock, by the way!'

Next season, 1957, Joe Dunphy took up racing seriously on the Triumph, eventually winning a non-experts race at Brands which upgraded him to the experts' classes. 'The standard of riding was unbelievably higher, though strangely enough my old bike was far from uncompetitive. There were a lot of Triumphs and Norton twins in the races then, but the riders were a lot better than I was. I was

driving a van for a living, and couldn't afford on my wages to race any further afield than Brands and Crystal Palace, but I had this dream to one day ride in the Isle of Man, so I managed to scrape up enough money to buy an old 500 Manx from John Surtees which I entered for the 1957 Manx GP. The conrod broke on the second lap, but I was hooked on the Island, and even though it took me five years to even finish in a race there, winning one on the TT course was my greatest ambition in those early days.'

In 1962 that ambition was fulfilled when Joe won the Senior MGP on Francis Beart's Norton which he had been offered on the recommendation of another racing friend, Roy Mayhew, sadly to be killed at Paddock Bend on a G50. It was the beginning of a successful partnership which lasted for the next five years, and which saw Dunphy riding the Beart-modified machines in the TT and Ulster GP, while Francis prepared the brace of Manx Nortons which Joe had purchased from Bob McIntyre's former sponsor, Joe Potts, in 1961 for short-circuit use. Before that there had been several years of club racing, which saw the name of P. J. Dunphy gradually climb its way up the results sheets, first on the Triumph, then with its 650 cc

K. German on a 350 cc Norton approaching Park
Curve, again in August 1963. It's so pleasant it looks
like a Sunday jaunt

engine slotted into a Manx frame to make one of the
first Tritons. For all his later victories, Joe Dunphy's
was no overnight success, but a classic example of
an aspiring clubman who eventually attained the
highest reaches of success in the sport through
dedication, hard work and perseverance—plus
luck.

'You always dreamed of being a professional
rider,' says Joe, 'but it always seemed there were
just a few making any money and the rest of us were
only making the numbers up. But I had to give it a
go, and after I'd scored quite a bit of success in club
racing I decided to take the plunge and bought the
brace of Manxes. This meant I had two competitive
bikes to go racing with, but the HP on them cost
more per week than I was making on the vans, so I

absolutely had to make a go of it. I was hungry!

'The big problem in those days, however, was
getting time off work to go racing, and getting
entries. It was very difficult getting accepted for a
national meeting then—seems daft today, doesn't
it!—so you'd keep on applying, keep on getting
turned down, until at last you'd crack it. Then you
had to show how good you were at that one
meeting you'd got into, so they never turned you
back again.

'In my case the breakthrough came at Crystal
Palace, but that's not the only reason it was always
my favourite short circuit—even more than Brands,
though you can't compare either of them to the TT:
that's something unique. The Palace was nice and
local, plus the fact you couldn't practise on it before
the event meant that it was the same for everyone: at
Brands you could cut your own groove in it on a
practice day, but the Palace was fairer for everyone,
so if you won there it meant more. They had two big
nationals a year there on Easter Monday and the

August Bank Holiday, and I never missed them. I suppose by modern standards it was a bit dangerous, but if you thought about the railway sleepers that lined the track and the lack of runoff area and the trees, you just didn't race at the Palace. I held the lap record or a share of it for six years, yet I only fell off there twice, and never through my own fault. The first time was when a borrowed Greeves Silverstone seized on me in practice—not the bike I rode for Francis Beart but another one—and the other was when I came out of the trees in The Glade and found bikes all over the track. I hit one of them and took off about 50 ft in the air before waking up in Beckenham hospital with concussion. I didn't break anything though; the only time in my career I did so was when I fell off at the hairpin at Cadwell at about 2 mph and broke my collarbone. That's ironic, isn't it?'

Was there a sense of occasion about Crystal Palace meetings? 'You bet: being in the middle of a big city and only doing the two meetings a year meant you really relished going there. I never quite got over the thrill all the years I raced there, and I think being so convenient to get to, a lot of people went to watch there who never would have gone to Brands Hatch or Silverstone. There was even a gateway leading directly from Penge Lower Level station into the track: can't get more convenient than that!'

The start line at the Palace used to be on the bottom straight of the 1.39-mile circuit, as it had been before the war, before a series of first-corner mêlées at Ramp Bend, coupled with the need to clear the old paddock site for the construction of the first stage of the National Recreation Centre, caused Bemsee and the LCC to move the start and finish to the Terrace (Top) Straight on the other side of the circuit, for the 1961 season. Did Joe prefer this arrangement? 'Yes, I did, because it gave you more time to sort yourselves out before the first corner, but even so this was always a bit hairy because the track was so tight. On a flying lap you'd take the left-hand curve leading into North Tower Crescent hard on in top, but then you'd have to brake like billy-o for the right-hander after. It was vital to line the left up correctly, cut it fine from right to left, then force the bike upright well before you would normally so as to be able to brake hard without being cranked over, else you'd be in trouble. You also couldn't drift as far over to the right as you'd like to ordinarily, because you had to get over to the other side of the road for North Tower, and at the same time you'd be zipping down through the gears

to bottom on the 350 or maybe second on the 500: you'd be pretty busy for a while!'

How was overall gearing at the Palace, compared to other circuits? 'It was quite low, the same as Brands' short circuit which saved quite a bit of swapping about in the early days. I actually preferred to use a four-speed box, because even with five speeds I had trouble working out which one I was in and with six—well, forget it! Plus Francis and I had a lot of bad luck with two of the Swedish Aargard five-speed gearboxes at the TT one year and I never really trusted them. You were trying to squeeze one or even two extra ratios into the space four normally occupied, and it was asking for trouble. It was only later when Schafleitner did it properly by adding a spacer to the casing that they were reliable—but even so, I didn't go for them personally.'

Anyone who has raced round the current Snetterton circuit will have an idea of how North Tower was on the Crystal Palace track, for the end of the back straight there is very similar. However, the next section could not be more different, for instead of the Norfolk circuit's open expanses, the Palace's traditional and unique parkland atmosphere asserted itself. Joe Dunphy continues: 'You had plenty of room coming out of North Tower so it was OK to drift wide, but then you'd do all the next bit in second, letting the bike find its own way through the tunnel of leaves that made up The Glade. There were thick trees and bushes on either side, and on a sunny day it could be quite dark there. However, there was never any trouble with fallen leaves and so on, because a fleet of LCC roadsweepers used to prepare it before each meeting, so the track was always in tiptop condition; that was another reason it was nice to race there. The surface was quite grippy in the wet, too—not like Brands which was a skidpan when it rained because of all the use it got. I was always pretty good in the wet, and won races on every track I raced at in damp conditions, including the Manx GP in the rain. But the Palace was extra good because there wasn't the oil and rubber left there from the meeting the week before which came to the surface in the wet, thanks to there being so few meetings there.

'After you came out of The Glade you'd start picking up speed and I normally grabbed third just after the apex of Park Curve, which was a fast right-hander leading on to the New Link, which was quite steep downhill: people sometimes got a bit carried away and likened it to Bray Hill, but it wasn't

anything like that. You'd be on your way though, and I'd get top halfway down the hill, tucking everything away nicely to get the last ounce of speed and every rpm going. People used to say I had a nice riding style, but it only came about from riding slow, underpowered road bikes for so long which meant you had to get flat on the tank to get anywhere. It was nice, though, going through that section: you've gone through The Glade, you're out in the open, the old bike's coming on song really well—I did get a thrill buzzing down that hill on to the old Main Straight.

'First though there was that little kink leading on to it, a right-hander which you'd take absolutely flat out against the stop, chin on the tank without easing the throttle. How fast you took it determined your speed on the straight, and it was a bit bumpy as well, so you had to grit your teeth and hold on tight if you wanted to stay tucked in.' At the end of the straight, which was the fastest part of the course because of the downhill approach, lay Ramp Bend, a tight right-hander and a favourite viewing position for spectators: was it a scratcher's delight as it always seemed to be to an onlooker? 'Definitely—it was a great outbraking place, but not in the way most people tried. I used to hug the wall on the left till quite late, and as people peeled off early I'd go round them on the outside. If you were having a dice with someone and he rushed past you up the inside, as most of them did to try and steal your line, you could always cop them on the way out because they'd be drifting too wide. I'd just steer inside them and invariably ended up in front going up Maxim Rise, where it was just about impossible to pass because you'd be swinging the bike about from left to right through the sweeping Esses on a tight line, with not enough space to get alongside anyone, let alone pass him.

'You'd be very active all the way up the hill through Maxim Rise and The Alley, under the bridge leading into the paddock, into South Tower Corner, cranking right over from one side to another, before throwing out the anchors for the right-hander leading back on to the top straight. You could make an incredible amount of ground up under braking at South Tower—even quite good riders used to cram on the stoppers so early it was a joke. Maybe they used to get disconcerted by all the sleepers round the outside and the wall of people

It's 1958 and it's raining as Mike Hailwood crosses the line to win the 350 race. He also won the 1000 cc event that day on his Manx Norton

sitting in their deckchairs that confronted you as you roared round the last curve under the bridge. Personally, I never used braking markers on any circuit except the TT; at Brands and the Palace and suchlike it was all instinctive, and you gradually learnt how late you could brake by instinct. If someone else passed you and got round in one piece, then you were braking too early. I wouldn't let that happen a second time if I could help it!'

Apart from riding Francis Beart's machines in the TT and Ulster, Joe was largely self-sponsored throughout his career, apart from a short period when he rode for Tom Kirby. 'Roger Hunter was

In this shot one can see just how close the houses were. Fine if you were a fan but, sadly, so many were not

riding for him then and always got faster bikes than I did, which upset me so much that after a short while I packed it in and went back to my old Beart-prepared Nortons on the short circuits. But one day at the Palace Roger and I were both on Kirby G50s, though mine was an old nail compared to his, and he kept passing me down the straight in the 500 final, only I'd get him back on the corners. On the last lap I practically went into the sleepers at South Tower I braked so late there, but though I led him away towards the line, his bike accelerated so much better than mine he started to pull alongside. Just as his wheel was level with mine, he missed a gear—so I won anyway, even though I thought I'd had it. I packed up riding Kirby's bikes after that.'

Was that Joe's best race at the Palace? 'No, believe it or not it was a race I didn't actually win that gave me most satisfaction, the time I had a great

A determined Dunphy, who won three races at Easter that year, leads the pack into South Tower Corner in August 1963

chase after my old mate Griff Jenkins on my 500 Manx at the Easter meeting in 1963. He was riding for Charles Mortimer at the time, and he drew a front-row grid position for the final, while I was right at the back. I usually made quite good starts and this was no exception, but after I got my bike fired up I had to sit and wait at the back because there was no way I could get through the crowd of people pushing. From where I was I could see Griff tear off in the lead, and in a ten-lap race I didn't think I had much chance of catching him. Anyway, once I got going I tried my best, and I was catching him hand over fist but just ran out of time. He won by a fifth of a second, but I broke Surtees' lap record which had stood for six years and I'd only previously equalled. I was really pleased with my ride: I'd lapped the Palace at over 80 mph for the first time ever, and got beaten so closely by my best chum. I didn't mind!'

With so many good riders vying for success, some of those races in the heyday of the Palace and Brands scratchers looked positively hair-raising. Were they as rough and tumble as they seemed? 'Believe it or not, no—not to us, anyhow, because we all knew and trusted each other, which also made it jolly good fun. They were wonderful times—very competitive, yet friendly at the same time; one minute you'd be out there rubbing elbows with each other, the next you were back in the paddock enjoying a cup of tea and a laugh. There was just one rider at the top level who used to play rough: he and the others know who he is, but I'd rather you didn't name him because he's still quite active in the bike world. If you were outbraked for the hairpin at Brands fair and square, you knew it and accepted it: maybe you'd get him back at the next corner. But this bloke played dirty: he'd come up the inside of you totally out of control, all crossed up, and you knew if you cranked over for the corner as was your right, he'd take you down with him—an accident was inevitable. It was well out of order and very dangerous, but fortunately he was the only topliner who played foul and in the end he was a bit too clever for his own good—not on the track, however.

'Even hard cases like Croxford and Cooper played by the rules. I remember Coop hooked me off in the

The Glade again and Rex Butcher (no. 7) will eventually lose to Stan Woods (no. 22) in this 1971 250 cc race. Both rode Yamahas

rain at Oulton one day when I was leading and almost bound to win—I liked the wet, remember. I was so mad I wanted to get up and stick one on his chops, but he'd broken his arm or collarbone or something, so fortunately I calmed down and let it be. About a week later I got a letter in the post from Coop apologizing for the accident and enclosing a cheque for the damage to my bike. I reckon that says a lot for him, and also for the respect we all had for each other.'

Joe Dunphy was a most exceptional racer, able to scratch round Brands with the best of them and undisputed Prince of the Palace at the same time that Minter was King of Brands. Yet he was also able to attack the quite different demands of the Isle of Man TT course in the efficient, thoughtful way

that so much endeared him to Francis Beart, on whose machines he capped a fine succession of TT placings with second position in the rain-swept 1965 Senior, behind Mike Hailwood's battered MV. 'Francis' own bikes weren't very fast but they were dead reliable,' says Joe, 'while for the short circuits he was able to prepare me engines that had all the power I needed and got me to the finish even if I used all the revs I was supposed to and a bit more besides. What he did with the Greeves showed how versatile he could be—we won and set up lap

South Tower Corner and a 1971 500 cc race. Barry Ditchburn (354 Broad Yam) leads Jim Harvey (496 Kirby Metisse)

The final conflict—August 1972 and riders stream up Maxim Rise with Ray Jenkins (no. 104) leading Mike Quaife (no. 108)

records all over the country with that little bike in 1963, including at the Palace where I broke Surtees' 250 cc NSU record which had stood for ages. I have a lot to thank Mr Beart for.'

Though much less heralded at the time than Derek Minter's concurrent retirement from the track, Joe also stopped racing at the end of 1967. Why?

'I'd just lost interest for one thing: it was costing me more and more to go racing, and yet the rewards were ludicrous. I was getting 25 quid total for four bikes' start money at Brands when blokes I was beating were getting £150 for three machines. Complain and they told you to get lost, so what were you going to do then—not turn up at the next meeting? They had loads of Brands scratchers anyway, so one more or less didn't make any difference. The TT was no better: I got the grand sum of £15 start money the first year I did the TT after winning the Manx the year before, and the

Joe Dunphy

North Tower Crescent, September 1971—Rex Butcher leads Paul Smart, John Riley (no. 143), Brian Wackett (no. 103) and Clive Offer (no. 17)

boat fare was more than that. Yet at the same time they were getting 40,000 for a Brands national and thousands in the boarding-houses for the TT. Now they complain because the crowds are non-existent—but they have themselves to blame.

'The other reason I packed up was equipment. The old Nortons were worn out and it'd have meant getting an Aermacchi for the 350 class if I wanted to continue. But the biggest single factor for me getting out was that Avons had stopped making racing tyres and there was no way I could get on with Dunlop triangulars, which were the only alternative. They were designed for Bob Mac, whose style of riding suited them: look at the old films and you'll see that he used to throw the bike into the corner very suddenly, from upright to full

lean instantly, unlike most of the rest of us who were much more gradual. To me, I didn't have enough rubber on the road with the triangles, and having always ridden on Avons, especially the Green Spots which were super-sticky and that you could wear out in an afternoon at Brands, I was in trouble. I was two seconds a lap slower at Snetterton on Dunlops, and that's an awful lot. I did gather up all the Avons I could lay my hands on, even part-used and half-worn ones, and raced that way for a while, but in the end they all wore out and I had to use Dunlops. I packed up soon after, cold turkey: one day I was a professional motorcycle racer, the next one I'd retired and sold my leathers. I didn't even sit on a motorcycle of any kind until I was dragged out for a couple of laps at the Minter Day do at Brands a couple of years ago. Now I'm selling my business and will have a bit more time on my hands—well, I reckon this classic racing game looks OK, and I might pop down to a couple of meetings just for a look-see. . . .'

Mick Grant on Macau

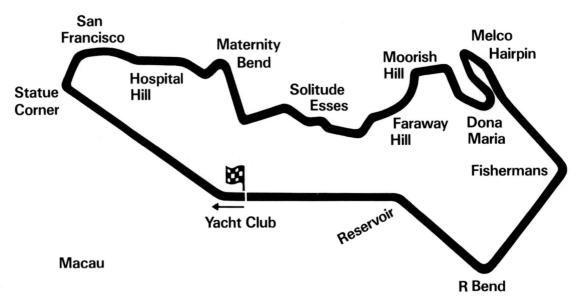

There is nothing else in the motorcycle racing calendar quite like the annual Macau Grand Prix, held each November in conjunction with a series of car races on the 3.8-mile Guia circuit, which twists and turns its way through the streets of the tiny

Riders mass for the start of the 1982 Macau GP, right by the jetfoil terminal where visitors arrive from Hong Kong

Portuguese dependency on the shores of China. An hour's ride by Boeing-powered jetfoil across the Pearl River from Hong Kong, Macau is no longer the slumbering relic of colonial rule straight out of a Hollywood movie that it was until recently. But in spite of the economic boom of the 1980s, the four square miles of land that comprise this province of Portugal, over which Chinese control is increasingly directed, has a much less frenetic pace of life than its dynamic British-controlled neighbour.

All of that changes in mid-November when the two- and four-wheeled racing caravans hit town, accompanied by crowds of visitors from all over the Orient. With no airport in Macau, the competing cars and bikes must first be air-freighted into Hong Kong, then ferried across to Macau on a fleet of junks. Though Macau's legal casinos probably represent at least an equal attraction to the gambling-mad Chinese, the Macau GP is one of the most important events in the Far Eastern motor sporting calendar, second only in two-wheel terms to the Suzuka 8 Hours and Japan GP. This explains the regular participation not only of factory-backed

Mick Grant with his faithful mechanic Nigel Everett and the local Suzuki wrenches at Macau before his last-ever race in 1985

riders from Japan with the latest works machinery, but also of an often formidable circus of European riders, mainly composed of British competitors, put together by travel agent Mike Trimby, who has worked closely for many years with the organizing Hong Kong Sports Car Club.

Macau as a place has often been compared to an Oriental version of Monte Carlo, and its races to the annual Monaco car GP. The similarity certainly exists, and was undoubtedly in the minds of a group of sports car enthusiasts from Hong Kong when they applied to the Portuguese Governor of the colony to hold the inaugural Macau GP over the Guia circuit in 1953. One of the participants in that début event was Teddy Yip, a Hong Kong high-roller whose enthusiasm has done much to ensure the race's continuation annually since then, even through the dark days of the Cultural Revolution in China, which spilled over into Macau in the form of some quite bloodthirsty riots. In 1967 a motorcycle GP was added to the programme, run initially as a single 100-mile event on the Saturday, as a curtain-

raiser to Sunday's car race. Later, this was commuted to two 50-mile legs, both run on the same day, before in 1983 the second bike race was switched to the Sunday as well for the simple reason that many of the local fans were not sticking around to watch the heavily-sponsored car event!

To begin with, the Macau bike GP was a benefit for Japanese riders, who generally managed to beg or borrow works-prepared machinery that was more than a match for the superior course knowledge of the locals. Names like Kanaya, Takai and Araoka dominated the list of winners until 1976, when that globe-trotter *par excellence*, Chas Mortimer, recorded the first European victory. The following year saw the floodgates open from Europe, since when the non-Oriental contingent has rarely comprised less than two dozen riders, latterly also including American and Australasian stars like John Long and Wayne Gardner.

Winner of that 1977 event was Yorkshireman Mick Grant on the factory water-cooled KR750 Kawasaki. Since then, whether mounted on the Green Meanie or on works Honda or Suzuki machinery, the veteran star has amassed a Macau record which is second only to Ron Haslam's, with two wins, a second, a third and a fourth to his credit. In a racing career spanning 20 years, including factory rides for three of the four Japanese teams as

Mick Grant

well as Norton and Duċati, Mick Grant has scaled the pinnacles of racing success, with victories in the Isle of Man TT and Ulster GP, at the Dutch GP and innumerable British short circuits like Scarborough and the like. Yet Macau's annual GP was his most enjoyable race: why?

'It's a funny thing about Macau,' reflects Mick. 'We all go there at the end of the season and say it's all for fun, and the racing isn't serious, and maybe to most of the Europeans it isn't. But what we don't realize is that to the Orientals it's a GP like any other—Holland, Silverstone, Italy, the rest. So victory there is just as important to them as in a "real" GP, and after Chas Mortimer won there in 1976, when I went there for the first time the next year on the Kawasaki, I wasn't really prepared for how seriously Asami, who was the local ace there, wanted to reassert himself.

'I'm usually terrible at learning new circuits, but for some reason I just felt at home at Macau from the very beginning, and in fact I equalled the lap record in my very first practice session ever there—I couldn't believe it. I actually won the race by lapping everyone but the second-place man, who was Stan Woods on the Suzuki, and I'd even have

Banzai! The local headbangers on their 250 cc production bikes depart at the start of one of the supporting races at Macau. This is Yacht Club Bend, taken at over 160 mph by the bigger bikes. Statue Corner is in the distance

lapped him if I hadn't made an insurance stop for a quick half gallon of petrol near the end—it was run as a single 100-miler in those days. Anyway, afterwards we went straight to Japan, and when we arrived at Kawasaki I found myself getting the full red-carpet treatment, with everyone from the president of the company down turning out to greet us. After that, I realized how important the race is to the Japanese, so though I always treated the circuit with a lot of caution, same as I would any road course like the TT or the North-West, I also tried my best to do well. In spite of that, I've always had a terrific time when I've gone there, almost like a holiday, because like all the other Europeans who go regularly, I've made lots of local Chinese and Portuguese friends who know how to show us a good time. For me, it's the most enjoyable race on the calendar, and doing well at it makes it twice as good.'

Given that the organizers are based in Hong Kong, and many of the spectators come in specially for the race, do the Macau locals participate with enthusiasm in the event? 'You can't believe how keen they are,' says Mick. 'The first time I went in 1977, we kept the bike in the workshop of the local Kawasaki dealer, Mr Tak. When it suddenly became obvious after the first practice that we had a chance of winning, you'd have thought it was the culmination of his life's work. From then on one of his men slept literally under the bike to prevent any funny business—apparently there's a lot of betting on the race and the local Tongs aren't above a little monkey business to make sure the favourite doesn't win! Mind you, even after I started coming with Suzuki, it was the same: all the locals feel it's an honour to get involved, and nothing is too much trouble. One night at about 11 pm we needed a burette; it took about half an hour to explain what

that was, but ten minutes later we had a brand-new one, probably because they'd knocked the local chemist out of his bed to get it. Ask for a snack, and back they come in a jiffy with a bag of delicious fresh prawns—it's that sort of thing that makes racing there so great.'

How about the local riders, though? Having personally tangled with one the time I rode there, they do seem to present a hazard. 'That's right,' says Mick, 'and apart from the nature of the circuit, they're the single biggest problem you have to contend with. They generally make up over half the field, and though there are some quite experienced ones like Kiki Kwong from Hong Kong or Foreman Ho from Indonesia, most of the rest are having their

Kai Man Wong's race comes to an early end after he drops his TZ500 Yamaha on the slippery corner in front of the San Francisco barracks

only race of the year, which they see as the passport to fame and glory. Macau's the only place I've been to where you have to cope with lapping the same bloke every three laps, which isn't so bad in itself, except that each time you pass any of the Chinese locals you must be prepared for him to do something totally unexpected and silly—like fall off in front of you for no reason whatsoever. You've got to be very careful and play safe whenever you come up behind them, which really typifies the whole approach a European rider has to adopt at Macau.'

Does that mean Mick's approach to racing at Macau differs from his attitude to the Isle of Man or the Ulster? 'Not really, because with any road circuit you have to come to terms with the lack of runoff and so forth; it's just that each of them has its own special problems. At Barcelona, for example, you had to contend with the abysmal standard of marshalling, which is actually pretty good at Macau, even if they do insist on waving blue flags at us, like the cars have, to warn someone you're overtaking them! Apart from the local riders, the other main factor you have to watch out for at

Picturesque—but dangerous. Riders head out towards the South China Sea through the Solitude Esses

Macau is the road surface, which besides being pretty variable also tends to have muck left on it from cars and trucks, not to mention that they don't always remove all the animal droppings that get there one way or another.

'Mind you, they've cleaned up the piggeries recently, though coming from a farm area myself, that never bothered me as much as it did some other people! The local café just past the start line used to have the restaurant upstairs and the family's own private pigsty below, with all the oinking and ponging going on underneath. Being the only place near the pits where you could get a sandwich and a cold drink between races when they used to run both legs on the same day, you either held your nose or went hungry!

'They've cleaned that up now, but in a way it's a pity, because it was all part of the atmosphere which makes Macau unique. People liken the race to the Monaco GP, which is correct, but now the town's getting like Monte Carlo too, with all the skyscrapers and new hotels and suchlike. When I first went there in 1977 there were only two hotels of any repute, one of which was actually of ill-repute—the Sintra, which had a brothel in it! Needless to say, the European riders were always booked in there. . . . Now there's half a dozen new

hotels and more going up each year, yet you still have your heart in your mouth when you arrive to check in, hoping that a car team hasn't shown up with twice as many hangers-on as they expected and bribed the manager to let them have your rooms!'

Though exactly twice as long as the Mediterranean circuit, Macau's Guia course resembles the Monaco GP track in more ways than just its location. Both circuits fall into two halves, with a fast series of straights beside the sea, before the road dives up into the narrow streets of the hillside town, to twist and turn its way back to the start of the seafront section again. How did Mick plot his way round the Oriental round-the-houses circuit—and having raced both two- and four-stroke machines there, which was most suited to the unique demands of the track?

'For a while the big four-stroke F1 Suzuki and Hondas were the thing to have, but then the 500 cc GP bikes improved so that they were just as fast, but a lot less of a handful round the back section,' he says. 'Last time I raced the F1 bike there was in 1982, and I was pretty exhausted at the end of the second leg after lugging it around the tighter corners. By contrast, the next year I set up a new lap record on the 500 when I won the second heat from Ron on the works Honda: unfortunately he'd opened up a big gap by taking the first heat while I was still getting the bike dialled in. You might expect the four-stroke would be the best bet, because of its much wider powerband, but the extra weight cancels all that out. Really, the old Kawasaki triple was ideal, with all its mid-range torque.

'Anyway, on a flying lap you get the best bit first, which is the high-speed right-hander just past the pits, called Yacht Club Bend. They've built a new hotel on the outside now, so you can no longer see round it—this makes it even more daunting than before, if that's possible. You're now approaching a flat-out corner hard on in top gear with what looks like a solid wall in front of you, and believe me when I say it takes a big deep breath to actually get round there as fast as you should, no matter how good a rider you are.

'I remember the last time I rode the big four-stroke Suzuki at Macau in 1982, I felt sure I could take Yacht Club flat out in top. So I tried it in practice, and just completely lost the front end doing so. To this day, I don't know how I stayed on: everything was on the deck, but somehow I stayed aboard and didn't come off—definitely my closest shave in bike racing. It's one of those corners where

The aptly-named Hospital Hill

each time you go through, you kick yourself afterwards because you're sure you could have done it quicker. On the 500 GP bike, I approach it flat out in sixth, stay tucked under the screen but just ease it for a fraction, take that deep breath, then get back on the throttle again. Definitely one of the most testing corners of any circuit I've ever raced on—it feels like 200 mph, but realistically I suppose you're doing 160–165 mph through it, and there aren't many circuits in the world nowadays where there's such a demanding corner that you take that fast.'

How did Mick gear for Macau: was it as high as the Isle of Man? 'Not quite, in spite of that long run along the seafront, and Yacht Club Bend is the reason for that. Round the back I've always found that with the RG500, being very torquey, standard

American champion Randy Renfrow cranks his RS500 Honda through Moorish Hill en route to third place overall in the 1986 Macau GP. Chasing him is German Superbike ace Peter Rubatto on a 750 Suzuki

gearbox ratios are OK, though you do end up using the clutch a lot because of the many slow bottom-gear corners, and the front wheel spends a lot of time in the air.'

The track's pretty wide along the seafront: did he use all the road on the exit from Yacht Club? 'No, because though there is a lot of runoff, it doesn't pay to drift out too far because of all the dust and bits of rubber the cars leave on the outside of the track. Getting through there is a bit like the school exams: you're glad it's all over, and relieved you did OK. Going along the next part is a bit like the school holidays, though: you can relax and take it easy—but you can't go to sleep, because the right-hander at the end of the Yacht Club Straight, which is called Statue Corner (in front of the wedding-cake Lisboa Hotel, where most of the gambling high-rollers stay) is one of the few corners at Macau where you can go straight on without coming to grief.

'For that reason, Statue is a good place to try to pass someone—but at the same time you have to keep an eye open to make sure nobody's trying to sneak up on you, either! If you leave it too late, you can take the slip road, which will only cost you time,

rather than a trip to the hospital. Touch wood, I've never fallen off at Macau, and it's not a place I'd ever want to. But at the same time, I've lost track of the number of times I've sat it out with someone going down into Statue. It's amazing how quickly you can get round it if you have to!'

It must be difficult judging your braking from such high speed for such a slow corner? 'Very difficult—although it's a very slow corner, it's one you have to commit yourself for. I do use markers at some places, but only for slower turns. Coming down from very high speeds for a first-gear corner, like at Statue or for Sulby Bridge on the Isle of Man, I do find it very difficult to judge the braking distance ideally. It's a real test of ability, as well as of nerves and the old kidology, sitting it out for a corner like that under braking with someone like Roger Marshall or Ron Haslam. We've had a lot of laughs about it afterwards—but at the time you feel there's nothing more important in the whole world!

'I use bottom gear for Statue and come down the middle of the road, which is quite wide on the approach, unless I'm trying to outbrake someone, in which case I'll go for the inside all the way. Then the road narrows quite dramatically, plus there's a lot more armco on both sides of the road than there used to be, for the cars, so I generally end up just tipping my shoulder on the bit that juts out on the inside as I just slip the bike round the apex. The racing line is literally only about six inches wide, so there's not a lot of room; when you see corners like that, you can appreciate how the locals who only race once a year get themselves in such a mess. It requires a lot of experience to judge a corner like Statue correctly, braking from such a high speed even on their slower bikes, then having to funnel off into such a narrow gap.

'Next there's a short squirt under the footbridge across the track, up to this bloody awful junction called San Francisco, after the old army barracks of that name which are on the inside on the right. It's a crossroads with six roads all coming in from different directions, each with its own surfaces and bumps and lumps and angles, yet you have to get the bike cranked hard over to the right and keep the power fairly well on to keep your momentum going up the hill that comes after. Plus there's more high armco on the outside, and always some car or lorry that's dropped its sump there, so you have a couple

of inches of cement dust to contend with— definitely not a place to take liberties with. No question it's my least favourite corner on the circuit, and no wonder they call the next bit Hospital Hill, because a lot of people end up making the trip up it in a white van to the Macau hospital, which is very conveniently situated at the top of the hill on the left!

'Mind you, most of the Brits call it "Spook Hill" instead, because it looks a bit dark and eerie going up there in the back of one of the bicycle rickshaws at night with a bit of drink on, and some poor old boy who looks like Fu Manchu pedalling his heart out to get us home! Anyway, on the 500, I just slip it into third before San Francisco, but ease the throttle

Mick Grant

A group of riders prepare to tackle Faraway Hill in the 1986 GP. Note the absence of any straw bales whatsoever!

going over the bumps and stuff before getting a drive on once I'm pointing up the hill. If the bike's pulling right, it'll go up Spook Hill on the back wheel, because it's quite steep—quite a good sensation, actually. I'll get fifth gear on the way up, and I actually get right round the apex of the right-hander at the top before I knock it, then come down four very quickly. This corner doesn't have a name, but it's absolutely blind, and a real teaser, especially if you don't know your way round very well.'

This unnamed corner marks the start of the twisting round-the-houses section of the circuit, with constant gearchanging on a two-stroke GP

Ron Haslam has won more races at Macau than any other rider. Here he gives the revolutionary ELF3 its maiden race victory in the 1986 event as he lines up to pass German Klaus Klein, on a 750 Suzuki, on the exit from the tight Melco Hairpin

bike, many short squirts from one first-gear corner to another, and all the time the constant surroundings of unprotected stone walls and the usual solid furniture of city streets. Back to Mick Grant: 'I come down four gears very quickly to bottom and brake hard for the left-hander after the fast right, which also doesn't have a name but does have a high stone wall covered with creeper on the outside. The road's really narrow here, and then there's a short squirt down to Maternity Bend, another tight right with the local hospital for expectant mums beside the track. I'll get up to second then down again to bottom on the 500, but you've got to be extra careful because there's a surface change in the middle of Maternity, and since you're going so slowly, when the power does come in it can be quite vicious.

'I remember the second time I won overall, in 1984, I had a great dice with Roger Marshall on the

works Honda in the second heat. I passed him before the start of the last lap, but I must admit he surprised me by getting past me again at Statue the last time. Coming out of Maternity I thought we were both down: he got the power on a touch too hard and too early, and the Honda came round so far it was literally almost broadside on to me, yet because the track's so narrow there, I couldn't get by him because his bike was taking up all the road! He sorted it out somehow, but we were both almost off a couple of times that lap before I finally squeezed past him at Fishermans, three corners from the finish; it was a grand scrap!'

After Maternity, the road heads out towards the China Sea—but about 200 ft up with only a low stone wall protecting the outside of the corniche road. Next come the Solitude Esses, a series of four corners with Teddy Yip's car team's garage on the left—one of my own Macau memories was of seeing the mechanics clad in bright red Marlboro overalls interrupting their work on the team's race cars to follow the bike GP: did Mick notice that too? 'Yes, but I also noticed that the times I was well out in the lead, they'd give up and go back to preparing the cars, but if there was a close dice for first place,

Macau's building boom in evidence at Melco Hairpin, as Eero Hyvarinen's 500 Honda leads Kenny Irons and Steve Parrish, both on 750 Yamahas, and Ernst Gschwender's Suzuki 750 in the 1986 GP

like between me and Roger that time, they'd stop there till the end. You could always tell how far you were in front by how much interest they displayed!

'Anyway, you come out of Maternity on the back wheel, so long as there's no sideways Honda in front of you, and I just get third gear before the left-hander leading into the Solitude Esses. This is a very deceptive corner, and a lot longer than it seems from the map, but with only one narrow line round it. I come down to second and peel off quite late for it, then I short-shift into fourth, off the power, for the Solitude Esses themselves, simply getting through the double left/right as best I can, standing on the footpegs and swinging the bike from side to side under me, just barely in the powerband and without any heroics at all. Then the road straightens out and I can get on the power again going downhill round the long left-hander at Faraway Hill. But then you have to brake quite hard for the next sharp right, which is the start of Moorish Hill. I take this in bottom, but you have to be careful again putting on the power on the way out, this time because the road is usually pretty dirty from all the vehicles that come in and out of the police workshops on the right, plus the next little straight is quite heavily shaded from trees and so forth and there's always a few leaves on the track, which all makes it very slippery, to say the least. I've had my fair share of slides there—definitely a place to approach with caution.'

Moorish Hill is pretty steep: does the RG500 get out of bottom gear before the unnamed but very tight right-hander at the end? 'Only just. I'll get second, but then down almost at once for the next corner. The surface is much better here, so you wheelie coming out, then go up to third for the next part, which isn't so much a straight as more of a long, curving left-hand approach to Dona Maria Bend. For some reason this is a mini-Daytona: it's quite heavily banked, so in spite of being pretty tight, you can actually get round it quite fast, with the bike cranked over at an amazing angle. Again it's first gear, then a short blast up into third again, straight-lining the downhill approach to Melco Hairpin, where the road suddenly widens quite a bit at the last moment, so there are several different lines of approach. It's always difficult braking downhill, which you have to do here, though you have the consolation of knowing it's the only other place on the course at Macau besides Statue where you can go straight on if necessary, into a sort of courtyard which they keep clear for you just in case. Mind you, the real worry is not to overbrake and lock up the front wheel, which always seems to happen to a couple of people. As hairpins go, Melco's the tightest I know apart, perhaps, from Governor's Bridge at the Isle of Man—and that includes anything at Scarborough, too! I've only ever had my foot down there once, which was on the old F1 Suzuki. That was a bit short of steering lock, but I can honestly say I reckon the sense of balance I got from trials riding helped in getting round here in one piece.'

Melco Hairpin marks the end of the street section of the Guia circuit. Is it all a series of quick blasts back to Statue Corner from now on? 'Sort of, though coming out of Melco there's a left/right jink which may not look like much on the map, but is quite pronounced on the bike. I use a lot of clutch coming out of the hairpin, even though the exit is quite steeply downhill, then short-shift into third to keep everything nice and steady through the jink. After that, you cram it on hard down to the seafront,

past the duck farms on the left, where tomorrow's dinner is still probably quacking around in the mud!

'Fishermans Bend is a 90-degree right with a narrow approach where the road's pretty bumpy and rough, and I actually brake on a particular bump about one-third over from the left, which is a good marker. The important thing here is to brake as hard and as late as you can, so you can get the power on again as soon as possible for the next bit, which is the first of the fast seafront straights. I just get into top coming down the hill from Melco, then come down to second for Fishermans, get off the brakes before I lay it in, drive through the corner and up into fifth gear along the quite useful straight beside the sea to what they call R Bend—I've no notion what the "R" is for.

'This is the bend where in 1982 Digger [Wayne Gardner] passed me on the way in without the benefit of a front brake on the big Honda four-stroke—the master cylinder had broken off in his hand! I couldn't believe how much faster than me he was going, and for a minute I thought it was me that was going too slowly. Then when he laid it down in front of me, I knew who was doing the right thing! Ironically, this was the first year they'd put up armco on the exit to stop you going in the sea, which was quite a regular occurrence before, especially for the cars—over the cobblestones they used to go, then splash! He'd probably have been better off doing that—I mean, most Aussies can swim, can't they?—but as it was, he was lucky to escape with just a sprained wrist.

'Anyway, if you take R Bend upright, it's very much a do-or-die effort on the brakes, so you can get the power on early again for the next bit. It's quite bumpy on the way out, so like on most road circuits like the TT or North-West, I avoid using all the road. The classical GP line isn't always the right one on circuits like these, where it's more important to avoid the bumps and get the power down early than observe the ideal outside/inside/outside trajectory. I take R Bend in second, then accelerate hard up through the gears to fifth for Reservoir Bend, which after all I've just said is the one corner at Macau where you should earhole it, short-circuit style. It's very fast, taken in fourth gear on the 500, and though it's not as fast as Yacht Club, it's just as important because it governs your top speed down the first part of the main straight: you have to line it up dead right and go through hard on the power as fast as you can. However, this time you can see round a fair bit, because there are only spectator banks on the outside, a bit like at Assen, rather than

Mick Grant sweeps into R Bend by the South China Sea on his last-ever race in a famous career, at Macau in 1985 on the Heron Suzuki 500

a solid wall, so it's not quite so daunting. Then you're up into top, past where we get our signals, and it's time for another deep breath in time for Yacht Club Bend again.'

In view of the generally excellent standard of organization, does Mick think Macau should ever become a round of the TT F1 world championship, or suchlike? 'Definitely not. For one thing, the race can stand on its own feet, and for another it wouldn't be fair on the privateers who had to pay their way over and back. But I think it would spoil the whole atmosphere of what is basically a fun race, even if some of us take it a bit more seriously than others. I go really because I like the place itself

so much; you can keep Hong Kong, which is much too commercialized, whereas I suppose Macau is the way Hong Kong was 30 or 40 years ago. It's a place we can go to race at the end of the season and enjoy ourselves, even if a couple of the lads went a sight too far in 1985 and got themselves arrested for throwing a firecracker into one of the brothels. My worst experience there? Nothing to do with the racing, but going out for dinner with some of our local friends once and having the usual eight-course Chinese dinner by the harbour in one of those places with a tin roof and a dirt floor. One of the courses was frogs' legs, which I quite liked, but a couple of dishes later I was daft enough to say, as a sort of joke, that I was glad they hadn't given us the rest of the frog as well. "Don't be so sure," my Portuguese friend said to me with a smile, "you've just eaten it!" That's Macau!'

Ron Haslam—Duke of Donington

Rocket Ron—equally at home on two or eight wheels

Donington Park would never have become a racing circuit in the first place if not for the efforts of one single-minded and determined man, Fred Craner, who in 1931 persuaded the Shields family to permit a race meeting to be held on the perimeter paths of their Midlands estate. Nor, conversely, would Donington exist today, reborn and flourishing as one of Europe's premier racetracks, other than for the stubborn determination of another such achiever, Leicester building magnate Tom Wheatcroft. More than any other circuit in this book, Donington's existence is owed to a single individual—and not once, but twice over, at that.

Fred Craner was a former bike racer whose enthusiasm to see motorcycle racing take place around the grounds of the stately home persuaded Donington Park's then owner, Mr J. G. Shields, to permit an initial meeting to be held along a two-mile gravel course on Whit Monday in 1931. Though paradoxically officially in Leicestershire, Donington in fact lies 20 miles from Leicester but only six from Derby and 12 from Nottingham, yet its proximity to these large towns doubtless helped explain the massive crowd of over 20,000 which watched the six races, embracing 58 riders, run at that inaugural meeting. Its success was such that the organizers

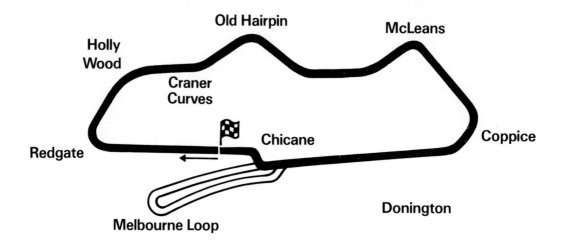

swiftly ran out of tickets, from then on, entrance fees were collected in washbasins to help speed up the huge traffic jams which resulted! In view of the nature of the track surface, it was not perhaps surprising that speedway ace Squib Burton dominated the day's proceedings on his 350 Raleigh. However, by the August Bank Holiday meeting in 1932, by which time the leading riders of the day were now Donington regulars, the path track was surfaced with tarmac throughout, raising speeds from Burton's first lap record of 46.5 mph to more than 60 mph. That winter, many alterations were made, resulting in the emergence of a 2.19-mile circuit broadly similar to that in use today, but with the start just before what is now the Old Hairpin. In 1933 the first car race meeting was held, though in pre-war days Donington was always primarily a bike circuit, and until the advent in 1937 of London's Crystal Palace track, from similar path-racing origins, Donington was the only road-racing circuit on the British mainland, and consequently heavily used for testing and suchlike. Its location in the Midlands, heart of the British car and bike industry, made it invaluable.

In 1934 the circuit was altered again, with a short extension built at the end of the main straight, and a new corner, Redgate, used to rejoin the old course; the start was relocated to just before this new bend, though the paddock was still rather inconveniently located outside the Old Hairpin, near the Shields'

domain which now took in paying guests from the wealthier teams for bed and breakfast. The new circuit measured 2.55 miles, but in 1938 it was further extended to a distance of 3.13 miles by the addition of a steep drop down to the 180-degree Melbourne Corner, before rejoining the pit straight again. This was done primarily to host the four-wheel car GPs, starring the all-conquering Mercedes and Auto-Union teams, in 1938–39, but it also brought a lesser-chronicled benefit to the bike world, in the form of the first British motorcycle GP, in August 1939. With the war storms gathering, it was surprising that the German DKW factory would have sent a supercharged 250 cc machine with which Ernie Thomas won his class at the meeting, with Freddie Frith pulling off a 350/500 cc double. A week or so later, the world was plunged into war, and Donington was requisitioned by the British War Office, who erected dozens of 'temporary' buildings, many of which are still in use today—just as at Brooklands—and used the circuit as an enormous vehicle park, with new access and other roads defacing the site.

A slightly fraught moment for Paul Iddon on the Krauser-BMW (no. 21) when he discovers that his gearbox has just blown in the middle of Redgate Corner on the first lap of a BoTT race. Amazingly, nobody hit him, but Rob Sewell on the John Player Norton (no. 149) must have had a narrow miss

Riders stream down Craner Curves into the Old Hairpin at the start of an international 350 cc race. Looks like Tom Wheatcroft made money on this one!

Desultory efforts were made after the war to reclaim Donington for motor sport, but the bureaucrats managed to fend off all attempts until they were faced with the massive will and determination of millionaire builder and car enthusiast Tom Wheatcroft, whose uphill battle against all the odds eventually saw the circuit reopen in only slightly modified form in 1977, under his control. Appropriately, that first meeting was for motorcycles, on the 'new' 1.97-mile circuit; to bring the circuit up to required length for car and bike GPs, Wheatcroft added a further extension in 1985 to further his claims for at least a share of the two major British motor sporting events, so that it now measures 2.1 miles and is generally reckoned to be the safest British racing circuit of the present day.

Though several riders, many of them locals, shared bike racing honours at Donington before the war, there is no disputing the man who, since racing resumed at the Midlands track, has made

Donington Park his domain: Ron Haslam. At first mounted on the Pharoah Yamahas of sponsor Mal Carter, then as long-serving member of the Honda Britain race team, Rocket Ron comes, as TV and circuit commentators have never refrained from pointing out, from nearby Langley Mill, a Nottinghamshire mining village only 15 miles or so away from the circuit. With literally dozens of victories on almost every kind of motorcycle to his credit at Donington Park over the years, it would seem likely that it is Ron's favourite racetrack. Is it?

'Yes, it must be,' says Ron, without hesitation. 'I've always gone particularly well there ever since I had my first ride at Donington on a TZ750 Yamaha at that first meeting in 1977. I won the main race and set up the first lap record for the new circuit that day, and to be honest I've not really looked back there since. Obviously the fact that it's my local track and I've done lots of testing there over the years helps—I've even driven my late brother's LCR "worm" outfit there, though I had trouble remembering not to follow the solo racing line and run the sidecar wheel over the grass: I spun it once in the Mallory Esses because of that, and the passenger said if I'd been a couple of inches further over he'd have been climbing a tree! Plus coming from just up the road means the Donington crowd has always seemed to give me that little extra boost that can make a big difference to your performance on the day, and I must say too that I've always been very fairly treated by the organizers over the years. I really admire Tom Wheatcroft for his professionalism and what he's put back into the sport. Even getting Donington going again at all was a terrific feat, but ever since that first meeting he's gone on improving the place all the time. I think it's shocking that after all he's done for bike racing, the ACU took so long to give him even a share of the bike GP, at least every other year. It's a much better circuit for motorcycles than Silverstone was.'

How does Ron rate the circuit as such? 'That's why I like it so much—it's safe, reasonably fast and quite tricky, but if you do come off it's most unlikely you'll hurt yourself badly, because they've put a lot of thought into runoff areas and such. Yet in spite of that you've got to keep thinking and working the

Kenny Roberts on the factory Yamaha 500 sweeps out of the Old Hairpin in 1981

whole lap, instead of just getting behind the screen and trying to get the most on top end all the time like at Silverstone.'

Apart from his three-wheeled forays, Ron Haslam has ridden a huge variety of solos at Donington, from those privateer 350/750 Yamahas to the NR500 four-stroke GP Honda in testing, and CB1100R production Hondas to the modern NS500 GP triple. How would he approach a lap of the 'old new' circuit, before the installation of the latest extension, on the GP two-stroke with which he tied for fourth place in the 1985 World 500 cc Championship with Honda Britain team-mate Wayne Gardner, as well as starring in the defeat of the US team by the British Commonwealth squad, of which he was the leader, in the 1985 Transatlantic Challenge at Donington?

'Well, believe it or not, all the years I've raced at Donington, I still don't know all the names of the corners,' admits Ron sheepishly. However, even he does own up to knowing possibly the most famous corner on the circuit, the first one after the start line which is located on Wheatcroft Straight: Redgate Corner. A tight right-hander named after the lodge of the same name which once served as a gateway

to the old estate, Redgate has been the scene of several spectacular first-corner tangles; what has been Ron's recipe for avoiding these over the years, as he has indeed managed to do—apart from concentrating on the lightning starts which have justly earned him his nickname?

'Starts at Donington are a problem,' says Ron. 'Some riders swear they always go up the inside, then when I've looked at a race on telly afterwards, I see them running on to the grass on the outside to avoid someone who fell off on the inside of them! It all depends on the start you get. I do get good starts more often than not, so if I'm first away, no problem—always go for the inside, because then everyone else has to go round you. Then if someone does try to do that under braking, you'll see them; soon as you see them, accelerate a bit to try to stop them—in other words, play for the first corner. On the other hand, if you have a bad start and find yourself at the back, then you must go round the outside, because everyone else is busy diving for

The ebullient Graeme Crosby pleasing the crowd as usual on the 1000 cc Yoshimura Suzuki on the short straight between McLeans and Coppice

the inside. When that happens, you get a road block, so best thing is to take a risk and go round the long way, because otherwise you've lost contact with the leaders and you'll probably never catch up. You are taking a chance, it's true, because if anyone comes down in the pack you'll probably get mixed up with it somehow—but then you've already made your mistake by getting off to a bad start, so if you do end up paying for it that way, you've only yourself to blame. But at least you have a chance of making up for it if you go for the outside.'

On a flying lap, though, how would Ron line up for Redgate Corner? 'Down the straight on a flying run, I gradually cross over to the left of the track, and use the pit road, where you actually filter back on to the circuit after leaving the pits, as my braking point. I pick up the end of the wall, and depending on how well I'm going and on the surface conditions, I'll either brake just on that marker or maybe go a little bit past it. I'd just be getting fifth on the NS triple down past the pits with the old chicane, not hard on but just into it and out again, down to second gear for Redgate, braking hard all the time in a straight line. However, I won't get second straight away, else the bike will over-rev, because the approach is very quick, and you're filtering into the corner. So you have to take your time, and I'll collect second just as I'm about to peel off.

'Funny thing about Redgate, but just where you rush in there's a place where the cars especially turn off into the paddock on the left. Exactly on that spot, it's very slippery and you'll always lose your front wheel if you don't watch it—probably it's all the oil and rubber that's been laid down, especially by cars that pull off the circuit in practice to go into the paddock after they've got a mechanical problem. So as I lay it in, just as I get to that spot I ease up a little bit, just enough to stop the front wheel stepping out. In a hard race, it's quite common to see someone coming down on the second lap or so at Redgate, because they're really trying a bit too hard and forgot to watch out for that slippy patch on the way in.'

Which brings up the most contentious aspect of racing at the reborn Donington Park circuit—its notoriously tricky surface which has sent many a rider sliding off towards 'Uncle Tom's Sandpits' for no apparent reason. Almost from the first the track surface has been controversial, some claiming the circuit's location directly under the flight path of aircraft taking off from nearby East Midlands Airport is to blame, believing aviation fuel dropped from the planes is the culprit. Others ascribe the undoubted

The leaders in one of the 1984 Transatlantic
Match Races round Coppice Corner: Mike Baldwin's
RS500 Honda (no. 43), Eddie Lawson's V4 Yamaha
(no. 4), and Rob McElnea's XR40 Suzuki (no. 15).
Freddie Spencer on the NSR500 Honda, later to crash
at Redgate, is just behind McElnea

problem to rubber and oil deposited over the years, especially by cars, which have become embedded in the surface, while out of the many esoteric rationales, my own favourite is the local moss which is supposed to grow on the tarmac and swells up when it rains, leaving the track greasy long after it should have dried! Which of these reasons, if any, does Ron Haslam subscribe to?

'None really, because having ridden on the track continuously since 1977, I've seen what's happened gradually over the years, which is simply that it gets used so much, it's just plain worn out. When they first laid the surface down, it was really unusual—nothing like it anywhere. I rode it when it was brand-new, and couldn't come to terms with it at all easily. See, there was a drainage system in it, whereby the water drained down into gaps in the surface when it rained, so that the tarmac sat up proud of the water—just like a tyre with its drainage grooves, only in reverse. When the track was new, this idea worked a treat, though it was super hard on tyres—in the dry, you had to run the hardest compound slick there was, and even then the tyre would go off before the end of a 15-lapper and you'd come in with the tyre looking like it had had a

tread pattern carved in it; the surface would just rip them to shreds. But in the wet—well, it could be raining cats and dogs, and you'd never have to use rain tyres: intermediates were fine, because there was so much grip. The moment it stopped raining, you could fit a slick on the back—I mean literally the very moment, because no matter how much rain had come down, the track would have got rid of it.

'So to begin with, the circuit was fine, but then over the years it just got used so much, especially with cars and the trucks on it, that the surface gradually wore down and the edge went off it. Plus the gaps in the surface where the rain was supposed to drain got filled up with rubber and other muck—maybe the moss as well, though I'm not a gardener myself!—so that now in the wet the effect's quite the opposite of what it was originally: it's fantastically slippery and you must be very, very careful because even a slight shower can make the bike almost unridable in places with a slick tyre.

'Mind you, it's an ill wind that blows no one any good, because the thing is that there are actually some parts of the circuit which are still quite grippy in the wet, because they're off the four-wheeled racing line and haven't got polished up to the same extent as the rest. So someone who knows Donington well, like myself, has a big advantage in the wet, because we know where the good and bad bits are. For example, soon as it starts raining even a little, you treat the Chicane and Redgate as if you're riding on ice—it's that slippery there. Yet on most other parts of the circuit, it's OK to really lay it over,

Roger Marshall with the 998 Suzuki (no. 11) leads Ron Haslam's 1128 Honda (no. 2) at the Donington chicane in a televised race in April 1982, with Randy Mamola riding a 500 Suzuki and emerging-star Wayne Gardner's 1128 Honda close behind

so long as you're careful and avoid the worst patches—like in the middle of the Old Hairpin, for instance. So a newcomer, like the foreigners who come over for the internationals, or specially the endurance racing crowd when they had the 1000 km races there—he'd get to Redgate first lap in the rain, put the power on, get a huge slide that almost chucks him off—and that's him good as finished for the day. In his mind, the circuit's like glass all the way round—except it isn't! I reckon that's another reason to give Donington the Grand Prix—the top British riders all know their way round there backwards, which then gives them the same sort of advantage the Continentals have on the tracks they hold their GPs on. We didn't get to race at Silverstone except at the GP, so it was no advantage to us, quite apart from the fact that it's a power circuit and dead boring.'

So much for the dreaded track surface: back to Redgate—in the dry! What are Ron's lines on a flying lap, given that there is a choice between peeling off late up the outside or going in early to the inside? Is the late line, especially favoured by

Barry Sheene when he used to race there, the favourite move? 'Not really, because if you let someone nip inside you by taking the outside, your paths will cross in the middle of the exit and if he knows what he's doing, he'll knock you down to his speed, and it's very difficult to change line under power to avoid him, because the track surface is so slippy.

'If I know I have someone behind me, I always go down the middle of the road into Redgate, which apart from the chicane is really the only good place to pass at Donington, so most people make a big effort there to steal up the inside under braking. If I see that happening, I'll close the door by moving over on them, but not too tight else it makes the apex too sharp and I'll lose speed. Otherwise, if I'm on my own, Sheene's right—go in wide, take a big sweep at it, so you come out fast and get the power on quicker by being more or less upright early. I don't use a marker for peeling off here, just rely on my experience of the corner.'

Ron's cornering style must be the most distinctive amongst modern-day GP riders—flat on the tank, head cocked sideways under the screen, body moulded to the side of the bike and knee dragging the ground: did he consciously develop it? 'Not really—I just always tried to keep myself tucked away as much as possible in my early days, and as I started riding bigger and faster bikes, it sort of stuck.

The 500 GP bikes are so powerful nowadays, you mostly use the screen to stop yourself being blown off the back, anyway—well, not exactly, but almost. You think that, till you find yourself flat out down a long straight on the Honda triple and Spencer or Lawson comes breezing past with a few extra mph and bhp in hand on their four-cylinder bike! That made me try to tuck myself in even tighter, I can tell you.'

On a quick bike, there is not really much straight at all between Redgate and the first part of the Craner Curves, named Holly Wood; this essentially follows the pre-war course, but with literally acres of grassed runoff area replacing the sturdy stone gate pillars which pre-war Donington daredevils used to brush with their shoulders as they raced towards the Hairpin, as the tight right-hander by the entrance to the manor house was known then. Is this bit as hard work as it seems—judging by the number of riders who have displayed a sudden interest in collecting soil samples just here, including the unfortunate Tony Head on the works Waddon 250 who once gracefully unloaded on the warm-up lap of a televised race in full view of the cameras!

'It can be,' says Ron, 'because you take the whole section from Redgate onwards as a series of fast swoops where it's vital to match your line to your speed. Plus the top of Craners is a bit slippery even in the dry, so I tend not to take it as fast as I could, because the road also falls away to the left a bit. On top of that, the left-hander comes up on you a bit sudden, so if you take the right at the top too fast, it'll put you wrong for the left, and even more wrong for the Old Hairpin, which comes next. On a big bike, like the old 1-litre F1 Honda, you'll be struggling to get from one side to the other.

'So what I do is to come out of Redgate in second, go up through the gears to fourth, then short-shift into fifth on the NS500 at the top of Craner, so it's smoother going down the hill, not using all the power which would tend to unsettle you. Then I ease it going into the right-hander, which gives me the time to pull it over to swoop over to the left, and puts me on the right line for the Hairpin. I'm not a ballroom dancer, but this seems about the same sort of thing on a bike—slow, quick, quick is the way you get through this bit best. You have to sacrifice in one corner to gain in the next two. I like circuits which make you do that, rather than go everywhere flat out, all the time.

'Line is critical here too. Because it's slippery at the top and the road falls away, I tend to take the right very tight—knee in the grass, sort of thing. Then I follow the edge all the way down, much further than I would normally, before peeling off into the left. The reason I do this is that the road here is very much off-camber, and if you drift too far over to the left so that you have to take the left-hander tight in, you'll end up having to physically turn the front wheel to the left to get round there, which generally results in it tucking in and you landing on your ear.' Sounds like that is what happened to the unfortunate Tony Head? 'Yes. What you have to do is try to make a series of big sweeps, rather than apex the corners normally.'

Next comes the Old Hairpin, a right-hander in the bottom of the dip before the track starts climbing again through Coppice Wood—not much of which remains today—and under the long-gone Starkeys Bridge. 'It's funny that,' says Ron. 'The bridge hasn't

Ron Haslam

Hectic action at the chicane in the 1984 Match Races. Barry Sheene on a Suzuki leads the Honda-mounted trio of Wayne Gardner, Freddie Spencer and Wes Cooley

been there for ages, yet we all still talk about going up the hill under the bridge! Anyway, I come down two gears to third only for the Old Hairpin—it's quite a fast corner, in fact—braking as I cross over to the left unless I've decided to nip past someone by shooting up past him on the right, and then cutting across in front for the corner—it's the only other place you can really pass safely. I lay it in hard at the beginning, starting to make another big sweep of it, but then I remember to ease up a good bit in the middle of the corner where there's a real slippery patch, before laying it hard over again on the way out, so as to stop running out too wide on the exit. I try not to drift out as far as the rough marker strips on the outside of the track surface, but it doesn't matter if I do end up running over them—you don't lose any time; it's just a bit bumpy, but depending on my speed down the hill and how late I've braked, it might be unavoidable.

'Coming out I get fourth, then short-shift into fifth for "under the bridge", which basically is a long, long left-hander climbing up the hill away from the Hairpin. This is another long swoop, but as you lay it in, there's a big dip in the road where a lot of folk also lose it and blame the track surface. Instead of easing off to stop the back wheel stepping out, I short-shift into fifth which takes you off the peak powerband and has the same effect, except I can keep the throttle twisted full open earlier, because there's not so much power at the back wheel. On the NS500 the real powerband was from 10,000 rpm to about 11,500, but with the triple ATAC system it'd pull OK from 8000 revs which was just right. Hitting fifth early here means the engine's doing about 9000 rpm, just right so that by the time I'm ready for the extra power, it's coming on tap.'

Is the next part to McLeans, the right-hander at the top of the hill, taken as a straight line, near as

Ron Haslam's distinctive style displayed on the Honda Britain NS500 triple at the Donington chicane in 1985

possible? 'No—it's all one great long sweep. Really, you could say that the section from Redgate to McLeans is all a series of Esses; there isn't really a single piece of road you could call a straight line, just a whole series of swoops where rhythm is all-important. With McLeans, the trouble is that it's partly blind and you can never get far enough over to the left as you'd like; best you'll get is the middle of the road, because the little right-hand kink before it throws you off. Just as I come round the kink I start braking very hard, coming down through the gears to second. It actually takes quite an effort to do this corner right, because you have to pull the bike upright coming round the kink to be able to brake as hard as you need to do. It's a very underrated corner that not many people take as well as they might—they just get through as best they can, but if you really attack it you can save some time there, and the surface is quite good, though a little bumpy on the apex now.'

Next comes a corner where perhaps too many people have tried too hard: Coppice, scene of many a tumble into the straw bales and sandpit. 'That's right,' says Ron. 'I visited it myself once, some time back on the big four-stroke Honda, but it was quite a funny story. I was first away and after about half a dozen laps I had a good lead and was just stroking it to the finish, when I came down the little straight into the dip before Coppice to find yellow flags everywhere, so I slowed right down to see what was happening. I saw a couple of other riders sitting on the fence, nothing in the track, but even so I was just creeping round when—*bang*, down I go on my ear. I was hardly going any speed, so I didn't slide far, and by the time the next bloke comes along, I was on the fence myself wondering why I'd come off. Then he went down, just like me, dead slow, on his ear. Every lap a couple more would come off, pick themselves up and wander over to join us all on the fence—I'm afraid it got to be a big joke by the time there were nine or ten of us, and we were taking bets on who would be next. What was wrong was that the first guy's fuel tank had split just over the brow of the hill when he came down, and you literally couldn't see the patch till you hit it, even though the marshals had done their best to clear it up. We had a good laugh about it, especially since nobody was even slightly hurt.'

But a lot of people come off at Coppice even on a clean and dry track: why? 'It's the hill that does it,' says Ron. 'The classic thing that happens is that you go rushing up there on the left, then lay it over for the corner before the top of the hill, as you have to

do, but forget the front wheel's gone all light because you're cresting a rise, and lose the front end. Gary Lingham did that in front of me in the 1985 Transatlantic: his front wheel just pulled away from under him, not because the road was slippery or anything, but because he forgot he was coming over the top of a hill on a powerful, light bike and had to turn right before he was over the brow.

'What I do is to come out of McLeans and stay on the left, get up into fourth in the dip then back to third. I stay on the left-hand side till very late, by which time I'm almost at the top of the hill leading into Coppice and can even start to see the apex. Then I pitch it in, but not very hard, though as I do so I'm cutting across the track, which means I'm getting rid of the brow. Then when I see I'm almost over the top, I'll lay it in real hard, use all the tyre, and that way I'll not have lost any ground or have the front wheel walk away from me. I get fourth gear again just as I come out, ready to clip the grass with my knee on the little right-hand kink on the way out, leading on to the main straight. Just there is another little dip, which you can actually use to your advantage, because once you get to know where it is, you can get the rear wheel spinning on it quite safely, though the first time it happens to you, you'll get a surprise and sit up. But once you know it's only the dip in the road doing that, because the rear wheel is going all light as you hit the dip cranked well over, you can start to correct the slide in advance, just by getting a bit of opposite steering on at the right moment. What happens then is that the rear wheel lights up, then when it grips again, it really fires you off down the straight—believe me, it can give you quite an initial advantage over someone alongside who hasn't built up his wheel speed that way.'

There are more dips down the main straight as well, aren't there—some of which seem to produce quite spectacular wheelies for the unwary? 'That's right,' says Ron. 'It seems like you're riding on ocean waves, on a fast bike, but I use that to my advantage, too. I go down the straight about six feet out from the left verge, and I'm still in fourth just before the first dip. But then instead of coming over the crest at peak revs, which would send the front wheel into the air, I snatch the next gear just before the crest, which drops the front wheel just as it's starting to come up. Then as it drops, I hit top gear, which fires me harder down the other side. You are changing up early, it's true, but if you didn't you'd have to back off anyway, else you'd get a big wheelie.'

Chop! Classic racing can be just as cut-throat as the modern stuff, as demonstrated here by the evergreen Kiwi Hugh Anderson, seen closing the door on American Dave Roper's similar Matchless G50 in the 1986 Classic Race of the Year. The venue is the new Chicane, adopted after the Melbourne Loop was opened that year to bring the Donington track up to full GP minimum length

The main straight at Donington, called Starkeys Straight after the local name for the hill on which that side of the circuit is built, is the only place on the modern track where most bikes will get top gear. Before the new extension took riders through a chicane near the end and off down the Melbourne Loop, the circuit provided one of the most gripping sights in British racing, as riders sat it out under braking for the much faster old Chicane, one of the main passing places on the circuit but now sadly removed from the track plan. The fact that, according to Ron Haslam, it was also the most slippery place of all on a circuit not noted for its traction, made it even more of a nail-biter for most riders, especially with the finish line just 100 yards or so past the exit of the right/left Chicane: how did he tackle it?

'No matter who you were, if you were leading on the last lap with someone just behind you, it was guaranteed he'd try to come up the inside of you,' says Ron. 'No matter how late you braked, they'd match it—it was the normal move. So on the last lap, you'd always take a tighter line than normal, which meant they'd go for the wide line up the outside, for the run coming out. You'd have mucked yourself about going in so as to stop him creeping up the inside of you, so he'd have a chance of outaccelerating you to the line by doing that. It was a real cat-and-mouse game, though mostly if you led into the chicane, you should have won, so long as you didn't mess it up in the middle, usually by going in too deep on the right-hander before laying it over.

'If it wasn't the last lap, though, I'd come down the left-hand side of the track, pick my braking point by the dips in the road, come down to second and pitch it in real hard just before the kerb starts, lay it a long way over and power on gradually out. Usually I'd have to lift my right knee up and over the kerb to avoid hitting it, I'd be that close in, then the same the other side after flipping it over in the middle of the chicane. Since that was the fast line by a long way, as you'd expect, anybody just behind you would always make a big effort up the inside. Because of this, some riders, and particularly Randy Mamola, used to do something very risky, which is to go into the chicane on a tight line at first to discourage anyone coming up the inside of them, then just before they got there they'd pull over to the left to get more or less back on the normal line and keep their speed up into the chicane. I didn't hold with that, because if the bloke behind can't come up the inside, which he's been shut out of doing, then he's got to be going up the outside and has a good chance of getting clobbered when the one in front moves over, away from his committed line. I wouldn't say it was dirty riding so much as stupid—if he's a hard case, the bloke on the outside won't give way, and there'll be a collision, and it wouldn't be his fault, either.'

Donington appears to be a very physical circuit, with precious little time for any rest on a fast bike. 'It might seem so, but really once you start lapping quick you find it's all a question of rhythm and flow. You can tell riders who've raced there a lot: they get a nice swing going down the hill at the Craners, letting one corner flow into the next one. That's my favourite part of the circuit—I like the swinging back and forth and the sense of rhythm you get from doing it right. Riding the endurance race there in 1981 with Joey [Dunlop] on the big Honda Britain four-stroke was a great memory; I knew before the race that the rhythm we could set up on a big heavy bike like that would be a big advantage in a long race, and it was. We led all the way till the engine blew—real pity, that.' What were the big Honda four-strokes, on which Ron really made his name, like to ride there? 'They were very good, but there were lots more points to watch for. Obviously their wide spread of power cut down on the gearchanging a lot, because they'd pull from almost zero, but their weight distribution meant they pushed the front tyre a lot more, so you had to be extra careful going down Craner Curves and the like. You'd reckon to have the front wheel sliding about everywhere, as well as the back—corners like McLeans you'd take in a controlled two-wheel power drift, which once you got the hang of it was a great sensation. Being big and heavy, the bike would break the tyre away easier, but also more gradually. The modern light bikes with the same power are more difficult to power slide because they snap at you—they aren't so controllable. It took a bit more practice to do that on the NS500, and was even a bit frightening at first, whereas it was quite easy and actually fun to do it on the four-banger. But you did have to be fit to ride them: they were very hard work indeed to get from side to side in the chicane, for instance!'

Did Ron have any special memories of his many races at Donington? 'It's hard to say, really—I've enjoyed most of them. Funnily enough, it was probably a time I didn't win anything I'm most proud of—the 1984 Transatlantic, when I was really trying hard. Even though I fell off at the chicane, where there's a worn patch of tarmac right where you put the power on on the exit that you have to watch out for because it's so smooth and has very little grip, I was very pleased with the way I rode against the Yanks. I gave 101 per cent for six races, and that made me very happy, knowing that I'd really done my best. I've always tried to do that, not just at Donington but all the time I've been racing, but that weekend I felt I rode just about as well as I ever have.'

Dick Mann at Daytona

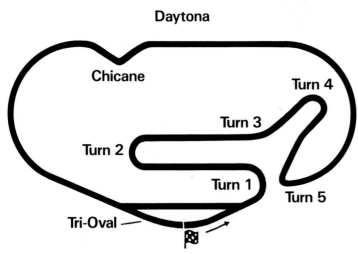

Daytona

As a nation, Americans like to see things in terms of superlatives. Occasionally, just once in a while, such hyperbole is justified: Daytona Beach, Florida, certainly deserves its self-awarded title of the World Centre of Speed. Car and motorcycle manufacturers have implicitly recognized this fact by tagging innumerable models over the years with the 'Daytona' name, password for performance and, yes, speed. The name of the Atlantic coast resort has become synonymous with pure, blinding, flat-out speed on wheels, first on the wide, hard-packed strand which stretches with only the occasional interruption from the Carolinas to Miami, though nowhere so wide nor so straight as at Daytona, then latterly on the purpose-built Daytona International Speedway, whose 32-degree bankings are the steepest in North America.

In half a century of car and bike racing, Daytona has witnessed more drama and history than most other tracks, apart from the Isle of Man, put together. It has also spawned more than its fair share of heroes, few of them comparable with two-time Daytona 200 winner Dick 'Bugs' Mann. Born in 1934 in Utah, the son of Mormon parents, Dick moved to Northern California and made his way to the top of the motorcycle racing scene through sheer hard work and gritty determination. He was

an official rider for more factory teams than anyone except Phil Read, was twice AMA National champion and the first man to score national wins in every kind of AMA event, as well as having raced at Daytona everything from a side-valve Harley on the beach to a TZ700 Yamaha on the banked tri-oval.

A narrow second to Brad Andres on the sand in 1958 and again in 1959 on a Harley, Dick repeated the feat on his beloved G50 Matchless in 1962 on the Speedway road course behind Don Burnett's Triumph. Yet no less than eight years later, he scored the first Daytona 200-mile win on a Japanese bike, setting a new race record average of 102.691 mph on the works CR750 Honda. The following year, at the age of 36, he made it two in a row on a factory Rob North-framed BSA three, upping his race speed to 104.737 mph—a record that was to withstand even the great Jarno

Looking like he can scarcely believe his luck, Dick Mann celebrates the first of his two victories in the Daytona 200-miler, aboard the CR750 Honda in 1970

Saarinen's Yamaha efforts in 1973. Modest to the point of self-effacement, Dick Mann is the doyen of Daytona riders; having raced with success on both beach and banking, who better to tell us about the World Centre of Speed?

'Daytona was never my favourite track,' recalls Dick. 'I liked the old Laconia road-race course best, a real old-fashioned street track that put a premium on riding skill. At Daytona there's only ever been one thing that counted, and that's how fast your motorcycle is. That and how much luck you have, because more than most other tracks, the important thing is to finish before you start figuring out how to win. Both times I won the 200 I did it coming from behind, outlasting other guys who were better riders or had faster bikes, just by running a careful race and changing my game plan as the circumstances of the race altered; 200 miles is a long way, and on such a fast track it's always been a feat just to get your bike to finish the race.'

Back in 1955, when Dick Mann first rode in the Daytona 200 on a privateer BSA Gold Star at the tender age of 20, it seemed that he had already learnt that lesson: he finished seventh, the first BSA home after the trio of factory A7 twins all retired—and in spite of falling off during the race and remounting. What was it like racing on the Beach Course? 'Pretty gruelling! Simple as the course looked, it was actually very rough, and there were a whole lot of factors you had to take into account that were unique to Daytona. We lined up for the start probably seven-eighths of the way back down the beach straightaway, not far from the exit from the South Turn, and in those days there was no official practice, not a single lap—nothing. Your starting position on the grid was chosen by lottery at a meeting the night before, and so you just lined up all across the beach like a motocross start, they dropped the flag, and everyone was away, all 80 or 100 riders in one massed start. Naturally, within two or three hundred yards on a damp beach you just ran into a giant blinding sandstorm of wet sand and water and vapour, but everyone kept right on going, flat out against the stop, mostly navigating by guesswork. If you were lucky enough to be able to see where the North Turn was, you turned left, but usually ten or 15 riders continued on down the beach aways and had to turn round and come back!'

Were the turns banked? 'Slightly, yes, and they were constructed from some clay-type material they brought in from out of state and mixed with the sand so that it packed down into a hard surface that was then blended in with the regular road that ran parallel with the beach. The turns were very tight, about the same radius as a half-mile track or even tighter, but the slight banking let you really keep your speed up once the first lap was over and the field strung out. But of course, all the traffic meant that the beach got torn up as the race went on and was very rough, so you had to pick a rut at the entry to the corner, about 150 yards out, then ride it all the way round. But then, just as you came off the beach on to the pavement, there was a big ridge, more of a kerb really, very sharp and very hard, which jolted the bike right up in the air. You couldn't use alloy rims on the bike, otherwise it would dent them, but another reason was that if you did, the ribs would fill up with sand and send the wheel wildly out of balance—the vibration would be unbelievable:

An alternative view of Daytona Speedway, as Mitsuo Itoh (nearest the camera, now chief of Suzuki's racing activities) and Isao Morishita line their 50 cc Suzukis up the 'wrong' way in pit lane for the start of the US GP in 1964. Luigi Taveri's Kreidler shares the front row of the grid

Racing on the Beach Course at Daytona involved setting up a pit out in the open on the sand

you'd have to stop and knock the sand out before you could go on. We went back to steel rims after that!

'It was quite a spectacle for the fans in the sort of makeshift grandstand they put up on the outside of North Turn, and at least they were safer than the ones lining the back stretch. There was no crowd control of any kind, and people and even dogs used to cross the road in the middle of the race more or less as they pleased, or else stand real close to the side of the road without any kind of barrier. The way the speeds went up towards the end, it was inevitable they had to move us into the Speedway: I'm just surprised it took them a couple of years after the cars did so to start holding our race there too.

'The first year we ran the full Speedway, in 1964, the motors just weren't powerful enough to let us run more than ten feet up the side of the bankings; mostly we ran on the flat apron at the bottom, or only a foot or two up the bank, because the distance you have to cover increases quite rapidly the higher you move up. There was no chicane, so you'd run the whole of the back stretch flat out, which at 130 mph let you get a little way up the hill on the East banking, but still no more than ten feet or so. People don't realize even today how much extra

ground they have to cover if they insist on riding the bankings high up on a bike that is slow enough to run all the way round the bottom—plus, the extra physical effort you need to stop it wanting to drop off down on to the apron is considerable. You're talking, maybe, seven motor lengths' difference between top and bottom all the way round, and that's quite a lot of distance, but if you have a faster motorcycle it's about an even trade to take the high line, especially since there are some bad bumps on the bottom coming off the East banking where the cars chewed it up right when the Speedway first opened and which they've never really smoothed out. Plus, on a fast modern bike, if you try to force it down on to the shorter line coming on to the straightaway, you're talking about having maybe 40–50 lb of torque in the wrong direction on the handlebars, just when the front wheel gets all light and you want to straighten up. It'll put you in a big wobble, so the best thing is to "let 'er ride" and go as high as is comfortable, but no higher than absolutely necessary.

'I remember riding the factory 350 Yamaha at Daytona in the late 1960s, which was very fast but had its engine much too far back so there wasn't enough weight on the front wheel. Coming on to the straightaway off the banking, the front wheel would start to lift off the ground, and with a strong side-wind the wheel would go lock to lock every so

Above *Dick Mann's legendary flying start in the 1970 Daytona 200 on the factory Honda*

Below *Bugsy's Beeza: Mann on the three-cylinder BSA cranks into Turn 2 in 1972, the year after he won the Daytona 200 on a similar bike*

Hurley Wilvert (no. 39) and Dave Aldana (no. 10) round Turn 4's horseshoe in the 1975 Daytona 200

often down the back stretch: you could clearly hear it going ''clack-clack-clack'' as it hit the stops. Fortunately, the speed was so great that as it touched the ground again it would straighten up—but it was pretty unnerving!'

Almost as unnerving must have been the prospect of racing round the steep Daytona bankings in the rain, as happened in the past until the AMA saw sense. Today Daytona is the only banked track in the USA where wet-weather racing for professional riders is not permitted. Curiously, it is apparently considered perfectly all right for amateurs to ride there in the rain, though—on the same machines the pros race! 'That's crazy,' says Dick Mann flatly. 'I was always a pretty good rider in the rain, and won a lot of my races on wet tracks, though I was never as good as Roger Reiman who in my opinion is the best rider I have ever seen in the rain.

'Anyway, Roger won at Daytona in 1965, the year they ran the race in the rain, and how there wasn't someone killed I shall never know. There was a thick wall of spray 20 ft high and thick as fog. You didn't dare to go much higher up the steep bankings—only our second year on them, remember—to avoid slower guys in case you got in a slide and came down on them. We lost a few people, but fortunately nobody was seriously hurt, though it could have been a giant catastrophe. The infield section got flooded, too—there were some long puddles half an inch deep which were lethal when you hit them at speed. Fortunately, it dried up during the course of the race, but after that we could

see that Daytona was not a place to race at in the rain, so the next time they tried to do so, there was kind of a riders' lobby—not a strike exactly, but that was next on the list—and we had our first-ever rain postponement. Strangely enough, it was the pressure from the British riders, who were by then starting to race at Daytona regularly, that tipped the balance: without them, I doubt the AMA would have listened to us.'

Was the start always given with the field lined up in pit lane? 'Yes, but with the difference compared to today that you'd have that first full lap round the bowl. You might think that would allow the field to spread out more instead of all trying to funnel together into Turn 1, which is a slow, narrow and tight left-hander on to the infield, but it's safer nowadays, because you're all bunched up and only doing 60 mph. In the old days you'd be drafting [slipstreaming] each other in packs at very high speed. In the F750 days when I had my two wins on the Honda and BSA, people would get used in practice to running 150 mph over the finish line before they braked and dropped down into Turn 1, because they'd be running on their own. But on the first lap of the race, the draft from 40 other motorcycles would let you run 160 mph, and the result was always some pretty spectacular accidents in Turn 1 at the start of lap 2 as people got sucked along faster than they'd gone before in practice. Every year someone would go down and take three or four out with him, so in the end they decided to make Turn 1 just as unsafe but a lot slower off the start, which means the field strings out sooner nowadays.

'There are two ways of approaching Turn 1: the high and the low. If you have a real fast bike, but one which isn't so nimble, like a Superbike, you can stay high across the finish line, then drop down gradually into the turn and make one big sweeping curve out of the whole thing, with a tight exit, which means you can get the bike upright sooner for the drive out. But on a better-handling machine, or on a slower bike, the best bet is to stay low, practically on the grass, then you can brake in a straight line, drift out to the right entering Turn 1, and tight-apex it. I always took this line because our bikes just weren't fast enough, even in the F750 days, to make it worthwhile staying high up, but braking was always a problem; they used to have distance marker boards then which I used, but it was always a test of judgement, especially coming down to bottom gear as you braked after travelling at high speed for so long.

'A lot of people fall down in Turn 1 under braking

Come in, no. 8—your time is up! Pity the poor backmarker who suddenly finds himself overwhelmed by the leading pack in the 1970 Daytona 200. Mike Hailwood's BSA three (no. 50) leads Gary Nixon on a Triumph three (no. 9), who partially obscures Cal Rayborn's Harley. Kel Carruthers' 350 Yamaha (no. 75) and Ron Grant's 500 Suzuki (no. 61) are about to give poor ol' no. 8 a hard time, as they enter Turn 5

midway through a race because they lose concentration when they're tired and forget that Turn 1 has some really strange factors which will get you if you're not careful. It's difficult to see even if you walk out there to show someone, but in fact there's a rise in the pavement, so that when you're braking hard from high speed and coming down through the gears, the front end gets all light. If you wait till the last possible moment to brake, you'll usually fall. I'd brake *very* hard to begin with, then ease off as the front end got light, then hard on the brakes again before getting bottom gear, laying the bike over in the kind of false apex I'd made for myself by drifting out to the right, and turning sharp left. I'd always run a real high bottom gear for Daytona, too, though one problem people had to watch for, especially as tyres got wider and better and you could lean over more, was that you could lean the bike over too far to the left in Turn 1 and ground the gear lever, which would knock the bike out of bottom gear on a left-foot change.'

There is now a quick right/left flick after Turn 1, termed the Turn 2 chicane, but prior to 1985 Turn 1 was followed by a short straight (now even shorter) to Turn 2, grandiosely termed the 'International Horseshoe', a 180-degree right-hander of even

radius. 'I'd switch the power on early coming out of Turn 1,' says Dick. 'It was always a consistent corner, so you'd figure on powering out of there a little sideways with the bike sliding slightly so as to give you a lot better run down the back stretch behind the pits to Turn 2. On the BSA three, which was easily the nicest bike I ever rode round the full banked speedway, I'd get third gear along that short straight, then down to second for the horseshoe. I'd drift wide out to the grass exiting Turn 1, then if I was running on my own, cross over gradually to the left to take the ideal line round Turn 2—outside, inside, outside. But there was also a very good line if you were lapping slower riders, which would be to stay over to the right all the way down, and hug the inside all round Turn 2. It was a little slower, but that way you'd be on the inside of the slow guys, which was a lot safer than either criss-crossing their lines, or trying to ride round the outside of them. That was

Reinhold Roth demonstrates why the Double Axel is named after a German after gassing his 250 Honda too early exiting Turn 5

taking a *real* chance!

'My fast line round Turn 2 was to actually go in very deep, braking very late so that I overshot what would be the ideal place to start turning in. But then I'd make an early apex for myself, turn the bike round and power out very early, clipping the true apex as I did so. Each year you could do it faster, because each year Bill France [proprietor of Daytona Speedway] would want to have a new record speed, so he'd make the racetrack a little faster! Each of the corners at Daytona have a history to them, where France added pavement so as to let you make the turns quicker, and on Turn 2, for example, each year he added pavement on the exit, so you could gun it harder and earlier and drift out wider and wider as you did so. Lots of people still don't take advantage of that, but there's no doubt you're cheating yourself of time if you don't.'

The fast, sweeping left-hand dog-leg at what used to be called Turn 3 (now Turn 4) has always been Daytona's most testing corner. Going through there under power without backing off the throttle has always been a mental barrier to be overcome—

More lapping drama as the leading bunch of Agostini (no. 10) and Roberts (no. 1), both on Yamahas, Nixon (no. 9) on a Kawasaki and Suzuki-mounted Barry Sheene overwhelm Alex George's Yamaha at the exit from the chicane on lap 7 of the 1974 200-miler, won by Ago on his Daytona début

hasn't it? 'I guess so,' muses Dick, 'though in our day it wasn't so wide nor so fast as it is today, which probably made it easier. I'd take it in third on the BSA, after gradually crossing over to the right after Turn 2, hitting fourth gear briefly, then coming back one for the dog-leg so you could run through there on the power—just pull it straight back one gear without shutting the throttle completely, and driving through. I wouldn't use all the road at Turn 3, because I wanted to get right over to the left again for Turn 4, which in some ways was a more important corner; you can save a *lot* of time here by doing it properly.

'The trick is to go very, very deep into the turn on the left for Turn 4, braking very hard and very late indeed. I'd use second gear if it was oily, because then you'd do the whole turn quite wide and concentrate on staying aboard, but otherwise I'd get bottom gear just as I started to turn into the bend, then get the power on really early and drive hard through the real apex of the corner, staying on the right-hand side of the road as I did so. Not only did this let me avoid all the oil and rubber that'd built up there as the race progressed, but it'd put me in the right position for Turn 5 [now Turn 6, a tight left-hander leading on to the banking] which was the key to how soon you could get your top speed on the bank. With the non-sticky tyres we had then, you could accelerate so much more quickly if you had the bike upright, but even without this I'm certain this is the quickest way round Turn 4 up to the point you start braking for Turn 5, because it's shorter. I was always very conscious of shaving yards off a racetrack's length if I could do it. There are three or four bike lengths saved by doing Turn 4 my way, rather than the classical sweeping British-style line people use nowadays, and if that lets you get the jump on another guy, as well as save time through the turn, it has to be right.'

Turn 5 used to be a much tighter entry to the banking than it is today, before the Frances re-routed the course so as to lead riders more

Freddie Spencer gives the V4 Honda NSR500 a victorious début in revised form in 1985 in the Daytona F1 100-miler. Here he sweeps through the first part of the Tri-Oval banking, past Hap Eaton's TZ750

gradually—and therefore more quickly!—on to the banking. 'Even nowadays this is a corner you must take with great care, because it's all too easy to switch the power on too hard and too soon, and spin out. There's a step in the pavement right where the infield meets the banking which can completely unsettle the bike and flip you over, and a lot of very experienced riders have forgotten that. I'd use bottom gear again after briefly grabbing second on the short straight down from Turn 4, then feed the power in real carefully as the corner opened up: you *must* wait before doing so because the turn seems to tighten up a bit on you, plus there's always a lot of oil and rubber laid down from the cars. Definitely the easiest place on the racetrack to come to grief.'

Daytona lore has it that the 'hot tip' coming on to the banking is to run right up to the wall exiting Turn 5, then drop down on the banking, thus supposedly gaining vital milliseconds by improving acceleration, and doing the same thing coming out of the chicane. Does Dick subscribe to this view? 'No, even on the triples, which were fast enough to run where they do today on the Superbikes, I'd always come out gradually, and aim for the centre of the banking, which is where I'd run all the way round unless I had to pass someone. Again, you're saving distance, which I thought was more important than playing helter-skelter! The wind could be a factor in how close I'd stay to the wall on the way off the banking though, and I did try to keep track of it at Daytona by watching the flags from time to time by the pits, because it could quite often change on you during the race. I was never very good at that sort of thing, and it used to amaze me when riders would come in and say they knew where they'd finished because they'd been watching the scoreboard! I always had to concentrate 100 per cent on where I was going just to stay in contention, and usually depended on how the bike was behaving out in the open on the banking to tell me if I was doing the right thing. We always thought the wall gave us more protection if the wind came from the sea, so we'd run right close to it, but it was nothing I would ever want to have to prove!'

Did Dick ever indulge in that favourite Daytona pastime of drafting bikes that were slightly faster than his own? 'I drafted everything! If a bike came past going 80 mph faster than me, I'd try to get his draft! I felt it was important back in the 1960s when we rode unfaired bikes, and it's important now when streamlining has become quite sophisticated. It'll always be important, I guess, because when it comes down to it, everything we've just talked about in terms of getting through the infield quickly is completely unimportant compared to your speed on the banking, and if you can increase that beyond what it ought to be by drafting someone, then that's vital, either to increase your top speed so as to stay with someone, or to pick up extra momentum so you can slingshot a bike of equal performance. The only thing I can really say is that it's a matter of judgement and therefore of practice. Just remember if you're drafting a two-stroke to always stay slightly to one side in case he seizes it! Back in the 1960s we tried not to think about what would happen if that occurred, because at those sort of speeds you'd have difficulty avoiding an accident that happened 100 yards in front of you on the banking, let alone right there by your front wheel. I had many near misses.'

The chicane at the end of the back stretch on the

Fast pitwork is an essential element in 200-mile race success at Daytona. Here, Kel Carruthers (with hair!) holds the overflow tank while Yamaha US personnel refuel Don Castro in the 1975 race. He finished ninth

tri-oval was only added in 1974, the year of Dick's final ride in the 200-miler aboard a TZ700 Yamaha. 'It was really necessary,' says Dick, 'because by then the bikes had grown so fast that turning off the back straightaway on to the steep banking at 160 mph-plus meant that it was reminiscent of pitching it into a turn on a half-mile dirt oval. The back end was threatening to break away at any moment, and there was a big strain on tyres and suspension that I don't think they were then ready to accept. Plus, installing the chicane gave you somewhere else you could try to outbrake and overtake someone, which Daytona badly needs. I only raced there the once with the chicane, which for years they used to build right up like a wall of straw so you couldn't see the exit till you were actually into it.

'I found the chicane deceptive, because it was difficult to realize just how fast you could take the first part, and therefore how late you could brake. You can stay on the brakes all the way through the gradual left-hand lead into the chicane, coming down on the Yamaha to third gear or maybe second. I'd figure to finish my braking just as I laid

Alan Shepherd sweeps round Turn 2 the wrong way in the 1964 250 cc US GP at Daytona, which he won on his factory MZ twin

the bike over to the right for the first part, drift out to the left in the middle, then get it upright as soon as possible and get the power on hard for the drive out. Again, there's a bump where the paved section of the chicane meets the banking again, but since you're not laid over, this doesn't upset the bike like it does in Turn 5. Doing the chicane at Daytona well is all about judgement and timing.'

How would Dick summarize Daytona? 'Very definitely it's a paradoxical track: all the minute details which wouldn't make a scratch of difference in the Isle of Man become magnified at Daytona and make all the difference there. Plus the race at Daytona isn't about lap times: it's about finishing, and you have only to look at the countless number of people who have led the Daytona 200 only to drop out through either rider error or mechanical problems to realize that—far more than in other races. It's so very easy to race hard at Daytona, but so very difficult to finish. Because the accent all the time is on speed, riders get carried away and forget that the most important factor about the race is that

it is long and very gruelling: the 200 miles is what makes it. It can take you several years to figure out how to win the Daytona 200; in my case it took 15 years and then I won it twice in succession. Both times I had bikes that were fairly competitive but very far from being the fastest things in the race, yet I was able to bring them into Victory Lane by going just fast enough to win and yet outlast all the faster machines. Each time I really *thought* my way to the chequered flag, and I was really pleased with the way I ran the race. I should have won again in 1973, when I ran the same bike I won on back in 1971, but painted up to look like a Triumph instead of a BSA, but because of internal team problems I never actually got to ride the bike in practice, which meant I had to start from the back of the third wave, in 80th place on the grid. I can honestly say that was my best race ever in my whole life: I didn't make a single mistake, I rode the whole 200 miles at absolute maximum speed, skidded the tyres in every turn, never missed a passing manoeuvre and finished fourth, exactly the same distance behind Saarinen who won as I had started behind him in the third wave. After that I had the Yamaha ride, but then I didn't actually retire, just decided I wouldn't race any more till I had a good ride: I'm still looking!'

Round Brands Hatch with Derek Minter

Though John Surtees almost certainly won more races there over the years, for most racing fans in the 1950s and 1960s there was only one King of Brands: Derek Minter. Riding a wide variety of bikes, from the little Starmaker-powered Cotton Telstar up to the musical, magical four-cylinder Gileras, 'The Mint' became the man to beat at the Kent track, whether on the 1.24-mile short circuit or the 2.65-mile Grand Prix one. Both distances were reduced by 0.04 mile in 1976 when the inside paddock was extended for the GP car circus and Paddock Bend altered, and at the same time many of the corners received new, car-inspired names; it was only after a wave of resentment on the part of Brands motorcycle fans that a new name was concocted for the short straight on the GP circuit between Hawthorn and Westfield corners, so Derek Minter Straight now honours the man whose name became synonymous with that of Brands itself for bike enthusiasts everywhere.

Now an independent haulage contractor living as before at Blean, just outside Canterbury, Derek has not raced since 1967, when a number of outside pressures, not least a start-money dispute with Motor Circuit Developments, then owners of Brands, hastened his retirement. 'They effectively wanted me to take a cut in start money,' recalls Derek, who obviously still feels strongly about the way in which he believes he was forced out of racing, 'and that was at a time when they were still getting gates of 50,000 for a national. I told them I wasn't having it, and that I'd rather pack up altogether than accept their terms when I knew my appearance could put an extra 8–10,000 people through the gate. It wasn't as if I had anything else to fall back on: I was a full-time racer earning my living from the sport, and it certainly wasn't getting any cheaper to take part; why should I have paid out more to ride and

'Mint' is King! Derek with pop star Lulu after winning the King of Brands title once again in 1965

Brands Hatch

Clearways

Dingle Dell

South Bank

Stirlings

Westfield

Druids

Bottom Bend

Paddock

Hawthorns

received less for doing so? That and the impossibility of ever getting a works ride was the last straw, so after the October meeting at the end of 1967 I packed up for good. Still won two races at that last meeting, though!'

Derek Minter began racing as a Canterbury youngster in 1954 on a 500 BSA Gold Star. Over the next 13 years he was to become acknowledged as Britain's leading short-circuit specialist, who also proved his worth at the Continental GPs and in the Isle of Man, where he became the first man to lap the Island at over 100 mph on a single-cylinder machine, in 1960, on a Lancefield Norton. Two years later he gained his solitary TT victory in controversial circumstances on a private 250 Honda, defeating the might of the factory team. The embarrassment this caused made him effectively

Phil Read leads the charge into Paddock Bend in the 1973 Race of the South aboard the 500 MV Agusta. Pat Mahoney's Kawasaki (no. 8), Paul Smart's Suzuki (no. 2) and Peter Williams' John Player Norton (no. 5) give chase

the only leading rider of that era to be passed over by all the Japanese manufacturers for a works ride, a fact which obviously still rankles. For this reason, GP success mostly eluded him—while at his beloved Brands, on the other hand, he was well-nigh unbeatable, riding Manx Nortons tuned first by Steve Lancefield, then later by Ray Petty, and carrying his favourite number 11. The white helmet with a single green stripe, tucked behind the screen of a fairing with white upper and black lower halves, seemed to be colour-coded with the chequered flag of victory, so often did 'The Mint' snatch yet another win, often when all the odds seemed stacked against him.

'I think this was one reason I was so popular with the crowds,' recalls Derek. 'For one thing there were a lot of good riders around, any one of whom could have won, whereas when Surtees used to ride at Brands, for example, there wasn't so much competition and he used to win three races in an afternoon pretty regularly. I had a lot more rivals to cope with, and on top of that I could never get a good start no matter how hard I tried. I could start

smashing when I used to practise it, but when it came to the race I used to have a lot of what we'll call "tummy-trouble"—I never could get away properly. People used to think that I liked to come from behind to make a show of it, but that wasn't the case at all: I simply could not make good starts however much I practised them. I remember I had a good start once with the Cotton, and a couple of times with the 250 Honda, but generally I'd be last away and that'd be it. It never used to worry me, mind—I used to enjoy coming through the pack even if sometimes I left it a bit late; as it was, my bad starts really made a race of it for the public, and I don't think I'd ever have been so popular with them otherwise.'

Minter was the first man to lap the Brands Hatch long circuit at over 90 mph, on the 500 Gilera in April 1963, and his 500 cc short-circuit record of 56.8 sec, shared with the late Mike Hailwood, both on Manx Nortons and set in 1960, stood for nearly 12 years before being beaten by a certain B. Sheene on a Yamaha in 1972. How did the man whom most Brands regulars, such as myself, came to admire as the man we would most like to emulate, find his way round this home of the mid-1960s 'scratchers'?

'The first lap at Paddock I'd usually go up the inside if I was in the middle of the pack, so as to minimize the risk of someone sliding off and taking me with them; usually though I'd be almost dead last so it wouldn't matter! On a flying lap, however, I'd always be out to the left-hand side as I approached the corner, then just as soon as I got over the crest of the slight hill leading into it I'd make a beeline for the apex on the inside—there was always a bump there, so you had to be careful, though. The TV cameras generally used to park themselves at Paddock of a Sunday afternoon so as to catch a few people sliding around on their ears for the evening news, and a lot of riders did indeed come a cropper there. The reason they mostly did so was because they'd go into Paddock up the right-hand side or in the middle of the road, which would mean they had to lay the bike over much further to get round and they'd run out of grip. A lot of corners at Brands are off-camber, and Paddock's one of them; they used just to lean over too far and either ground something or lose the front end by going off the edge of the tyre—even Ago got caught out there once, I remember.

'I usually used a six-speed gearbox in the 350 Manx and a five-speeder in the 500. Going into Paddock on the 500 I'd change down twice from

Future GP star Roger Burnett drops through Paddock Bend in an early ride on a Steve Wynne Ducati 750 in 1984

top just past the hump—the crest of that rise—notching third just by the gate where we used to pull in after practice on the left. A bloke used to stand there with his flag, and I often wondered if he knew how I used to hold him in my sights, because just where he stood was my peeling-off point! I'd hold third all the way through the corner *and* down the hill, then notch fourth in the dip, and if you kept it screwed on hard you'd have enough momentum to carry you up the other side to Druids all in fourth gear—I'd be getting about 7000 rpm in top before I had to brake for the hairpin.'

Most people's memories of racing at Brands in the 1960s include seeing riders rounding Druids up to three abreast, literally rubbing fairings. Was it really as hectic as it looked at the time and still does in all those photos? 'It could be, but only if you were going round there with riders you didn't know and couldn't rely on to know what they were doing. With people like Read, Hailwood, Dunphy, Jenkins, Butcher and so on, you could depend on them not to do anything stupid, and even hard triers like Degens and Ivy usually didn't present a hazard; it was the inexperienced bloke who'd get mixed up with the top-liners occasionally and found himself in over his head—they were the ones you had to watch out for. Mind you, we all used to overcook it

Minter has a rare ride on a Seeley-AJS 7R at Brands in 1966. Here he leads John Cooper (Norton) into Druids, with Peter Williams (AJS) on the outside. Dave Degens (no. 12) is about to incur Derek's displeasure by cutting up the inside!

occasionally, me included. I think I'm right in saying I must have fallen off at least once at every corner at Brands at some time or another! We used to have to ride really hard to win races back in the 1960s, and it was just inevitable you'd overdo it once in a while. You just treated it as part of the game, really, and I'm glad to say Ray Petty did too. He knew if I'd bent one of the bikes it wasn't because I'd done something stupid, just that I'd been trying that little bit too hard. He was a smashing bloke to go racing with. One of the reasons I managed to lap Brands Hatch as quick as I did was because he and I used to go practising there a lot in the middle of the week. He used to time me using different lines through different corners on different laps, until we found the quickest way round; if they'd done any resurfacing work, or some new bumps or ripples had appeared, next week Ray and I would be down there sorting out the fastest line. He was a great deal more than just an engine tuner for me.'

So going back to Druids, what was 'The Mint's' chosen line through there, out of the many available

to him? 'There was only ever one fast line round Paddock, but at Druids even the fast blokes used to approach the corner on all sorts of different lines and it didn't matter—not there, anyhow. But it made a big difference to the exit. I used to go up the hill on the left, brake really late, and go across the road still braking, because that would enable me to hug the inside on the way out, and take the shortest route down the hill to the left-hander. If you couldn't brake hard while cranked over, you'd never win a race at Brands Hatch: it was quite a common sight to see the good riders in a two-wheel drift on the way into a corner.'

But didn't a lot of people shoot up the inside to 'cut him off at the pass', thus spoiling his line when their trajectories crossed in the middle of the corner? 'Yes, there used to be charmers who did that, and they could spoil your line and even get inside you for a while, but you'd always get them back again on the exit because they'd run wide on the way out. Sometimes they'd see you nipping inside them again as you started down the hill and they'd turn the power on too hard while still cranked over and slide off—I remember Mike Hailwood, of all people, doing that one time. My way, I'd stay tight in to the right kerb all the way down the hill to the left-hander and being upright much sooner meant that I could get the power on quicker, and in any case I'd

Derek Minter

Above *Who says the 'Brands scratchers' are gone for ever? John Ruth (750 Norton) leans on Dutchman Cees van Maris (Seeley-Norton 850) on the entry to Druids in a 1984 Battle of the Twins race*

Below *At the exit from Druids, Kork Ballington's 500 Kawasaki (no. 7) leads Graham Wood on a Yamaha (no. 18) and Suzuki-mounted Kiwis Dennis Ireland (on the inside) and Stu Avant in October 1982*

have less ground to cover—all because I took a wide line going into Druids, and braked really late.

'I could always reckon to outbrake almost anybody, and one reason, which only a few people knew about, was that when Ferodo were about to pack up making the original brown linings, I spent a whole day at Oulton Park testing the replacement product—what people later called green linings. To me they weren't really satisfactory, but they must have been cheaper to manufacture or something; anyway, I was crafty—I acquired all the remaining

The first lap of the 1977 Transatlantic Match Races, and Americans Kenny Roberts and Steve Baker have already opened up a huge lead as they sweep through Bottom Bend—now renamed Graham Hill Bend after the father of a modern bike racer!

brown linings for Manx Nortons and the like and kept them at home, so whenever I wanted a brake relined I just took the complete wheel and my own linings to Ferodo and they did them for me. Even when I finished I had enough linings left to do me for another two or three years—I gave them to Ray Petty in the end.'

What gear did Derek take Druids in? 'Always bottom, then I'd go up two to third for the left-hander, then up another one or two, depending on how you were going, for the back straight. But Bottom Bend was the one corner at Brands on either the long or short circuit I never really could get on with. There were a lot of ripples there you couldn't avoid, and the bike used to skitter and hack to one side however carefully you'd set up the suspension. A lot of people used to fall off there; it was definitely my least favourite corner.'

Clearways is another corner that has caught a lot of people out. 'That's right—and again it's because the further over you drift out to the left on the exit, the more the road falls away from you. The approach is tricky too: I used to knock it back a cog to third for the left-hander at South Bank on the short circuit, then try to straight-line the next bit as much as possible, automatically hooking back another gear as you did so. The trick was to aim for a point on the outside of the circuit halfway between the two right-handers that make up Clearways, then sweep her over into the second part of the turn, staying as tight in as possible. Once you could see the straight in front of you it was safe to drift out towards the middle of the road, but it's much quicker to stay over to the right coming past the pits than use all the road as most people did. But if you turned on the power too soon or drifted over too far at Clearways you'd be on your ear in no time—the back end would just step out and there'd be no chance of getting it back. I remember too there was a little ripple about three feet out from the inside of the corner which would set the bike hopping about unless you stayed in close. Anyway, then I'd be off up the main straight and into top gear, starting to cross over to the left just after the start and finish line, ready for my appointment with the chap with the flag at the entrance to Paddock!'

So much for the short circuit—nowadays known as the 'Indy' track, for some obscure reason. How about the longer GP version? 'Bottom gear would be too low for South Bank,' recalls Derek, 'even though we'd have higher overall gearing for the long circuit. So I'd take it in second, then we'd be back into top for the long straight under the bridge

Above *Ron Haslam gives the ELF3 its first-ever victory in the 1986 Macau GP*

Below *Barry Sheene sweeps his 500 Yamaha out of Donington's Old Hairpin in 1981*

Paul Smart takes his Imola-winning Ducati 750 up Druids Hill the 'wrong' way in the 1972 Hutchinson 100 meeting, run on the Brands Hatch circuit in the reverse direction

Above *Griff Jenkins leads John Cooper round Druids on their Manx Nortons in 1967*

Below *The field pours through Statue Corner at Macau in 1986. Anyone got a Chinese dictionary?*

*Eddie Lawson prepares to lap Marco Papa's RS500
Honda on his works V4 Yamaha OW81 in the 1985
Imola 200 at Acqua Minerale*

Above *Hugh Anderson in action on the 125 works Suzuki that took him to two world titles*

Below *TT maestro Tony Rutter sweeps his works Ducati 750 through the Gooseneck on the IoM*

Left *Ago reaching for the sky at the bottom of Bray Hill on the TT course*

Above *Derek Minter leads John Cooper at Clearways on their Manx Nortons in 1965: 'Old Moon-eyes obviously thought he had me weighed up . . !'*

Above *Start of the 500 cc race at Mallory Park in 1968. From left to right on the front row: Hailwood (297 cc Honda six); Read (V4 Yamaha 250); Agostini (500 MV three); Cooper (Seeley G50)*

Below *Kenny Roberts on the 500 factory Yamaha at Laguna Seca in 1983*

before notching back two gears for Hawthorns—that's a lovely corner, a fast sweeping right-hander that tightens up on you at the exit. You had to leave it really late before peeling off—sometimes I used to think I'd run out of braking space, and there were some bumps on the way in which would unsettle the bike. It was a real sorter; you had to be good to get round there fast, and the bicycle had to be properly set up too. On the other hand the next corner, Westfield, was about the only completely straightforward bend on the whole track; I'd go up into fourth from Hawthorns, then back into third for the corner, then up one cog as we plunged down the hill towards Dingle Dell. I'd just clip the apex on the right in the dip, then over to the left for the right-hander, braking really hard and late, coming back two gears as I did so. That's where I broke my back in the accident with Dave Downer, but I'd rather not talk about that because it was a really tragic incident that I don't care to dwell on.

'Afterwards you had a short squirt up the little straight to Stirlings, which I understand is sort of banked a little nowadays [it is]. It wasn't like that in my day, so it was quite a tight corner to get around. I'd take it in second on the five-speeder, then change up two going under the bridge to Clearways—when they first built the long circuit it seemed like you were going to bang your head on the parapet: if I hadn't been flat on the tank I'd have felt like ducking my head! I usually held it in fourth all the way round Clearways, taking great care to hug the inside coming out of the corner so as not to run along the off-camber section, then off away to the end of the lap.

'From my point of view Clearways was a much easier corner on the GP circuit than on the short one, but I know one person who might not think so, and that's John Cooper. He once fell off in quite a big way coming out of the corner on the long circuit. He'd been following me for a bit, trying to learn any tricks I had—you always had to be careful who was behind you when you pulled anything extra-special because if they were any good they'd pick it up at once and you'd have given the game away. Worst of all, they'd remember it for next time, as well! Anyway, old Moon-eyes obviously

Spaniard Victor Palomo does it all wrong on his TZ750 Yamaha at Druids in the F750 world title round in April 1978

Above *French sidecar-ace Alain Michel stops for adjustments after spinning off at the entry to the GP circuit in his Seymaz-Yamaha outfit in 1978*

Below *Derek Minter displays his effortless style on the 500 Petty Norton, here fitted with a Fontana front brake*

thought he had me weighed up, because he'd keep trying to overtake towards the end of the race coming out of Clearways—practising his last-lap effort, I suppose. Well, that was all right because what he didn't know was that I wasn't entering Clearways at my normal speed—until the last lap. I must have come into the corner a good ten miles an hour quicker than I had before in that race and of course he tried to pass me again, only this time he was going so much faster than before without realizing it that I'm afraid he fell off, and that was the end of him, for that day at least!

'My favourite corner was undoubtedly Paddock; I adored taking it, getting my braking and peeling-off points just right, following just the right line, and so on. You have to peel off for it blind, because you can't quite see the apex till after you've committed yourself, and I think that's one reason why so few people used to get it right consistently. A lot of

Italian multis in action at Druids in October 1966, as Remo Venturi leads team-mate Frank Perris on the final racing appearance in Britain of the Gilera fours

people fell off there, myself included. One time I remember doing so was after I'd been to the Belgian with the Nortons and had run there on them with smaller tyres—only a 2.75 on the front and a 3.00 at the rear for a bit more speed at Spa on what was then a very fast track. Anyway, I came back to Brands the following week and used the same tyres, but unfortunately for me it was raining that day and there was a small river flowing across the track at Paddock. I arrived there in the lead and it just aquaplaned on me; I lost the front wheel and finished up at the bottom of the hill all in a heap. I was so surprised because I'd deliberately chosen to use the smaller tyres to cut out the risk of aquaplaning—maybe it was even wetter than usual. Being built in a hollow, Brands was always very treacherous when it rained, because the surface water would drain off in every direction; there were at least four places where you'd have miniature streams running across the track, and this could be very tricky.

'But I really liked Paddock. I don't think anyone ever passed me in a race there. They might have pulled alongside but by the time they'd get to the

'I used too much back brake and the rear wheel stepped out!' Minter recovered from his famous moment to repass Phil Read and win the race

apex, I'd be gone. I don't really know why they changed it—must have been to give the cars more runoff, I suppose. When they went through their armco phase a lot of places got very dangerous for us lot, including parts of Brands—I remember Cooper broke his leg at Paddock quite badly as a result of the armco, and I think he gave up after that. It didn't really affect me so much because I retired just as the car boys were getting up on their high horses, but I think apart from the steel barriers

Brands has always been quite a safe circuit for bikes.'

Did 'The Mint' adopt any conscious style when he rode at Brands Hatch? 'I always tried to keep my knees in close to the tank and my weight on the seat, and tuck myself away as much as possible, even going round corners and along short straights. I don't approve of this modern habit of riding with the knees out hanging off the bike. If it steps out you've nothing to control it with, whereas if the front or back end went away I could control it with my knees against the tank. A typical example of this was that famous picture of me going into Druids all sideways. It was my first meeting after breaking my back, and I was going round together with Read. I said before that I always braked very hard and late for Druids, but this time I used too much back brake and the rear wheel stepped out. Luckily for me all I ever used to have on my Nortons was 20 degrees of steering lock, which was the minimum allowed, so when the back wheel went away it only went 20 degrees before the forks hit the lock stop, by which time I'd released the back brake, held on tight with my knees, and caught it. Next lap I actually passed Read again and won the race; mind you, that episode really frightened me afterwards, because being my first race back after my big accident I was only too well aware of the specialist telling me that if I fell off again I could be paralysed for life.'

Riders of today will claim that they have to sit off the bike in order to exploit the greater grip of modern tyres. 'Well, I think that's all rubbish. I used to ride the way I did, yet lean the bike over as far as anyone, given the section of the tyres; I'd love to have a go on a modern racer with a fat set of slicks, but I bet you I could ride it the same way as I did my Manx Nortons without being disgraced. Mind you, I did use to stick my toes out a bit going round corners—it told me when I was about to go too far

over, but on the other hand it meant having my boots repaired every week and a pair rarely lasted me longer than a month!'

What does Derek Minter consider to have been the main reason for his remarkable run of success at the Kentish track? 'Though I did practise a lot there, so did most of the other leading boys I rode against; we all had as good a knowledge of the circuit as each other. I think the real reason I did well there was that I had superior machinery, and it made a big difference to your confidence at the start of a race to know you had an edge in that department. I never touched the engines myself on the Manx Nortons, though I did do the rest of the bicycle myself at home. All the time I rode Nortons I only ever had two tuners, Lancefield first, then Petty, and I reckon they were the best in the business. I never checked a tappet clearance or mag timing or anything: I had two really good people to look after the engines, and that's what brought me so much success at Brands Hatch and elsewhere.'

Surtees concentrating hard in the class of '57

Phil Read at Spa–Francorchamps

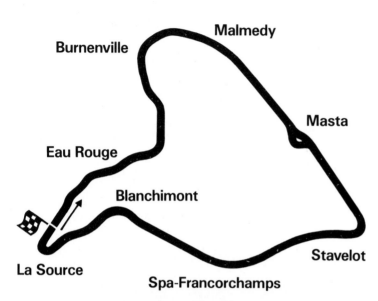

It may come as a surprise to know that, next to the Isle of Man Mountain course, the oldest motorcycle racing circuit in the world still in current use—albeit in modified form—is the Belgian track at Spa–Francorchamps.

Nestling in the beautiful, heavily forested Ardennes mountains near to the German border in the southern part of the country, the Spa circuit is for many people the epitome of a true road course, utilizing public roads in everyday use and legendary for the ultra-fast speeds permitted by the many flat-

Cordial team-mates and the best of enemies: Phil Read (left) and Yamaha colleague Bill Ivy in 1968

*Start of the Sidecar GP at Spa in 1972, won by
Enders/Englehardt on their works BMW, at an average
speed of over 110 mph*

out sections, interspersed with challenging corners
whose names are almost as well known to British
enthusiasts as Ballaugh Bridge or Leathemstown.
First used in 1921, the Spa circuit was roughly
triangular in shape and did not actually run through
or beside the elegant watering-place of Spa at all,
but instead between the southern tip of the
neighbouring town of Francorchamps and the two
smaller villages of Malmedy and Stavelot. The
original circuit measured 14.12 km (8.774 miles) in
length, and remarkably enough was used for all
Belgian bike GPs (except for 1923 and 1936, when
tracks at Dinant and Floreffe respectively were
employed) between 1921 and 1978, when
primarily in response to pressures from the four-
wheel world it was shortened to a length of
6.947 km (4.317 miles). In doing so, some of the
character which made Spa one of the most
respected circuits in the world was retained, but
sadly the section incorporating Malmedy and
Stavelot was omitted by means of a new purpose-
built road effectively cutting the old circuit in two.
Nevertheless, the Belgian GP is today still held on
what most road-racing enthusiasts the world over
consider to be its true home, and by modern
standards the new track is still a considerable
challenge and quite fast, in spite of the insertion of
an idiotic 'lay-by' type chicane just before the La
Source hairpin.

Over the years Spa has represented a happy
hunting ground for British riders, with six victories
each to Jimmy Guthrie, John Surtees and Eric
Oliver (the last in successive years in the Sidecar GP
from 1949 to 1956), five to Mike Hailwood and
four to Jimmie Simpson. But the man with most
classic victories to his credit there is, not
unexpectedly, Giacomo Agostini with eight wins,
registered in consecutive years in the 500 cc class
between 1966 and 1973. Strangely, there was no
350 cc Belgian GP after 1959, the four-race
programme instead featuring a 50 cc race as a
regular event from 1962 onwards; in view of the
ultra-fast nature of the circuit this must be
accounted a disappointment—though the reason is
not hard to decipher in view of the importance of
the tiddler category in the Benelux countries.
Nevertheless, local man Julien van Zeebroeck's
performance in averaging over 100 mph on his tiny
production Kreidler single to win his home 50 cc GP
in 1975 should not be underestimated, though this
pales beside the feat which many enthusiasts
regard as the ultimate achievement of the brilliant
rear-guard action fought by Phil Read and the MV
Agusta team on behalf of the golden era of four-
stroke GP motorcycles, against the modern
generation of two-strokes. For at Spa in 1974 Read
and the 500 MV literally pulverized the Japanese
opposition on the world's fastest GP circuit; lapping
at over 130 mph from a standing start, he arrived at
the end of the first lap so far in front that pit
observers felt convinced there had been a horrific
pile-up which had eliminated the opposition. Such

was not the case, for by the end of the second lap Read and the red and silver Italian four-cylinder fire-engine were a stunning 13 seconds in front, going on to win comfortably from arch-rival Agostini's works Yamaha four en route to a second consecutive world 500 cc title. Even more remarkably, Read broke Ago's lap record by over four seconds, becoming the first man ever to lap the Spa circuit in under four minutes at a stunning 133.34 mph—the fastest lap then recorded in any GP anywhere in the world.

The following year, 1975, Read and the MV won again at Spa, this time thwarting the challenge not only of Ago's Yam but also of Barry Sheene's new works RG500 Suzuki. Though it was Sheene who ended up with a new lap record, Phil did record the fastest-ever race average for a GP of 133.14 mph en route to the chequered flag. Who better then than

Read scorches into the lead of the 1974 Belgian 500 cc GP on the MV four, leaving Agostini's Yamaha (no. 4) trailing

the man whose controversial racing career reached perhaps its finest hour at the Spa–Francorchamps circuit to relate how he used to ride the doyen of Continental Circus tracks?

'I always thought of Francorchamps as "my" circuit,' says Phil. 'I only won three races there [the other was on a 250 Yamaha in 1968] but that was because they never had a 350 event while I was racing and stopped holding the 125 race for half a dozen years in the 1960s when I was on the Yamahas, else I'm sure it would have been more. Most people assume that because it's so fast the guy with the quickest bike will always win, but that isn't so—look at my MV wins, for example, when my machine was giving away a good 5 mph and more to the strokers. What you really needed was a bike with a wide spread of power to cut down on unnecessary gearchanging and to enable you to take some of the flat-out kinks with just an easing of the throttle rather than have to mess about with the gearbox in order to keep the engine on the boil. In this respect the MV was an ideal bike for the circuit,

Rod Gould on a Yamaha leads Agostini's MV through Eau Rouge at the start of the 1972 350 cc Belgian classic. The MV won, of course

Christian Leon wheelies the factory RCB Honda endurance racer out of the hill above Eau Rouge, en route to a mid-1970s victory in the 24 Hours race

and I also pride myself that over the years I really learnt how to get through the many tricky sections as quickly as anybody.

'Anyway, the first time I went to Spa was in 1961 after I'd won the Junior TT on a Lacey-tuned Norton. I hadn't really considered doing the GPs at all till the TT win came along, but then Joe Ehrlich offered me a ride on his 125 EMC and was able to get a very good start-money offer from the Dutch and Belgian organizers, so I took my brace of Nortons along as well. I did very well at Assen, especially considering it was the first time I'd ever raced abroad, let alone in a GP, and ended up with two fourths and fifth. So we went to Spa the following week and of course I was expecting my run of good results to keep up—but sod's law always brings you down to earth with a bump and I retired in both the 125 and 500 events.

'In spite of that, I was absolutely captivated by Francorchamps. It was an awe-inspiring circuit, running through pine forests in a beautiful setting in the heart of the Ardennes that looked like a postcard someone sends you from abroad with "wish you were here" on the back. It was even then much faster than the Isle of Man in spite of also being run on everyday roads, but quite different in character because you could scratch at Spa in a way that would be madness on the Island. Take the first corner after the start and finish line, for example—Eau Rouge. It's a downhill left-hander with a dip in the apex, followed by a right and another left as you climb the hill with thousands of people sitting on the bank in front of you. Because it was a very difficult corner to get right and was also situated in full view of the pits, everyone made a big effort there to impress the opposing teams as well as the trade reps and any possible future sponsors who might be watching, quite apart from the sea of spectators. They always seemed to get huge crowds at Spa, often 100,000 or more spread all round the circuit.

'So there were certain places at Spa where you could really earhole your way round, but there was also hardly a corner on the circuit that wouldn't bite back at you if you took liberties with it. At Eau Rouge you had to get lined up dead right for the left-hander, else you'd be hopelessly wrong for the right, which in the early days when I first rode there before they resurfaced the track for the car guys was also off-camber. That meant that you couldn't actually put the power on hard till you were through the right and just going into the second left around the corner and out of view of the pits. Lots of people did, of course, and the result was some spectacular entries into the hay bales, but it was all a question of momentum and power spread: if you could rush through Eau Rouge proper, which was the first left-hander, fast enough on the right line, you wouldn't need to switch the power on till it was safe to do so. Later on, when they recambered the right-hander properly it wasn't such a problem, but you still used to see the occasional showman who'd practically run over the toes of the people standing at the end of the pits road on the right before sweeping dramatically into the left-hander; it really wasn't necessary though—they only did it to break up the people in the pits a bit, I think!'

Given that the start line and indeed the whole pits area was situated on a fairly steep downhill slope, did Phil adopt the now fashionable paddle-start technique? 'No, I was always a traditional run-and-bump man, even with the 125 Yamaha: I just thought that that way you were certain of having enough speed up when you let the clutch out, and don't forget that with the Yamahas we were

Swiss-Hungarian Gyula Marsovsky leads Dieter Braun and the rest of the Yamaha-mounted pack battling for second place in the 1971 Belgian 250 cc GP through Stavelot

running some pretty high compression ratios which made the chances of the back wheel locking up even greater.

'I don't remember much about that first meeting apart from one thing: it was my first encounter with the Latin loo! Assen was no problem, because the Dutch are like us in that respect, but Spa was another matter. I was a bit of a shy lad in those days, so when a very shapely Belgian blonde walked in to fill a can of water from the tap just as I was relieving myself after a couple of the local beers, you can imagine my reaction! Communal toilets were just one of the many things you had to get used to when you joined the Continental Circus, and that first Spa meeting was really my initiation into a quite different world from what I'd been used to. I remember there were people there like Paddy Driver, Mike Duff, Bob Mac and Hugh Anderson— lots of the old names who were real hard, professional privateers who let you know how you stood with them and weren't afraid of a good party or a few laughs. It all changed so much when the Japanese teams came into GP racing in a big way, and though I'll readily admit I made the most of things when they did, I can't say I cared for all the politics and back-biting that developed as a result. I played my full part in it all, because I had to if I wanted to safeguard my position and my career, but there's no question things were better in the old days before Honda, Suzuki and Yamaha came along—we were all just a lot poorer, that's all!'

Was the racing better too—from the spectators' point of view? 'In a way, yes—because though the handful of works bikes usually won if they finished, there'd be some terrific racing further down the field because everyone else was so evenly matched as far as the bikes were concerned. Also, those old G50s and Manx Nortons were pretty fast, reliable machines, and in those days it was common for 90 per cent of the field to finish an hour-long GP, instead of less than 50 per cent nowadays in a race lasting less than 45 minutes. That had to be better—

though of course in the mid-1960s you had the best of both worlds because there were bitter battles between the works bikes for victory and quite good finishing records down the field.'

Riding a classic British single at Spa must have meant a lot of flat-out running? 'Yes, with a four-speed box, especially, riding a Manx or G50 there was a piece of cake compared to later on; really only La Source required any clutch-slip, and you could do Eau Rouge in top, then nick it down a gear in the dip and hope you'd be going fast enough to keep it on the mega going up the hill—second would be too low. Later on with the six-speed 250 Yamaha I'd come back two or even three gears to keep it on the pipe going up the slope; it's probably just as well I never rode the 125 V4 Yam there because it had a very narrow powerband. We used to rev them to 17,000 on the last lap, but normally the limit was 16,000, with the power coming in between 14,000 and 14,500 rpm—it was very hard work to get the best from them. By comparison the MV was like a road bike: on the 500 you had a 5–6000 rpm rev band, which meant that I'd nick it into fourth (on a

Roberto Gallina exits Stavelot on the factory three-cylinder Laverda 1000 he shared with Nico Cereghini in the 1975 Spa 24 Hours

five-speed box) just going into Eau Rouge, ease through on the overrun, then notch third in the dip just to carry me up the hill. Just at the crest, where the front wheel started to paw the air, I'd slip it in fourth, then away along the straight out into the country. Remember that the circuit was so fast we'd be pulling a very high gear: third on the 500 MV would be good for over 120 mph, for example, and we had to have special 21T engine sprockets made for the Norton, the track was so fast, compared to only 19T or maybe 20T gearing for the Island.'

The straight after Eau Rouge must have been quite fast if you were coming on to it in fourth gear, surely? 'Yes, but not as quick as elsewhere because you were actually climbing very gradually uphill all the way. You actually reached the summit of the hill just before the next tight left-hander which I never did find out the name of, but which was a vital corner. It was a second-gear turn going downhill, and how fast you could get through it determined your speed down the slope and round the next corner, which is really called Burnenville but which all the Brits used to call the "Cocoa bends" or the "Co-cos", for obvious reasons! On the map it looks like two corners, but really it's the longest right-hander in the world; it just went on and on and on— made Gerard's at Mallory seem like a hairpin in comparison! There were a couple of farm buildings on the outside bang on the apex, and you'd give a sigh of relief each time you'd get past there in one piece because it was a place you really didn't want to fall off at—you could be sure it was going to hurt if you did. On the Norton I'd be flat out in top gear— around 140 mph—chin on the tank and cranked over for what seemed like ages with the rear tyre scrabbling for adhesion. The Cocoas were certainly one of the most demanding corners I've ever ridden round: on the MV I'd knock it back a gear, but that would still be 140 mph, though much more comfortable.'

Talking of falling off, did Phil ever explore the natural habitat of the Ardennes flora and fauna? 'Not once, I'm glad to say. I never fell off anywhere at Spa—though I did have one very close shave I'll tell you about in a minute—which was just as well. After Jackie Stewart had his big shunt there in 1964 or so, he wound all the car guys up and they insisted on the circuit being lined with armco. That may have been fine for them but not for us; bike racing was very much the poor relation of the cars in those days, so what had been quite a safe track up till then for motorcycles suddenly became very dangerous. It was obviously impossible to line the whole track

with straw bales, and it was a bit of a death trap after that, I'm afraid.'

After Burnenville came the Malmedy crossroads, which, riding round on a road bike at the time, never seemed much of a corner: was it then? 'Well, remember you were coming out of the Cocoas at nearly, if not at, maximum speed, so what looked a gentle swerve actually became a tricky kink at speed—Spa was full of those, but the trickiest of all came next. After Malmedy there was about a three-mile straight down to Stavelot [actually 4.75 km— about 2.95 miles] which was completely flat out as fast as you could go on the tallest gearing your bike would possibly pull—except for one little problem called the Masta kink. Masta was a little village— more of a hamlet, really—where the road did a sort of narrow left/right S-bend. You could take it absolutely against the stop on a 500 Manx Norton *if* you knew what you were doing. You had to be lined up exactly right to do it flat on a British single, and of course on any other 500 or even a 350 it was a real white-knuckle affair, especially as there was a house bang on the racing line on the way out, and picking the bike up enough to miss the steps that came down from the front door into the street— there was no pavement—could be a real struggle. You had about a 50-yard margin to play with in terms of the precise moment you peeled off for the left-hander going in, and again when you flicked it over to the right in the middle of the kink. It required very precise and careful timing, and you could always tell who the really good riders were, the ones who were trying really hard, by how well they did Masta; if you knocked it off when you didn't have to you could lose 500 revs just like that, which you might not see again till just when you were coming down into Stavelot, so it was crucial to do it right. Each lap as you approached the kink you'd say to yourself: "Right, this is it, this is it, I'll do it flat this time . . . *whooooooops*!", and then you'd chicken out and ease the throttle just that little bit!

'I remember in 1964 I finished second to Mike Hailwood on the MV in the 500 race on a good old G50 Matchless—a very good bike that was, too. Anyway, after one of the practice sessions we were all sitting round having a smoke and a chat when Mike came in, just off the MV. He was as white as a sheet and shaking. We asked him what was wrong and he simply said: "Masta. I've just taken it flat out—but never again, *never*!" We knew he had done it too, because Mike didn't make things like that up, so there were lots of nods of sympathy, but I little thought that a couple of days later I'd have my

Phil Read about to swoop past Rosner's MZ under braking for La Source to take the lead on his works Yamaha and win the 1968 250 cc Belgian GP. The East German was second

biggest scare on a racing bike at exactly the same place. It was in the 250 race, and Redman on the Honda four and I on the Yamaha were having a big tear-up for the world championship. Anyway, the Honda always started faster, so off he went into the lead, but then I steamed past him coming out of the Cocoas and he tucked in behind me to try to grab a tow. Mike Duff, who was my team-mate then on the second RD56 Yamaha twin, was right up Jim's chuff as well as we approached Masta. Just as I was peeling off into the first left-hand part, the Yamaha seized on one pot. I always rode with my hand on the clutch, of course—it was suicidal if you didn't— so I whipped it in just as I felt the bike tighten, but not in time to stop the back wheel stepping out as it locked up. Fortunately, the faster you're going the longer it takes for the back to come round, if you think about it—your own velocity helps keep it in line—but I still had a hell of a job fighting it into submission and of course there were the houses on

the outside of the exit to worry about too. Anyway, I just managed to miss everything, but as I toured to a stop I saw this Honda leaping back on to the track in front of me from the middle of the surrounding countryside! Redman had apparently just managed to avoid ramming me when the bike nipped up, but only at the cost of running off the track at 140 mph or so, brushing telegraph poles and missing the wall of a house by less than a foot before he eventually rejoined the circuit. How he stayed on I'll never know, because of course he daren't touch the brakes on the grass, but anyway he made it, though not surprisingly he was pretty detuned and couldn't catch Mike Duff who won the race for Yamaha. Whew!'

Presumably Masta on the MV would have been a case of notching it down a gear? 'No, not at all, the only bike I ever had to do that with was the RG Suzuki I rode in practice there in 1976 before I retired from GP racing for good at that very meeting. With the MV all I needed to do was just ease the throttle, and this was what made it such a great bike for Spa or indeed anywhere else. It had such a wide spread of power you could afford to ride it on and off the throttle, because if you lost 500 revs somewhere you knew you could pick them up as soon as you opened her up fully again, instead of paying for it all the way along the next straight.

'Because the circuit was so fast you had to modify your style—like, for example, you didn't sit up for corners except for La Source and maybe a couple of others: you could lose quite a bit of time if you did, so usually it was just a case of a quick peep over the screen, then back down with your chin on the tank again at once. The straight bits were only a problem with one bike I ever rode there, which was the V4 250 Yamaha when we first had them—1966, I think. We'd started off running the bike, which was a lot heavier than the twin and had to have quite a few pounds of lead clamped to the bottom frame rails to make it handle even halfway decently, with the same front brake as the 250 twin.

Agostini cranks the three-cylinder 500 MV into La Source en route to yet another GP victory at Spa in 1968. He averaged over 200 km/h for the first time that year

It was hopelessly inadequate, so they turned up at Spa with this huge new 4LS device that had two enormous air scoops cast into the brake plates which certainly worked a lot better. But going along a fast straight I suddenly felt the bike veering off to the right, so I hoicked it back, thought "hm, funny" to myself, then a couple of seconds later it was trying to turn left! What was happening, of course, was that the air scoops were so big they were catching the slipstream and forcing the handlebars over. Soon as we cut them off everything was fine!'

Watching at Masta once in practice I remember being impressed by the way that Ago went through there every lap just raising a puff of dust from the straw bale protecting the steps of the house on the exit down into the street. Did Phil do that too? 'No, I tried to stay away from the straw bales in more ways than one, but that was typical Ago—it was just the Italian way. Their natural habitat in those days were all the seaside courses like Riccione, Rimini, Cervia and Cesenatico, which were all lined entirely with straw bales. The past master at showing off in that

way was old Provini: he used to get the crowd into hysterics just by rushing down the straight and lining up for the corners about three inches out from the straw bales, then leaning into them and brushing them with his shoulder on the way in and out. All the bits of straw would flutter up into the air and the crowd would go mad—pure bravado.'

After Masta there was another long straight to Stavelot, a fast right-hander at another crossroads: was this a straightforward corner? 'Yes, fairly, except that again momentum was important, because there was a downhill entry and an uphill exit, so on anything except the MV you had to try to keep it wound up through the corner. We did it in top on the Manx and G50, but though Spa was always a pretty smooth circuit when I raced on it, there was only one bump which really mattered and that was on the way into Stavelot—it could really unsettle the bike if it wasn't set up properly. That brings us to the only man who ever questioned my riding ability—Geoff Duke. I rode for him on the Gilera fours in 1963, and in practice Geoff decided to carry out plug chops at the end of the Masta straight. So he and a mechanic went out to Stavelot, and for about four or five laps in succession I'd cut the engine and coast into the crossroads by the entry to the village while they checked the plugs. Of course, this meant that I wasn't getting any practice at doing the corner properly, and to make things worse the Gilera was a real pig to ride—definitely the worst-handling bike I ever sat on there, including the Yamahas. Anyway, after they'd done enough chops I did half a dozen laps straight off, but going into Stavelot each lap I'd hit this bloody bump and the whole bike would start hacking about, so of course I was pretty slow through there, especially not having had many laps to find a possible way round it. Back in the pits after practice Geoff comes up to me and starts tearing me off a strip in front of everyone: "You were absolutely useless through that corner," he says. "Useless: what's wrong with you?" Charming! It was no good telling him it was the bike that was useless, that because he wouldn't let us change the way it was set up it was practically dangerous—that was just the way things were in the team. It was all very dispiriting, knowing you had a hell of an engine sitting in a camel of a chassis, being told to go out and ride your hardest, it was OK, you were well insured! Seriously! I actually finished second to Mike's MV in that race, but Spa didn't place a premium on handling as other circuits did.

'Anyway, after Stavelot there was a left-hand curve going up the hill again which you took flat out accelerating hard, then two rights which were awfully tight—but you couldn't afford to lose momentum because it was all uphill. This last third of the circuit between Stavelot and La Source was where you could really make up time if you knew your way round—bit like Glen Helen on the TT course, or the Milntown section.' Wasn't this where the heavily forested part began, too? 'Yes, but at first it was open on the right, then the trees started to close in till it could get very dark in there on a dull day, which placed even more of a premium on course knowledge.'

The Ardennes are famous for their sudden changes of weather. Was this a problem on a circuit as long as Spa? 'Well, it's true that it could be raining on one side of the circuit while it was warm and sunny on the other, but if you kept your wits about you it wasn't a problem, especially back in the 1960s when everyone used treaded tyres. I always used to glance over towards Masta after I got on to the straight above Eau Rouge, which is the highest point on the course, and you could see quite clearly if there was any sign of a rain cloud on the horizon so you'd be ready for spots on the screen if there was. Same thing going down towards the Masta kink from the Cocoas—look over towards La Source to check if it was cloudy there. If it did rain it was the same for everybody; you just knocked it off and hoped nobody would find more grippy parts than you did. I can see the point of slick tyres with the power of modern bikes, but I sometimes think it's a pity we don't all ride on multi-purpose tyres nowadays.'

In the midst of the pine forests there was a very tricky corner, Blanchimont: what did Phil think of it? 'It was the last major corner before La Source, and nothing like as fast as a lot of people seemed to think—every time I rode at Spa there'd be some hotshot off there. You'd be back a couple of gears on most bikes, especially on the very high Francorchamps gearing, and it was a late-entry left-hander which you had to be careful not to run too wide on the exit from. But once again you were still climbing slightly, so it was important not to lose too much speed; again, the MV was ideal through there.'

Then came La Source—one of the most photographed corners in the world, and one of the slowest, no? Read grins with pleasure at the memory. 'Aha—a very interesting corner, La Source. In fact—a terrific corner, actually; a great place for outbraking, or playing another rider out by

Read accelerates out of La Source at the end of the first lap in the 1974 500 cc Belgian GP—'One of my greatest moments in bike racing.' No sign of Ago!

pretending that you couldn't pass him under braking all through the race, first up the outside, no good, then trying up the inside, still can't do it— then the last lap when he thinks he's got you taped and brakes in the same place as before you just whistle up the outside of him on a faster line—and goodbye, Charlie! I used to work to the marker boards for braking there, but things were a little complicated by the fact there was a left-hand curve just before the hairpin, and you actually didn't see the corner till quite late.

'I remember I ran out of brakes there once with the 250 Yamaha; the hydraulic brake pipe had severed, so when I went for the front brake I had nothing—the most awful experience a rider can have, in my book. Luckily there's an uphill slip road, but the trouble is that they used to wheel a big metal barrier across it to stop people watching for free. I practically locked the engine up I came down the gears so quickly trying to stop, with the rear end fish-tailing as I stamped on the rear stopper. Would you believe my front wheel just kissed the barrier as I finally stopped—more or less upright! I take it back—*that* was my worst moment at Spa, not the Masta business!

'I also remember the last lap of the 250 race one year—it must have been 1972. I'd been dicing for the whole race with Rod Gould on the works Yamaha, me on the private bike I'd won the title with the year before. All the way up to the last lap I'd been weighing him up for a big outbraking effort at La Source, and sure enough I just managed to hold on long enough to get past him on the inside on this last corner. Then we set off down the finishing straight, which isn't a straight at all but a long curve to the right. About halfway to the flag I saw this thing start creeping up the inside of me—it was Rodney's front wheel. So I moved over a bit, then a bit more, then a bit more still, till I was practically running into the pit barrier, but still this bloody wheel kept creeping up till I couldn't move over any more and that was it—*zap*! I'd outridden him into La Source but he'd outpowered me on the works bike down to the finish. In the end we were both surprised to find out we were dicing for second place because Saarinen was so far in front we hadn't seen him!'

What was Phil's greatest moment at Spa? 'Well, of course it was the first win there on the MV. I'd had a frustrating Dutch TT and was neck and neck with Ago in the championship—him on the Yamaha, of course. I'd got myself in the mood to ride on the limit for the whole race if necessary, and was fired up enough to clear off from the two-strokes at the start and stay there. In the event, that's what happened. It was just about my perfect race, especially in view of the circumstances, because I broke the four-minute barrier for the first time—

which was the equivalent there of doing a 100 mph lap on the Island in the 1950s—in spite of the fact that the MV was actually slower than the Yamahas and Suzukis on pure top end, which you'd think would be disastrous on such a fast circuit. I must say that the end of the first lap that year was one of my greatest moments in bike racing; I'd lapped at over 130 mph from a standing start, I was seven seconds in the lead after only one lap, and the echo of the MV's marvellous exhaust note bouncing off the pits as I swooped down to Eau Rouge with everyone standing on their feet and cheering and waving even made my eyes mist up a little. Eau Rouge was always my favourite corner at Spa anyway—getting it just right was a big thrill, especially in front of the sea of people on the bank and in the pits with the commentator getting all worked up, and so on. You could actually see the spectators on the grass in front of you standing up to cheer and applaud, and that day I really must say I felt proud of what I did. Spa played quite an important part in my career one way or another, quite apart from being just about my favourite circuit anywhere, and that day was probably the most satisfying I ever had in racing. No wonder I like the place so much!'

Up the famous hill with Chas Mortimer leading Dieter Braun and Gyula Marsovsky all aboard Yamahas in the 1971 250 GP

Kenny Roberts: Lord of Laguna

Kenny Roberts—keen amateur photographer as well as ace rider

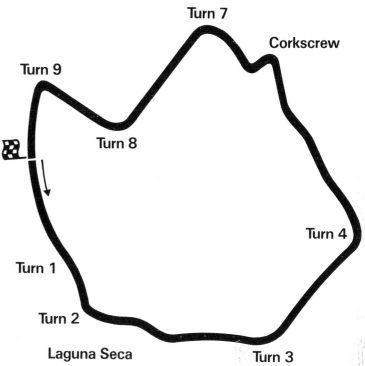

Few riders have ever so totally dominated the history of motorcycle racing at one of the world's major racetracks as has Kenny Roberts at Laguna Seca. Since the first bike race was held back in 1972 on the picturesque, challenging 1.9-mile Northern California circuit, laid out among the sand dunes of the Monterey Peninsula, the three-times 500 cc World Champion and twice AMA Grand National title-holder has won the main event at the annual July meeting no less than seven times, out of a total of 13 times 'at base'. If that isn't incredible enough,

Kenny has been second twice (on one occasion winning one of the two 100 km legs that have given the so-called Champion Spark Plug 200 its name), third once and retired three times—on two out of the three occasions with chain problems. Even then, he has won no less than a staggering 65 per cent of the individual races he has taken part in on what is in effect his home track, coming as he does from nearby Modesto, California. Kenny Roberts may be known as 'King Kenny' the world over, but in California he is the unchallenged Lord of Laguna!

Originally developed as a sports car course in the mid-1950s by the SCCA, Laguna Seca hosted its first bike meeting in 1972, when the late, great Cal Rayborn scored one of his many notable victories over faster, but thirstier and less reliable, two-stroke opposition on the thundering XR750 Harley-Davidson road racer in the inaugural 125-mile

The first wave of riders leaves the grid at the start of the Superbike final at Laguna Seca in 1983

AMA National event, ironically sponsored by Kawasaki, who were favourites to win. But Yvon 'SuperFrog' DuHamel, team leader of the Green Meanies, unloaded spectacularly while in the lead, a feat he was to repeat no less than three more times in the next few years on the Monterey track. However, if Laguna is far from being the gritty little French-Canadian's favourite ribbon of tarmac, it certainly must be Kenny Roberts'; starting with third place in that inaugural race on a small Yamaha, he has made the annual July classic his own, winning into the bargain in 1978 and 1979 on the only two occasions since the mid-1960s when the USA has hosted a world championship road race, when Laguna was one of the qualifying rounds for the F750 world title. If and when a United States GP is held again, the betting is that it will be Laguna Seca that will host it. Not only is it the leading track in California, hotbed of US road racing, but it is the only circuit in the USA which traditionally attracts large crowds: compared with the 30,000 or so vacationers who line the Daytona Speedway each March for the 200-miler, Laguna Seca's attendance for the annual July meeting, when traditionally the American riders who have latterly dominated the world 500 cc scene return for perhaps their one and only back-home race that year, has steadily inched towards the six-figure

mark. What is more, the crowd is considered remarkably knowledgeable about road racing, still a relatively less important side of US two-wheeled competition compared to the established dirt racing scene.

Kenny Roberts is in no doubt where the credit lies for the success of the annual Laguna Seca meeting as a motorcycle event: promoter Lee Moselle. 'Lee's the only promoter in the USA I've worked with who knows or cares about road racing,' says KR. 'I first got involved with helping him promote the deal in 1979, after Sears Point was sold, which is where he'd been before. I'd just won my first world championship in Europe, but the organizers at Laguna couldn't see what a good thing that was to hang the meeting on—they didn't think it was worth the money to bring me back from Europe in mid-season. They didn't realize that it was costing me money to come, we had to bring the mechanics back, the bike back—everything. Well, Lee was the only one that figured it out, so when he went to work at Laguna Seca, I made a deal with him, just two weeks before the race, to come back and do it, and I won it. What's more, he had a lot bigger crowd than the year before, and that was the start of the growth in interest in big-time road racing in California—Lee Moselle made Laguna into a big race. From getting 20,000 for the race, he's taken it to 90,000 or more, just because he wanted the stars to come and made sure they did by paying them a guarantee. I know he's had real fights with the AMA about this, because they say he shouldn't pay me or

Randy Mamola or Eddie Lawson or Freddie Spencer to come from Europe—they figure it's un-American or something, because the guys that stay at home and race in the States don't get start money—but that's BS. The reason Laguna is big time is because the fans *know* that all the top US riders will be there and will really go for it, not like at Daytona where you might have a couple of guys on factory bikes and 75 on street four-strokes going 50 mph slower and spending all they've got just to make up the numbers. Laguna is an honest race, because Lee promotes it honestly. He drags me and Randy Mamola and Eddie Lawson round the TV stations in the Bay Area saying: "Hey, these guys are back from Europe just for one weekend, they're the best in the world and you can catch them in action at Laguna Seca." He gets local media who give motorcycle racing less coverage than arm-wrestling to sit up and take notice, and he's built Laguna into the premier road race in America,

KR at Laguna's Turn 2 with the Yamaha: 130 mph in fifth gear

which is what it is. I'm happy to have helped him do that, because I felt when we started out together that this was a cause worth building. When in 1983 they had so many people going through the gates that they ran out of tickets and had to start giving pieces of paper out, that's when I knew he'd made it. Now all we need is for the AMA to recognize that, and give Lee Moselle the support he needs to run a US GP—at Laguna Seca.'

Does Laguna have the facilities to host a round of the world championship—again, remembering the 750 title round in the late 1970s? How about the track length, too—at 1.9 miles Laguna is just under the FIM minimum circuit distance for GPs? 'That didn't matter when they needed rounds for the 750 series, and it shouldn't now,' says Roberts firmly. 'Misano in Italy is hardly any longer and they run there, even though the track's in real bad shape. Laguna has everything a track needs: apart from the real pretty location [a stone's throw from the Pacific Ocean, in one of the most scenic parts of Northern California], you've got good hotels, good pits, good golf courses, a nice atmosphere and a track laid out

in such a way that the riders like to come and race there. You have personnel at the racetrack that make it a little more enjoyable than the regular places, like Daytona, where they throw you out of the pits if your passes aren't visible and you get this feeling of hassle all the time. Laguna is just an enjoyable event, especially now it's no longer a dusty bowl in the infield—they've got grass, there's a lake in the middle, they've moved the guard rails back and, above all, they didn't say: "Hey, we really want to make a lot of money at this"—they said: "Hey, let's build a really good racetrack and run a good event," which is what's happened. The key to Lee's success is that he's built a major race by working with the riders, with the media and with the sponsors, so that now it really is a big thing.'

Kenny Roberts' sentiments about Laguna Seca thus echo Barry Sheene's similar feelings about Scarborough—but how does KR rate the actual circuit itself after racing there so successfully for more than a decade? Is it a challenging track? 'I pretty much know everything there is to know about the racetrack by now,' states Kenny, 'but that's only happened because I've raced and tested

The 250-class riders sweep through the sand dunes of the Monterey Peninsula

there so much since I first raced there back in 1972. But I can recall real well that first time I rode there, back in the days when I didn't really know much about road racing—it was just something you did to get extra points for the AMA National series—and I knew a whole lot less about how to get round Laguna Seca. I was *lost*! That was the year Yamaha brought out the TZ250 with water-cooling, but Kel [Carruthers] built the bike I rode, which was like a new air-cooled version—sort of like an RD56, I guess. It was faster than the TZs, which is why he did it, but the swing arm was a couple of inches longer and the engine an inch more forward, so it had a wheelbase about three inches longer than usual. It was real hard to turn with, and I just couldn't figure it out: I knew it was pretty much front-end heavy, and at Daytona and the super-Speedways it worked real good, but at Laguna it was a definite handicap. You'd be going round the Corkscrew, and the front end would be going down while the back was still turning! Plus the track was so fast, you had all these real demanding corners which kind of flowed into each other, and I was still learning about road racing—with a bike that didn't want to turn corners. So I just rode round and came third, not really knowing what the hell I was doing, but at least I beat Kel: he was only fifth!' Carruthers

Roberts on the 350 Yamaha on which he made his Laguna début in 1971, finishing third

announced afterwards to reporters in best Australian that 'I got me ass blowed into the weeds!' Rayborn and second-place man, three-cylinder Triumph-mounted Gene Romero, proved that the day of the F750 four-stroke was not over, only waning. . . .

Kenny Roberts has another vivid memory of that first Laguna Seca bike race. 'I was coming over the hill into Turn 2, doing probably about 130 mph on that bike, and I was lapping a guy. He went from one side of the road to another as if he was even more lost than me, which I guess he was. Anyway, I dove on to the inside into the corner, and just then he decided he needed the inside line again, so we met at the apex and I just smacked into him real hard. I don't know what happened to him, if he came down or not, but when I ran into him, it broke my front-brake lever in two. I didn't know much about road racing, but I did know we weren't riding dirtbikes and I was supposed to have brakes I could use at the front. Fortunately, he left me just about an inch of lever I could still use, so I stayed in the race and came third—but after that, it got kind of scary thinking maybe you could hit someone at 130-plus going into Turn 2. I thought I was dead when it happened, that's for sure.'

Presumably after that the bikes got better, and Kenny got to learn a bit about road racing? 'Guess

so, but it took me a couple of years to figure Laguna out properly, so that it got to be an easier place to ride—usually I can learn a track much quicker, but not this one. Laguna is just one complicated racetrack, and being so short as well, it means you have very little time to rest on it mentally. It's not so tough physically because you have a couple of sixth-gear straights you can get a little breather on, but because it's so complicated, it's very demanding on your concentration—if you break that for any reason, you can go from 1:06 laps to 1:08 real quick. And a lot of guys who are quite good riders won't even get into the sevens at Laguna, because although it's a fast circuit, it's short and so complicated. There are bumps you can work with, pavement changes, places where you don't take the obvious line—I think Laguna's one of the better circuits in the world for the rider because it gives you the opportunity to work with something. They didn't just draw it out on a piece of paper and say: "There's your line, guys—go for it!", like at Silverstone, for instance—you don't have much to work with there. You do have a variety of things you can work with at Laguna, and your job is to put it all in a package which will give you a fast lap time. OK, the bike might not work well in Turn 9, which is real slow—but you don't want it to, because if it works good at Turn 9, it's not going to work well round the high-speed corners, which is where you get your lap times. If you're prepared to go 1:06 at Laguna, you have to be very, very close to a disastrous

mistake all the way round, because to get in the sixes, you have to be doing 150 mph round the turns. If you're doing that, and you get your line wrong by two inches going in, you're facing disaster coming out. Well, OK—you can always roll the throttle back: great—you just went from 1:06 to 1:09 real quick!'

Considering that a 1:08 lap time at Laguna Seca still comprises an average speed of over 100 mph, it is evident that the switchback track packs a stiff challenge into its nine turns. How does KR ride the circuit, beginning with the hilly start and finish straight? 'This is one of the sixth-gear straights you can take a little breather on,' says Kenny, 'but you can't relax too much, because the crest of the hill is at a kind of awkward moment, just after the bridge on the start line and just where you'd be in sixth gear. So I actually short-shift a little, and I'll poke sixth gear about 20 yards from the crest of the hill, which means the only problem then is that you can't see over the top of the hill, where the mountain starts to go away. It doesn't matter exactly where you are on the racetrack when you come over the hill, but when you come down on the

Above *Gary Scott with the XR750 Harley-Davidson (no. 64) and Gary Nixon on a Suzuki (no. 9) sandwich Steve McLaughlin at Laguna*

Below *Kenny Roberts and Eddie Lawson on their 500 cc GP Yamahas about to swallow up John Ashmead's Kawasaki superbike at Laguna in 1983*

other side, you've got to be lined up straight towards the white line which is on the outside of the racetrack. The mountain comes in a little bit after the crest of the hill, so that if you're pointed wrong, you run into the side of it, so the key thing is to start right and shoot over the top of the hill straight. Otherwise, if you're trying to turn on the brow of the hill, the bike will kick sideways because not only does the front end get light—I'll be pulling wheelies at 150–160 mph plus—but so does the back as well: you're almost taking off with both wheels at once. So if you're not pointed in the absolute right direction, when you try to correct, the bike will step out on you, and that'll be it: they'll pick you up in a little box.

'They call that Turn 1, even though it isn't much of a turn at all, but it is the key to Turn 2, which is one of the most important corners on the racetrack—where I hit that guy the first time I raced there. This is a fast left-hander, and if you don't come out of the hill lined up just right, you're not going to get into Turn 2 just right, and you'll lose time having to back off. Plus, the most important thing about Turn 2 is the kerb on the right-hand side on the exit, on the outside of the track to stop the cars getting off into the dirt. If you could go through the corner the way you wanted to, you'd need a foot of that kerb, so you can't do that. Instead, you have to cut it a little early so as to miss that kerb, which you can't do unless you line up Turn 2 with Turn 1. Turn 2 is a very fast corner, taken in fifth gear at about 130 mph, but it's only a fifth-gear corner *if* you enter it properly, and to do a 1:06 at Laguna, you've got to almost hit that kerb by inches and get right in its gutter if you want to get Turn 2 down. If you enter it too early, you have to physically force the motorcycle to turn on the exit, which is something it doesn't want to do at that speed, just to miss the kerb. On a 1:06 lap, I'll use the fact that it's a slightly banked corner to my advantage, and actually go over the white line on the outside of the track out on to the bare pavement so as to go in real late, past all the black rubber marks left by the cars and such, then get back on the throttle real hard just when I run on to the banked part, running out to just clip the kerb on the exit. That's the fastest possible way round Turn 2.'

After this dauntingly fast but subtle section of track, there is little time for the rider to draw breath before he enters another key section of the circuit, almost equally fast. Kenny Roberts: 'After Turn 2, you've a straightaway which has a change of camber, which is no big deal, but then you go to sixth gear and just as you've got maximum revs in top gear—about 12,000 rpm on the 500 Yamaha, same as you would going over the hill by the start line—you come into Turn 3. This is probably the easiest corner on the racetrack, with a nice camber to it; it's a pretty big turn, more of a dogleg than a proper turn, which you take in fifth gear, curving gently to the left, but it's the key to Turn 4, which is another fast corner, again a left-hander, and that in turn is the key to a fast lap time at Laguna Seca.

'You can take Turn 3 a lot faster than you might think, because the camber and the gradient are going to slow you down, so you can bury it in the corner and get on the throttle real early, just waiting in case the back end decides to step out a little, which it might do. But it's important to get a real hard drive out of the turn as early as possible, because that governs your speed up the next hill leading into Turn 4. I'll hold fifth gear all the way up the mountain, but then just as the engine peaks out in fifth at 12,000, you have a fourth-gear left-hander just over the crest of the hill, so you can't see the line you want till you get there: that's Turn 4. You mustn't get too hard on the brakes here, otherwise you'll upset the balance of the bike coming over the top of the hill, and that'll affect your exit speed on Turn 4, which has an even sharper hill leading out of it. The way the track goes, you have an uphill coming out of Turn 3, then it sort of flattens out a little, then gets even steeper out of Turn 4, and if you don't take this corner at the right speed so that you end up dropping off the power even a little, you can't get up the hill—you're gonna have to downshift and say goodbye to that fast lap time. So this is a really critical corner.

'So I go into Turn 4 a little wider than most people, flick it down pretty hard on its side, to the left, then gas it real early. There's a bump in the middle of the corner, so you have to be on the gas to be able to carry the power through when you hit it. You can't drift too wide, because there's rain gutters on the outside, but I come out wider than most people also, only because the closer you hold it in, the harder it is on the tyres, so I'll drift out to the white line usually and try to keep the speed up that way—really, if you don't come out of the corner at 10,000 rpm on a 500 Yamaha, you aren't going to cut a fast lap.'

Next comes one of the more spectacular sections for the spectator of an already spectacular race circuit, where the faster bikes pull huge wheelies at high speed, before pirouetting into the most famous corner on the track, beloved of photographers—the

Corkscrew. KR: 'I'll hold fourth gear after Turn 4 almost to the crest of the steep hill after it, then poke fifth just before the top, where it pulls a big wheelie. Really, that's not the crest at all, only a small flat area about 30 ft long where the road sort of goes down into a little dip and the thing wheelies over that. But as soon as the front wheel hits the pavement again, you've got to be hard on the brakes, because you're coming into the Corkscrew, which is what everyone calls Turns 5 and 6. The Corkscrew starts out at the very top of the hill, where you turn left, then drops steeply down the hill to turn right—it's like a chicane someone stuck on the side of a roller-coaster, and it takes a lot of practice and care to get right.

'As you crest the hill, you in fact have to be turning slightly right at the same time as hitting the brakes hard, which causes a lot of people to fall off at this point. Spencer came down here on the factory Honda one year, when he was too hard on the brakes at this point, or maybe he even committed the kind of error many novices make here, which is to get on the brakes before the front wheel is down on the ground again properly after the wheelie, in which case, of course, you lock up the front end and come down. So you have to be hard on the brakes here, but not too early and not so hard you'll lock the front wheel, and at the same time you're pulling over to the right to enter the Corkscrew, which is a second-gear left-hander dropping steeply down the mountain. You go from outside to inside going into the left turn, and then just as you hit the apex you crack the throttle hard, it does a little wheelie and starts off down the hill. But this is where you must be really careful, because after the apex of the left-hander, there's only about ten feet of pavement before it turns sharp right and the road drops away on the left. So above all, you must not have the bike leaned over to your left, still trying to make the first part of the chicane, once you crest the hill, but instead start trying to bring it upright as the road begins to fall away, and get the power on so that it pulls that little wheelie, which will help you pull it over to the right, because turning two wheels is harder than turning just one wheel. If you can get the front end kicked up just a little in the air, you can flick the back of the bike over to the right that much easier, and that's really the key to that corner, because it helps you go from flat over on the left to flat over on the right as quick as possible: without doing that, most people can't physically turn the bike enough with both wheels on the ground to take the Corkscrew right. Plus,

that allows you to get the power on much earlier to get out of the right-hander and down the hill, and if the back wheel does start to slide a little, it's no big problem because the weight's carrying you down the hill and you won't get out of shape.

'Getting out of Turn 6, which is the second part of the Corkscrew, is quite important, because if you run too wide, then you can't get back for Turn 7, which comes soon after and has a slight left-hand curve on the entry to a tighter, third-gear left. This is not a hard corner, except it's bumpy and some guys like to make trouble for themselves by going through the bumps rather than around them. The line I take there can only be taken if you take the Corkscrew right and don't run too wide on the exit where you start downhill, after which it flattens out a little, then starts downhill again so that you actually have to make a left-hand turn that's on the side of a mountain. It's not real steep, but it will carry you down there quicker than you want to go, which is exactly the way you have to take Turn 7—if you go into it thinking you've got the right speed, you've done it wrong! You've got to go into the corner thinking that you're a little hot, and then everything works out for you.

'As I come out of the Corkscrew I'm banked over maybe 25–30 degrees to the right, and I carry that line so it takes me where I want to go, towards the outside of the track. Then I lay it right over to the left at once, probably 50 or 60 degrees the other way without ever running straight upright, making a long, long corner out of it, running off the throttle in third gear, coasting downhill under a bridge, where it's hard to see the line. On the inside of the track by the apex are a lot of bumps where cars have roughed up the pavement, and you get guys who like to go through the holes 'cos if you drew a map of the circuit they'd show you the ideal line for that corner, except that line goes through that rough section. So a lot of people end up going through bumps for ten years before they figure out, hey, there are guys that are going round me on the outside faster. This is because there's a smooth line about four feet out from the kerb, and since you're going downhill, you can maintain your speed by taking this wider line just as well as you can by clipping the apex and running close in all the way round. If you run over the bumps, you can't keep your momentum up, whereas if you run round the outside, you not only pass people taking what's supposed to be the ideal line, but you actually come out of the corner in a better position than if you just try to give it a whole bunch of throttle and come out on the inside. But some guys can't see this, which is fine by me, 'cos I'll pass them there every time!'

After this, there's a tricky little downhill straight before Turn 8, another of those testing high-speed corners which make Laguna Seca such a challenge for the rider. How does Kenny Roberts take this one? 'A lot of guys fall off here, because of the camber, which is very difficult to get right. It's a very fast third-gear corner, still on the side of the mountain, but as you enter the corner to the right it's flat to begin with and then it goes into a terrific positive camber. So if you don't judge your braking right, and complete it before you get into the turn, your wheels will leave you because of the sudden transition from being flat to sharp camber. You can't brake into the apex like you can with most corners because of this, so you run away off to the outside of the track on the way in under hard braking, then get ready to flick the thing on its side without any brakes at all. Then the camber changes there and the corner is actually banked just on the apex, so that at that point you want to be hard on the throttle, because you get a tremendous amount of down-force on the back wheel, and you want to take full advantage of that to get a good drive out of the turn. But this will run you on to a line that goes a little bit off-camber, and just at this point there's a bit of a rise, too. When it hits that rise, the back end will step out if you're really going for it and start sliding just a little bit, but it's no big drama because you're going fast enough that it isn't going to come round on you. I've had it come round a lot on me at this point, but really, feet-off type things are rare there. However, if you've got a tyre in a race that's going away, you have to feather it just when you get to that rise, to wait for the rear wheel to catch up, because the camber change will make the back end all light. You gotta pay attention here, that's all.'

Next comes Turn 9, perhaps the slowest corner on the circuit, but one at which a surprising number of riders fall off: why so? 'It's because of the nature of the racetrack, and I guess human nature as well,' says Kenny. 'Being a very slow, bottom-gear left turn after so many fast, 150 mph corners, a lot of guys get to Turn 9 and think: "Wow, I've got to gas it hard, I'm too slow here"—and they spin the thing coming out. They feel, because the rest of the circuit is so fast and complicated, that they come to this easy corner and have to make up time on it, which you can't. With all those fast corners where if you get it right you can go from a 1:09 to a 1:06, why do you try to make up all your time at Turn 9, which is a low-gear corner? Even at the Corkscrew you can't

Battle of the Twins bikes at the entrance to the Corkscrew in a 1983 race

make up much time, only lose it—exiting and position is the key to doing the Corkscrew right, but at Turn 9 you've just got to cool it and concentrate on not getting taken out, and getting round the best way you can. Randy [Mamola] and some other fast guys like to come right down the inside, stay close in all the way round, then gas it on the exit, which might be fine on the three-cylinder Honda he used to ride, but the V4s take a bit more to get going. So I

use the whole racetrack, which means I can get harder on the gas and not force the tyres into making an abrupt corner. It's quite bumpy from all the cars braking there, but I'll take the perfect line, starting wide out then going to the inside and wide out again, aiming towards the wall on the exit and giving it a lot of throttle, which is why you get a lot of fish-tails: the back end is spinning so much in first gear, then you'll grab second and it'll spin again, and then you'll get to the wall and the bike has sort of spun itself out of the turn and you're gone up the straightaway to the start line for another lap. This way, my way, there's no chance of losing the back end, whereas the way Randy and those others take it, there *is* a chance for the back end to come round and spit you down the road. You get the thing sideways, your feet fly off and you've got to correct it again, so that's why I take a wide line at Turn 9—I let the bike do what it wants, I'm keeping my momentum up, and if I want to roll back a little and clip the wall or ease off a little if I get too close on the exit, I can still do that and maintain my speed. Turn 9 is a place to be real conservative, that's for sure.'

The many pre-season test sessions Kenny Roberts has carried out with Yamaha at Laguna Seca over the years must have helped his course knowledge grow, no? 'Yes, but sometimes you can't really run as fast in a winter test session as you can in the July race meeting, and cutting a 1:06 at Laguna means you've got to be hot, you've got to get in the groove. I do a lot of testing there though, sure, but the problem I've always had doing that there is the squirrels. Yamaha usually want to test there in the spring, which is when all the squirrels are coming out—guess they go to sleep in the winter or something. Testing at Laguna is a pretty scary deal anyway, because there's no runoff on any of the corners and when you're testing there's no hay bales, so if you come down you're going to hit the dirt first, but eventually you're going to end up in a wall or a guard rail without straw bales. Anyway, I remember tyre testing there one time, and there's this squirrel that makes his home in the apex of Turn 2. This one test session he wanted to come out of his home and get across the racetrack, and every time I bended off into Turn 2, going like 150 mph, I had my knee on the ground and this squirrel would stick his head up and come out of his

Roberts ignoring his own advice on the exit from Turn 9 in an effort to beat Suzuki-mounted Randy Mamola (no. 6) to the line in 1983 on his factory Yamaha 500. Team-mate Eddie Lawson (no. 21) leads the pursuing pack

KR showing the approved line through the Corkscrew to young Yamaha team-mate Jimmy Filice in 1983

hole right where my knee was going. It used to scare the hell out of me, so I went to the guards and asked them to scare him off, but they said they couldn't do anything, because Laguna's in the middle of a National Park and the wildlife is protected. I mean, never mind it's going to be squirrel squash when my knee hits him or I might unload because he wanted to play chicken with my front wheel—PROTECT ANIMALS, right? Well, eventually I ended up taking my pellet gun over to Laguna when I tested, and we'd go round in a truck beforehand and pop a few of them off. I figured— well, it was either them or me. You bend this bike into Turn 2, going 150 mph plus, and every other lap there's this squirrel popping his head up to say "hi"—no thanks!'

Local animal life apart, how does KR rate Laguna compared to the other tracks he has ridden on, especially in Europe? 'No doubt in my mind, Laguna Seca is a GP-calibre racetrack, and the sooner the AMA get themselves in gear and get a date for a world championship race there [now planned for 1988], the better for proper road racing in America—not this Superbike stuff, which is just a substitute. I think it's coming, but it's a long time coming. OK, so the track is short—but it has far more of a challenge packed into 1.9 miles than

Silverstone or Monza have in almost twice that. If you showed up at Laguna for a GP, you wouldn't know the track well enough to know how to tune it up right, because you'd be figuring it was wobbling when it shouldn't be, stuff like that. Well, there are places at Laguna it *has* to wobble, otherwise it won't go round Turns 2 and 3 fast. I guess because I pretty much do know everything about the racetrack, the only challenge I get riding there now is to set the bike up right for it, which is a lot different than for a European GP circuit. Plus, the secret to getting in the 1:06s at Laguna is split-second timing and good judgement, and no matter how long you've been racing at a track, if you can still pull that off and cut a good lap time, that's going to satisfy you. Without Laguna Seca, racing in the USA would be nothing.'

Superbikes at Laguna have everybody entering at different angles. Here Harry Klinzman (no. 31) leads Randy Skiver (no. 65), Carry Andrew (no. 41) and Larry Theobald (no. 20)

Barry Sheene on Scarborough

Barry Sheene: household name, but his own man

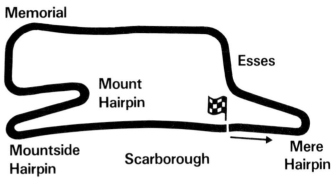

Scarborough's 2.41-mile Oliver's Mount circuit, so called after the hill on the southern side of the Yorkshire seaside town over which the switchback track winds up and down, is justly proud of its 'Mini-TT' nickname. It is well deserved, too, not just because of the 'street furniture' such as trees, lamp-standards and the like which line the course, but because of its unique nature as a relic from a bygone age of motorcycle sport. Actually, Scarborough is quite unlike the Isle of Man Mountain course from a physical standpoint; it is incredibly narrow, slow and runs entirely through wooded hillside apart

from the open section at the very top, whereas the TT is ultra-fast, mostly open, and has the biggest variety of scenery imaginable. Yet the two of them share the same implicit dangers of road courses, and at the same time present the same attractions to spectator and rider alike, being especially challenging taking into account the ultra-powerful nature of today's breed of racing machines. In fact, Scarborough is a famous survivor of a near-extinct breed: the path courses of the pre-World War 2 era, laid out along the perimeter paths and access roads of public parks or private parkland alike. Two of these, Donington and Crystal Palace, blossomed into fully-fledged race circuits, while others died a death in the course of time. Together with Wales' Aberdare Park and Scotland's Beveridge Park, Scarborough's Oliver's Mount course is the last of a generation of such tracks.

In view of this, it is surprising that racing only began at Scarborough immediately after the last war, when the Yorkshire town was host to one of the first British road-race events to be held after the end of hostilities. Strangely, the two-day meeting's schedule was modelled on the Manx GP, with racing held on Tuesday and Thursday, 17 and 19 September 1946—presumably as an extra attraction for visiting holidaymakers. The course was exactly the same then as it is today, only the surface changing over the years, and unchanged too since then is the keen support from local dignitaries for motorcycle racing in the town—with the huge

A bevy of Manx Nortons take the flag for the start of the 350 final at Scarborough in 1958. Mike Hailwood (no. 83) is first away

crowds of 40,000 or more which have on occasion lined the hillside to appreciate the unique viewpoint afforded by the natural grandstands, you don't have to be a hard-headed civic treasurer to appreciate the economic benefits to the town of the bike events. Not surprisingly, considering the narrow width of the circuit, Scarborough has always been a bike track, apart from a couple of races held in the mid-1950s for Formula 3 racing cars powered by single-cylinder motorcycle engines.

That first-ever meeting was dominated by Syd Barnett on his 500 Norton, who not only won the main event but also set up the first lap record at 57.49 mph. Sprint star George Brown, no mean road racer as well, wrested this from him in 1948 at 57.94 mph, doubtless treating the circuit as he did one of the hillclimbs such as Shelsley Walsh at which he was so adept; even so, to wrestle his big and powerful Vincent Black Lightning round the

course ahead of the more nimble 500s was quite a feat. The following year, Geoff Duke broke the outright record for the first of four times in all, eventually leaving it at 69.29 mph in 1955 on his four-cylinder Gilera 500, though it was Andrews' Norton which was first through the 60 mph barrier in 1950. By now, the Scarborough circuit was hosting two events per year, a national in July and the International Gold Cup meeting in September, attracting many of the leading stars of the GP world. In 1965, John Cooper was the first man to lap the circuit at more than 70 mph, on his 500 Manx Norton, though it took 'Moon-eyes' until 1971 to overhaul Dan Shorey's superb record of 14 race wins on the twisting track, when Coop won four races in a day to bring his score to 16.

The 1972 Gold Cup meeting was arguably Scarborough's greatest: not only did Giacomo Agostini visit the unique circuit for the first time (he didn't return!) and become the first foreign rider to win the Gold Cup on his three-cylinder 500 cc MV Agusta, but for the first time the track was lapped in less than two minutes by the great Jarno Saarinen on his TZ350 Yamaha, in the process knocking no less than 2½ seconds off the existing mark. It was an incredible feat, sadly not to be repeated in view of the Flying Finn's tragic death at Monza the following year, but it also emphasized Scarborough's popularity for the dozens of Scandinavian riders who have competed there over the years. The following year, the name of one Barry Sheene appeared on the list of Gold Cup winners for the first time, and in 1977 Barry made his own mark on the circuit's history by becoming the first man to lap it at more than 80 mph on his works 500 Suzuki. Britain's double World 500 cc Champion went on to win the Gold Cup no less than five times in all, and indeed his victory in the 1984 event was Sheene's last-ever two-wheeled race victory.

Scarborough's dangers have been emphasized many times over the years by the many serious accidents that have occurred on the circuit, tragically leading to the death of several famous names in road racing, such as John Hartle, Bob Smith, Neil Robinson and Ron Haslam's elder brother Phil. Yet at the same time as being a leading critic of the Isle of Man TT, Barry Sheene remained a staunch supporter of Scarborough right up until his retirement from racing in spite of its dangers and public-roads nature. How could he reconcile two such distinct attitudes—and was it not hypocritical to continue accepting large chunks of start money to race at Scarborough, while continuing to denigrate the TT?

'Not at all,' says Barry. 'People always accuse me of not having liked road circuits and gone out of my way to get rid of them, but in fact that's absolute rubbish. There are many road circuits I really enjoyed riding on, like Spa where I still hold the all-time lap record or Chimay in Belgium where I won loads of times—both of them road circuits with lap speeds of over 135 mph. What I didn't like were tracks like the TT or Ulster GP which were so ridiculously long you had no idea what the weather would be like on the other side of the circuit when you set off, and no way of remembering where all the bumps were and so forth. If you like that sort of thing that's fine, go and race there, but don't tell me I've got to as well because championship points are at stake—that's totally wrong. The only reason I ever rode one time in the Isle of Man [in the 1971 125 TT, when he crashed at Quarter Bridge] was because I wanted the points the year I was trying to win the 125 world title, and that's why I did my utmost afterwards to get it banned. The whole idea of the TT is ridiculous, to my mind: for me, racing is against other people, not looking at my wristwatch

as I go round, trying to keep track of some crazy time differential. Who needs it? And who needs to get to the Mountain and not be able to see in front of your face because it's thick fog, and have the race carry on as if the sun was shining. It was like that my first-ever practice lap in the Isle of Man, and I said to myself then and there: "This is the first and last time you're ever coming here, old fruit"—and it was.

'Personally, I raced because I enjoyed it, so I couldn't see the point of riding somewhere that I hated. Places like the old Nürburgring and Brno were the same, and both years I won the world championship I said in advance I wouldn't race in Czecho if I could get it wrapped up beforehand—and nor did I. With me, I either liked a place or I didn't, in which case I either raced there or I didn't; money never came into it, unlike some other idiots who would make a big noise about how dangerous a certain track was, then go and race there anyhow because they were being paid huge amounts to do so—that's hypocritical for you. All the time I was racing, people could never honestly accuse me of saying one thing and doing another. What's the

Derek Minter on a 500 Gilera leads John Cooper's Norton and Phil Read's Gilera at Scarborough in 1963

point? You only lose respect and, apart from anything else, the one person you can't fool is yourself.'

Did that mean Barry always rode within his limits at Scarborough? 'Definitely. I remember a couple of years before I packed up I said to Stavros [Steve Parrish]: "God, I'm disgusted with myself—I must be the slowest person in the world coming down the hill before the finish line." I just didn't feel comfortable over that bit, because I just don't like going downhill, but he said I was ridiculous, seeing I was fastest in practice by some way. In the race I caught him up, and afterwards he said he couldn't believe how slow I was down to the line—but that was it: I didn't like jumping in the air and coming down all crossed up, so I took it easy and made up time elsewhere. On any track, if I wasn't comfortable somewhere, I'd just slow down till I came to a bit I was happy on, and for sure that's why I'm still more or less in one piece.'

Isle of Man TT supporters would cite that as an example of the throttle working both ways, just as any Island rider worth his salt must learn to

Sidecar action at the approach to Mere Hairpin in 1963, as Deubel/Horner lead Camathias/Herzig, both on BMWs. Note the Swiss driver opts for a British-style right-hand chair

practise—but weren't the attractive financial inducements to race at Scarborough, made possible by the large crowds that continue to flock there even during British road racing's time of recession, an important factor in Barry's decision to go on competing there? 'That's rubbish too, and to prove it I'll tell you about the last time I raced there, in 1984. I was on £8000 start money, and the weather was pretty bad, though they still had a sizeable crowd. At the end of the day I went to Peter Hillaby, the organizer, and asked him what the crowd was like. He said it wasn't as good as if it had been sunny, but they'd still made money. I said: "OK, I'll just take five grand and you can keep the rest," and I wouldn't have done that if I didn't like the place and the people behind it a lot. If I like somewhere, I'll ride there, but if not, I won't. I started racing because I enjoyed it, and I was still enjoying it when I stopped. I couldn't see the point of racing somewhere I hated, and I hated the Isle of Man and I liked Scarborough. In fact, the year after I stopped racing, the only weekend I really missed bikes at all was that one, when I read the comics and thought—ah, Scarborough, wish I'd been there.'

Just why was Scarborough Barry Sheene's favourite race meeting? Was it the unique challenge of the circuit, and the fact that he was so good at it? 'It was the atmosphere—it was always terrific; to my

Path racing as it is practiced. Dan Shorey and John Hartle, sadly later to lose his life at this very spot, sandwich Bell's Matchless with their Manx Nortons as they exit from Mere Hairpin in a 1960 500 cc race

mind, just what racing is all about. I'd go up there for the weekend, stay in the same little hotel each year, do a bit of practice, walk around the shops in the evening, spend some time in the town—we'd have a lovely time. I remember the first time I raced there, in 1970: it was just the same then as later, and I thought it was great racing in this nice little town, then going to the riders' disco on the Sunday night, having a proper prizegiving and so on—the whole weekend was just everything I'd ever thought of racing as being—you know, the circus comes to town sort of thing. From then on I was a staunch supporter of Scarborough, and I didn't care who knew it.'

Having won the Gold Cup, first awarded to Jack Brett in 1951, almost twice as often as anyone else, Barry Sheene's Scarborough system is well worth

hearing about. What is his most memorable moment there, though? 'The first time I ever went there in 1970, I had a 250 Yamaha with bloody big carbs fitted to it, which made it a bit sudden on the powerband, but quite quick. Steve Machin was the star there in those days, but in the 250 race I was with him all the way—we were using a Bultaco frame which made it handle really good. Anyway, coming out of the last hairpin on the last lap I was just behind him, and I gave it a big fistful of throttle to try and catch him just where there's a big bump in the track. I had the front wheel come so far up in the air I thought I was in orbit, and then when it came down it did so so hard it broke the bottom fork yokes clean through! Somehow I stayed aboard but didn't catch Steve, so I was second in my first 250 race there, but beat him in the 125 on the Suzuki and broke Alan Shepherd's MZ lap record, which pleased Franco [Barry's father, Frank] a lot. That day I also had one of my few rides on a four-stroke, in the Gold Cup—a Kuhn Norton 750, which was pretty well prepared and quite a nice old thing. I led for a while, but then the clutch started slipping—all those hairpins, I suppose—but I still finished third. Seemed like a vintage racer compared to the Japanese two-strokes.'

Was the Norton the most docile and flexible bike Barry ever rode there, if not the fastest? 'No, the easiest undoubtedly was the 750 Yamaha, which was like a superfast road bike with the reed valves and a real doddle to get out of the hairpins, which is the real trick to doing well at Scarborough; with ten kilos of extra weight on the front end, it was a wonderful ride there.' What? Did Barry actually ballast his bikes to alter the weight distribution and keep the front wheel on the ground? 'Oh, sure. People are only just waking up nowadays to how vitally important correct weight distribution is on a bike to stop the front end washing out on corners, which at least means today the bikes are designed

properly from the start. But all the time I was racing, the engines would always be placed much too far back in the chassis, even for the normal run of circuits, let alone somewhere like Scarborough with so many low-gear corners. Throughout the last year I raced, in 1984, I ran two kilos of lead weight strapped to the front of the frame on my 500 Suzuki, so that we ended up with a 52/48 frontal bias to the weight distribution. But when I raced it at Scarborough, I used to run *eight* kilos of lead! Then I could belt it straight out of the corners at full throttle on low gearing and still keep the front wheel more or less on this planet.'

Though the Yamaha may have been his favourite bike for the Yorkshire track, Sheene did all his Gold Cup winning on Suzukis. 'Yes, that's right, and the 680 cc RG square-four actually ran the old Yam fairly close. People used to think that bike was a monster, which in a way it was, but you could do things with it that were impossible with other bikes, provided you set up the carburation and internal gearbox ratios right—other riders didn't, and that's

Chris Conn leads Bill Rae and John Nutter, all on Manx Norton 500s, at the Mere Hairpin in 1963

*Mike Hailwood riding the 500 Norton leads Alan
Shepherd on a 500 Matchless at Memorial Corner
in 1959*

why they hated it. They used to rev it to 11,500
which was completely unnecessary; I'd use 10,300
tops, which with the right ratios and usable power
from just over 8000 rpm was fine—I could lap
Scarborough without ever using the clutch on it.'
Maybe so, but it was the TZ750 Yamaha that Barry
used to set up the outright lap record, which he still
holds, at 81.82 mph!

How did he approach the start of a race at
Scarborough? 'Because the first corner [Mere
Hairpin] is so tight, I would always try my best to be
fastest in practice, so as to line up on the left of the
front row, get a good start, and hug the left-hand
verge all the way up to the first corner so that some
numbskull didn't end up centrepunching me.' Did
that ever happen? 'No, 'cos I was always on the left-
hand side of the road! I might get third before the
hairpin, but in any case it would be back to bottom

gear and just sort of flop the thing on its side to get
round the bend, which is extremely tight with an
uphill exit. The first lap, I'd use the clutch on the way
out, because staying on the inside on the approach
I'd have made the corner much tighter than on a
flying lap where you could get more of a run at it,
but after that, if the bike was set up correctly, it
would just motor out of the turn, with all that extra
weight I'd have strapped on to the frame helping to
keep the front wheel down.

'I'd get it upright as soon as possible coming out
of the Mere Hairpin, then go uphill more or less in
the centre of the road as I accelerated up through
the gears into fourth, on a six-speed bike like the
later RG500. That had a nice powerband from 8000
to about 11,500, which was a big contrast with the
first factory square-four 500 I rode in 1974, which
was sudden death—no power below 8500 rpm,
65–70 bhp at 9000, and 95 at 9500! You could
only rev it to 11,000—it was ridiculous. People
nowadays don't realize how easy modern GP two-
strokes are to ride in comparison with even ten years

Ralph Rensen on a 500 Norton is pursued by Ginger Payne's unfaired Matchless G50 round the first part of the Esses in 1960

ago: more power, sure—but also far more manageable.'

There is a left-hand kink in the middle of Quarry Hill, leading away from Mere Hairpin (the latter so called because of the little lake that lies beneath it)—did Barry take this hard on the throttle? 'Yes, I'd make up a lot of time there because I wouldn't ease off, but I'd still end up more or less in the middle of the road again for the Esses. Soon as I saw the first right-hand part of the Esses, I'd lay it over as far as I could, having knocked it down a gear to third just beforehand. But then in the middle of the Esses, just before cranking it over to the left, I'd put it up a gear so as to let the engine pull without getting all peaky, then use all the road on the way out. Lots of people fall off here, because they've either got the engine buzzing hard and putting out all the power it's got, in which case they lose the back end, or else they don't lay it over as hard as they could on the first part, and run out of road on the second. On slow corners, I used to virtually get the number plates on the ground, and at the Esses, you could crank it on your ear on the right-hander, so that you'd done all your hard work and could get a really good drive out of the left-hander. What's that about road racers going in slow and coming out fast . . . !'

The Top Straight runs along the peak of Oliver's Mount, with the North Sea just over the crest on the right, though riders hardly have time to appreciate this since by now they are on what seems to be the fastest part of the course: is it? 'Yes,' says Barry, 'because though the Bottom Straight is longer, it's much bumpier and isn't really straight at all, whereas this is the only really open part of the track where you can see where you're going. I used to gear the bike so that I'd get top gear about halfway along the straight, with the engine peaking out three-quarters of the way down it, because that's where you'd have to knock it off and start braking and coming down through the gears again for Memorial Corner. This is a great place for overtaking people, because the first left-hander is actually faster than it appears and you can brake so late you think you'll end up in the shrubbery—Granty [Mick

Grant] and I have had dozens of shoot-outs there, because of course the trick is to get inside the guy in front on the brakes, but at the same time not get too far over to the left so that you end up not making the corner and either having to back off or, worst of all, take both of you out. And at the same time, the guy in front is wondering how far over to the left he can dare go, so as to shut you out: real game of poker, that place!'

Memorial is named after the War Memorial standing on the right, and is really two corners, both left-handers, with a short, slightly curving straight in between. Did Barry try to combine them into one long corner? 'No way! I'd take the first left in second gear, then as soon as I was straight, I'd get it upright and gas it as hard as I could down to the next left. Almost everyone else takes the tourist route—drift

Phil Read accelerates his 500 Gilera four out of Mount Hairpin in 1963

wide out to the right, then set up to apex the next left—but that's a big mistake. I'd give a big handful of throttle in second gear soon as I could bring it upright, and straight-line it to the inside of the next left. When I got there, I'd get hard on the brakes, lay it right over on the inside and then just nick it into bottom gear as I did so. Then heave it upright again, and another big handful—the back end would fish-tail, the wheel'd spin, the whole bike used to jump about, but that didn't matter: as long as you just sat straight on the bike, you'd be OK. It was good fun, too, another reason I liked Scarborough: you could really race with people round there, in very close quarters in a way that not many other circuits let you. Some of the races were quite long and it's a very physical place, so that after about ten laps of a 25- or 30-lapper, you'd be absolutely knackered!'

Next comes a short straight leading up to Mount Hairpin, a 120-degree right-hander with an unprotected fall on the exit into woodland that I personally find the most daunting aspect of the

Scarborough track. Another place for demon outbraking manoeuvres? 'Yes,' says Barry, 'but if you approach it up the right-hand side of the road and aim for the apex, you'll stop anyone come up inside you and also prevent the risk of being centrepunched, which happens quite a lot there. I might just get fifth gear going up to the hairpin, but more likely fourth, but then it'd be hard on the brakes, stay over to the right and again just nick bottom as you lay it hard over into the turn. Then once again, get it good and upright before you gas it hard, and that mini-precipice won't enter into it—it's all in the mind! Mind you, I did actually fall off there once, in the rain—the only time I ever came off at Scarborough. It was the first lap, and I came round in the lead on the RG, and just as I came round the corner, dead slow, I saw this enormous, great, muddy footprint right in front of my front wheel, where I suppose a marshal had walked on the track in a muddy gumboot. No way I could avoid it, so down I went, and didn't even fall off the bike, just sort of toppled over on the right side. But a carburettor came off, so that was that—definitely my slowest-ever accident, though!'

The next section runs downhill, curving slightly to the left as it does so, and is thickly sheltered by trees: did this cause visibility problems? 'No, not half as much as the fog which I suppose was really a sea mist, being so close to the water, which is very common at Scarborough, especially in mid-September when they used to have the big meeting—the last time I raced there, they had no racing at all on the Saturday because of it. That downhill section is always slippery, even on a dry day, probably because of the trees, so I'd always make sure I straight-lined it without any heroics. I never rated that bit—don't like going downhill, remember!—so I'd always stay right over the left-hand side of the road, go as quick as I felt safe, under the bridge, then start braking for the next corner, Mountside Hairpin. Nine times out of ten, I'd look over my shoulder here, because I was always worried about some idiot coming up the inside and taking me out—a pair of wing mirrors might have been useful!—and if I saw nobody stuck right up my backside, I'd take a really wide line, coming down the right-hand side of the road before laying the thing on its fairing and cranking hard over into the left-hander, then get it upright as soon as possible and gas it as hard as possible for an early, straight drive down to the finish line. I'd have got fourth or maybe even fifth if I was feeling brave going down the hill, and again I'd just nick bottom

gear as I laid it over into the hairpin. If there was someone close behind me though—especially Granty, who was past master at sticking his nose up inside people where it wasn't wanted!—I'd stay right over to the left all the way into the hairpin, so as to shut him out; it's impossible to pass anyone round the outside anywhere at Scarborough, because it's so narrow.'

The next section down to the start line was Barry's least favourite part of the Scarborough circuit. Supposedly the Bottom Straight, it is actually a winding, undulating and, as always, narrow ribbon of tarmac that has been the scene of many serious accidents. What was his race-winning formula for survival? 'I'd get a really straight drive out of the Mountside Hairpin, then up to third gear, trying to stay as much as possible in the middle of the road. About then, the road curves round to the right, then there's a little jump followed immediately by the big jump. To take this I used to get right over to the left-hand side of the road, as far as I could, make sure I was upright and right on the power in third: that way, when the front wheel came up in the air, as it's bound to do there, it wouldn't do so too far, and by staying on the throttle I might have an exciting moment or two, but it would all stay under control. The big mistake a lot of people make there is to knock it right off the power as soon as the front wheel starts reaching for the sky, which means the front end comes down with a bang and they get all crossed up and into frightful trouble. I've never forgotten what happened to me there my first-ever time at Scarborough in that race with Steve Machin, which was caused by doing exactly that. As I say, I'm the slowest of anybody through that bit, because I don't like it.

'After that, the road drops away a bit more and it's more or less straight to Mere Hairpin. I'll get fifth gear on a flying lap, but there's another jump before the start line which is actually very nice, because you're really in control when you take it, and you can bring the bike across the line standing it on its back wheel, which is really fun; it's also a good place for spectators to watch. I might sometimes get sixth gear going down to the line, but whatever happened, I'd always pull it back one gear before I got there. That would steady the bike up a bit, so you could really accelerate hard through the start and finish area, where it's pretty bumpy. In fact, that whole part is a very gentle S-bend, so it's best to come up really close to the fencing on the right, drop it down a gear, then accelerate hard and let the bike drift out to the left. That way, you can let it leap and jump about when it starts to get a bit lively, without worrying about running out of road, because you've given yourself more road to use. Then immediately you're through there, you have to get hard on the brakes and come down the gearbox to bottom again for Mere Hairpin, where the rules are the same as for Mountside: take it high, wide and handsome if you're on your own, in which case you can drive it through there without using the clutch, or hug the inside to prevent yourself getting T-boned or overtaken up the inside if someone is close behind.'

Did the narrowness of the Scarborough track—scarcely more than three metres wide for most of its length—ever bother Barry? 'The only place was strangely enough on the Top Straight, because if someone wanted to be awkward and used all the road, you couldn't get past them in a straight line even though you might have the faster bike. It didn't involve weaving or anything out of order like that,

Walter Schneider and Hans Strauss squirt their BMW Rennsport outfit round Mountside Hairpin in 1955 en route to second place in the sidecar event

but if you went up the centre of the road and just varied your line slightly, it made it very difficult for someone to pass you—lapping backmarkers was sometimes a bit of a hit-and-miss affair, for that reason.'

Who was Barry's most respected rival for honours at Scarborough over the 15 years that he raced there? 'Definitely I'd have to say Mick Grant. He always wanted to win there so badly, which I suppose was natural coming from Yorkshire himself, so we had some great battles there over the years which were a lot of fun—we'd always have a laugh about it afterwards, as well as a lot of wind-up before! But I suppose the race I remember best was one I had with poor old Dave Potter, which unusually was one where they paid lap money to the leader on the fifth lap, the tenth, and so on. There was no way you could keep track of the laps at Scarborough, it was all so frantic, so I had my mechanic Don Mackay standing at the exit from Mountside Hairpin holding a board with a ''£'' sign on, which he'd show me at the appropriate moment!'

Was the Yorkshire track Barry Sheene's favourite circuit, out of the many he raced on in one of the

The two Scarborough scrappers, Barry Sheene and Mick Grant, seen here fighting it out at Brands Hatch on Suzuki and Kawasaki respectively

most illustrious racing careers on two wheels, lasting more than a decade and a half? 'Yes, I think so, mainly because of the atmosphere and the fact that the actual racing was so much fun, with the track being so tight. The only place I would say might rival it was Chimay in Belgium, which had exactly the same sort of atmosphere but the complete opposite sort of circuit—ultra-fast, also on public roads, but full of 150 mph blind hills— that sort of thing. I think one thing I particularly appreciated about Scarborough was the organization: Peter Hillaby and his helpers were always dead keen and very helpful, whereas with some organizers, they'll only do the right thing if the riders force them to. When I started GP racing in 1971 I went to Imatra in Finland for the first time, and the

paddock facilities were just disgusting—three toilets for everyone which were permanently blocked, no showers, and so on. I was really green: I went to the organizers and complained, and came away believing all their promises about how next year they were going to rebuild everything. I was really pleased with myself, till all the old hands of the Continental Circus told me how they'd been getting the same promises for years and years, without any results. I was really upset, so I decided to make sure that this time they'd have to do what they were promising, by setting fire to the bloody things and burning them down! Next year we went back, and there were hot showers for the first time, lovely clean loos—it was great. But they'd never have appeared if I hadn't forced the organizers' hands. One of the great things about the people at places like Scarborough and Chimay is that they treated us properly—and that's why I always did my best to put on a good show there.'

Paul Smart on Imola

Riccione, Cervia, Milano Marittima, Cesenatico, Rimini and Cattolica—nowadays the names of these Adriatic resorts mean nothing more to motorcycle racing enthusiasts than another page in a travel brochure. But in the 1960s and early 1970s, together with two inland tracks at Modena and Imola, they were reknowned as the venues of the annual Italian *temporada di primavera*, the spring series of races which traditionally opened the European racing season, when the Continental Circus was reunited after a winter's hibernation.

The seaside promenades and streets which once echoed to the howl of an MV four or the thunder of a pack of Manx Nortons now host nothing more exciting on two wheels than an occasional stage finish of the cycling Giro d'Italia. For in the wake of Angelo Bergamonti's death at Riccione in 1971, the Italian street circuits were gradually closed down, until today only one of those tracks lives on: Imola.

Lying 40 miles from the coast, Imola was never a true street circuit, but neither was it a purpose-built track. Instead it developed into what the Italians call a 'semi-permanent' course, which means that from its origins as a public-roads circuit immediately after the last war, when races for small-capacity bikes and scooters were run on the minor roads that wended their way up and down the hills forming the valley of the River Santerno, the Imola course was gradually improved over the years to its present role as a closed GP circuit for cars and bikes alike. However, because there are a number of property owners on the inside of the course, whose access to their homes across the track remains a jealously-guarded right, the 3.1-mile Circuito Dino Ferrari (thus named after the Commendatore's only son, who died in his youth in the late 1950s at Maranello, only a couple of dozen miles away to the north-east) can only be closed for specific race days, even though you cannot drive along the roads which comprise it as a matter of everyday course any more. It is a real anomaly, a sort of semi-road circuit which retains enough of its original

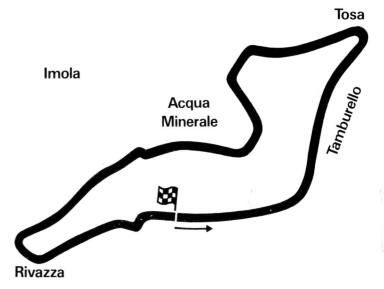

character, in spite of the efforts by the Formula 1 car circus to emasculate it by adding a quartet of chicanes to slow competitors down before the more demanding corners, to present a real and potent challenge.

The first meeting held on the circuit in its present form took place on 25 April 1953, before a huge crowd of 40,000. Imola's location, only 25 miles from Bologna, in the heartland of the Italian motorcycle industry, has always resulted in big gates; less than 30,000 for a major meeting is considered to be a flop. The big race at that inaugural affair was the 500 cc event, won by Alfredo Milani on the works Gilera four ahead of five of his team-mates, and indeed Imola would play an important part in the fortunes of the Arcore firm before they finally retired from competition. Such was the size of the crowd for that first meeting that the organizing AC Santerno had no difficulty in attracting substantial sponsorship from Shell for a big-money meeting the following year, and so in 1954 the first Coppa d'Oro Shell (Shell Gold Cup) was run off in April, leading eventually to the Spring series and ultimately to the famous Imola 200-miler of today.

Paul Smart after winning the F750 race at Rouen, France, in 1974 on his works Suzuki. You are invited to guess what the girl on the right is saying!

In spite of its open-roads heritage, Imola has proved a relatively safe circuit over the years. However, before the installation of the chicanes began in 1973, Imola was also a fast and difficult track which required a keen eye for the racing line. No less a rider than Geoff Duke fell off there twice in one day in the Gold Cup meeting in 1957, a day which also saw Bill Lomas bite the dust on the 350 Guzzi while trying to stave off the speedy Gilera fours of McIntyre and Liberati, and the first international victory of the fabulous V8 Guzzi, with Dickie Dale aboard.

However, no man is more closely associated with the name of Imola, in the minds of British racing enthusiasts especially, than Paul Smart. The Maidstone rider's victory there in the inaugural 200-miler in 1972 also marked the début of the 750 V-twin Ducati in competition, and over a decade later it still ranks alongside Mike Hailwood's comeback win in the 1978 TT as the Bologna firm's

greatest day. Yet for Smart, the son of a Kent café owner who started racing in 1964 on a 125 Bultaco, it was also his most unexpected success in a long and illustrious career which saw him win major races on both sides of the Atlantic.

'In 1972 I was riding Kawasakis in America for Bob Hansen,' Paul recalls. 'We had a deal that he'd release me to ride in Europe on non-conflicting dates, which is how I came to be available for the Ducati ride at all.' In fact, though, it wasn't Smart whom the Ducati factory boss, Fredmano Spairani, approached first: Flying Finn Jarno Saarinen and Paul's brother-in-law Barry Sheene had both turned down the idea of riding the, as they saw it, lumbering and uncompetitive V-twins. It was left to Barry's sister, Maggie Smart, to accept the ride on her hubby's behalf.

'Paul was racing at Road Atlanta when Ducati called me in California, where we were living,' recounts Maggie. 'I had to give them an answer right away, but there was no way I could get hold of Paul, so I made the decision and accepted for him. It was only a week before the Imola race that they called, and I knew he wasn't doing anything, the money seemed good, so I said yes. Then when he called me later that night after Atlanta he went mad. "I'm not riding that bloody old thing," he said, but I told him: "Well, you are!"—and so he did!'

Flying directly to Milan from Atlanta via New York and London, Smart arrived in Italy after a marathon 23-hour journey to find himself hustled straight to the Modena track where Ducati wanted him to test the bikes. What he found amazed him: a total of ten F750 bikes had been built, two for each of the four riders (Smart, long-time Ducati tester Bruno Spaggiari, Ermanno Giuliano and British importer Vic Camp's man, Alan Dunscombe), plus two spares. But Paul was less impressed with the bikes at close hand: 'They were fitted with skinny little TT100s and huge steering dampers they didn't need, because with a 60 in. wheelbase they wouldn't go round corners anyway. It felt pretty awful to ride that first time, even after I persuaded them to fit some racing tyres—it seemed so slow, even though the engine had lots of torque, but with the 90-degree vee layout it seemed to be firing every lamppost!'

Maybe so, but that Modena outing confirmed the Ducati's potential. 'After about ten laps I came past the pits and all the mechanics were hugging each other like I'd just won a race. When I came in I found I'd broken Ago's lap record on the MV—it was just a totally deceptive bike, faster than the works

Kawasakis and everything, even though it hardly seemed to be revving.'

So, brimful of confidence, the Ducati team came to Imola, a circuit which Paul Smart had not ridden at before, but which he soon came to respect and like. 'I've never needed more than four or five laps to learn a new circuit,' he says. 'I figured if you needed more then you shouldn't be there in the first place. Soon as I went round it the first time I knew it was my kind of place—lots of balls-out fast sweepers, tricky corners like Acqua Minerale where you had to keep your momentum up else you'd fall out of the revband and have to change down, blind approaches over the tops of hills—a real rider's circuit. The chicanes really spoilt the place more than any other track I can think of; now all the most demanding corners have one just before them to

The unmistakable style of the father of the modern manner of race riding en route to his most famous victory in the 1972 Imola 200. Note the Ducati's ground-clearance problems

slow you down, which is crazy—all the crashes happen at chicanes. The car people have a lot to answer for, and I never did understand at Imola why they didn't bypass them like they do at Silverstone.'

Was the fastest bit on the circuit the stretch past the pits? 'Yes—it'd be flat out in top gear, whereas now there's a chicane there before the pits that ruins it. The old Duke was really on her way there, and in fact that's where I passed Ago in the 1972 race on the MV, after he'd led the first five laps. The start was absolutely typical for Italy: as soon as Ago started, *then* they dropped the flag! He was riding a shaft-driven MV which was a one-off F750 bike, and he was taking it very seriously. Bruno and I were fastest in practice by some way, and I suppose it was the first time Ago hadn't been on pole position for an Italian race for five years or more. Anyway, the MV lit up and off we went after him. Ago's bike was very fast, but smoked a lot, and it also weaved like mad down the straights! Following it was quite an experience, but the Duke by contrast was steady as a rock, though you had to

Above *Start of the first leg of the 1973 Imola 200. Mick Grant (no. 85) and Bruno Kneubuhler (no. 86) have their works Ducatis to the fore, but Saarinen's Yamaha has already departed the scene*

Below *The field streams into the Tosa on the first lap of the 1976 Imola 200, with Roberts leading Baker, Cecotto, Rougerie, Palomo, Agostini and van Dulmen, all of course on TZ750 Yamahas*

Virginio Ferrari and Barry Sheene at Imola on their Suzukis in the 1979 Italian GP. Ferrari was second behind Roberts' Yamaha

send it a telegram if you wanted it to change line once you'd committed yourself for the corner—they don't like to do that. We used to wear the front tyres out very quickly, because they understeered so much.

'Ago found the MV a particular handful on the flat-out left-hander after the pits, called the Tamburello, and he used to ease off for it quite a bit, which was how I came to pass him there. It was a real sorter, but the Ducati would go through there flat out in top, though you had to get absolutely the right line and use all the road; Alan Dunscombe fell

off there in the race when he ran out of room on the right. Next there was another sweeper, not so tight and a right-hander this time, leading up to the Tosa hairpin. You changed down one gear just as you went round the sweeper, and used all the road normally so as to end up on the left of the road for the approach to the Tosa. For a good lap at Imola it was essential to use the entire road width all the way round—it was all a question of line and maintaining velocity.'

Did Paul take the shortest way round the Tosa, or try to make it a wide sweeper like some do at Druids hairpin at Brands Hatch? 'Normally I used to rush down the inside, keeping as close in as possible to prevent someone sticking his front wheel inside me, and braking very hard in a straight line, though if you were really on your way you'd have to start braking while still cranked over coming out of the sweeper. Normally it'd be a bottom-gear corner, but in the 1972 race the old Duke chucked out first gear after only a couple of laps; I was just accelerating away from the Tosa when it went "bang"— nothing. After that I had to do the slow corners in second, and since I knew the clutch wouldn't stand being slipped, I had to try to drive through them on the throttle. That meant taking a completely different line at the Tosa— high, wide and handsome, they'd have called it in America! After we passed Ago, Bruno usually caught me up there, but it was OK because the Ducati's engine was so torquey: there was a tremendously wide powerband from 2500 rpm up to 8500 that year.'

Next comes the steep climb up the side of the Santerno valley, which must have been tailor-made for the Ducati. 'It was,' nods Paul, 'because though the Tosa's not a particularly tight hairpin and you can come out of it quite fast, the hill's pretty steep and on a short-wheelbase stroker like the Suzukis I rode there the next two years it was quite exciting. But the old Duke just thundered up there as if the

Kenny Roberts' Yamaha (no. 2) leads Gregg Hansford's Kawasaki (no. 5) as they lap a pair of riders going up the hill from the Tosa in a 250 cc race

hill didn't exist, and with such a long wheelbase the front end didn't get all light as you crested the rise. That was even more important because the road curves slightly to the right just over the top, then you have a tight left immediately after, called the Piratella, which is very tricky.'

Presumably once again line was all-important here? 'Right,' says Paul, 'because you had to stay over to the left going up the hill, then know just exactly where to peel off for the right curve without being able to see the apex. You had to do it very late, so as to be right over to the right-hand side for the Piratella. Real tester, that. I'd only get third going up the hill on the Duke, because in those days before the chicanes you'd gear very high for the long, fast stretch past the pits. Then you'd come back one gear for the Piratella, crank hard over, then away downhill towards Acqua Minerale.

'The Ducatis in 1972 had one high-rise exhaust on the left and a low-down one on the right, because there was only one reasonably tight right-hander and the other ones where you might scrape the pipes were left-handers, so at somewhere like the Piratella there'd be no ground-clearance problems on the tyres we were using then. Mind you, my hanging-off riding style really suited the bike, what with the long wheelbase and the way it scraped the cases on the right. I got a lot of stick for that over the years, especially from Steve Lancefield

Renzo Pasolini dropping down to the Rivazza on the new two-stroke Aermacchi HD 250 in 1972

after he let me ride one of his Nortons: I won the race, but he told me off for hanging off and wouldn't let me ride it again. But it was my natural way of riding—I did it from the very beginning, and it just never dawned on me that there was anything wrong with it.'

Was there a particular reason he started riding like that in the first place, though? 'It probably started when I was riding on the road,' muses Paul. 'I was handicapped because I was a keen BSA owner, and all my mates had Triumphs. The only way I could keep up with them on a Shooting Star was to scratch like mad, and of course that meant everything grounded. So I suppose I used to try to keep it as upright as possible by hanging off. It was all dead serious in those days; a bunch of us used to go everywhere at full tilt—we went to all the ''caffs'', like Johnsons on the A20, the Ace and the Busy Bee. A lot of good riders came out of that scene—Crox, my mate Ray Pickrell, and of course Joe Dunphy: he was one of the Chelsea Bridge mob. Mind you, it was still a big step actually going racing, but there again all the lads in our mob

chipped in to get me an old van to do it with. Those were wonderful days.'

Back to Imola, and next came one of the most famous corners on the track: Acqua Minerale, so named after a mineral water spring close by, and the only tight right-hander on the circuit. How did Paul take it? 'For me, this was the most demanding corner on the track, because you had to get it just right, else you were off the power coming out. Second gear was too low, and third too high unless you really earholed round it. There was always a big crowd there, waving and cheering, and I remember the spectators at Imola were always just about the most enthusiastic you'd find anywhere; they knew their bikes, too. Again, you used all the road coming out, which put you on the left for the climb up the next hill. That was OK, because there was a long, long left-hand curve all the way round, up and over the hill, and you'd hug the inside as tight as you could, accelerating all the time, then rush downhill, to the Rivazza.

'It was on this long left sweeper that old Bruno almost came to grief in 1972. It was a bit difficult with him at first, because he was sort of the Percy Tait of Ducati, he knew the circuit and his bikes backwards, and of course he wanted to win the race himself. Spairani had a meeting with us the night

Paul Smart

Steve Baker, slightly crossed up on his 500 Yamaha

before the race, and it was incredible: there never seemed any doubt in anyone's mind that we were going to win it comfortably. He told us that he'd be showing just three signs—they were little wands with discs on the end like the *carabinieri* use in Italy, with different colour discs. Green meant OK, lap as you are now; red was danger, get moving; and yellow was slow down. That was our signalling system, no lap times or anything, and the only other instruction was to circulate together till the last five laps, when it was every man for himself.

'Well, of course, as soon as the five-lap board went out as we passed the start line, old Bruno went mad—smoking tyres up the inside of me at the hairpin, and suchlike. Two laps from the end he made a do-or-die effort in a very strange place, round the outside of this long left-hander at the top of the hill—it was about a 90–100 mph corner. There's just no way he could have pulled it off, so inevitably he ran out of road on the right. I remember standing on my footpegs, thinking: "I hope the silly ass doesn't fall off." There were clouds of dust everywhere, but he managed to get it back on the road again OK, but after that his engine

Above *Agostini leads the pack on his 500 Yamaha through the hills of the Santerno valley, on their way to the new chicane before the pits*

Right *Gilberto Parlotti on the Morbidelli leads Dave Simmonds' works Kawasaki through the Rivazza in the 125 cc supporting race at the Coppa d'Oro meeting in May 1971*

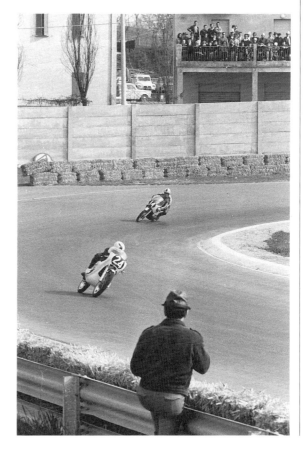

started misfiring. They said after the race it was because he was running out of petrol, but I had loads of juice left in my tank, so he should too. He almost certainly got some muck up his carbs after his little excursion, but anyway after that I was home and dry.'

Next came the Rivazza, the last major bend before the start-line straight. Another challenging corner? 'Definitely, because you'd come tanking round the long sweeper at the top of the hill, then start going downhill again quite steeply into a fairly tight right-hander—it was a second-gear corner. Lots of people fell off there under braking, because they'd be hard on the stoppers going downhill and would lose their front wheel, so judging the speed of approach and tyre adhesion was more important than line. Then it was hard against the stop for the short squirt to the top hairpin, which was a simple two-part left-hander that you'd apex in the middle, and then it was off down the straight again, up through the gears, round a flat-out right-hand curve and over the line.'

Was the Imola win Paul's biggest day? 'Yes, it was, I suppose. I won more money at Ontario in 1973, but the Imola race was more satisfying in a way because I hadn't gone there expecting to win it. I cleaned up about 5000 quid that day—all in readies: lots of those big, old, tablecloth-sized Italian notes with loads of noughts all over them stuffed into my helmet bag. We'd agreed the night before to pool our winnings, and that's what happened, but Spairani had also said: "Whichever of you wins the race will keep his bike, of course"— and he was as good as his word. It's a lovely old thing, and in a way I wish I'd had it when I rode for them the next time in the 200 there in 1975. They gave me one of the short-stroke bikes with 60-degree heads and so on, which was still pretty good, but I was lying eighth in the race when it started to ring and lose top-end power. With a Ducati that's a sure sign that it's used up its clearances, so I came in and let old Farnè rev it up a few times in the pits. He sent me back out again, but

sure enough the next lap it locked up just after the Rivazza going into the hairpin and threw me off. I thought I'd broken my leg, but in the end it turned out only to be pulled ligaments and bruising. That didn't stop them plastering me up to the hilt!'

Was Imola Paul Smart's favourite track? 'Well, I never had any real favourite circuit—for me, it was all a question of whether it was raining or not: if it was, they could stuff it! I loved racing in the States for that reason: if it rains, call it off and set a rain date—that's how it should be, too. But as corners go, I like Acqua Minerale very much: it was real Isle of Man stuff, where you had to keep the power on and your speed up, else you'd lose seconds a lap. I did love riding at Imola before the chicanes—all those fast corners and sweepers. Big race circuits were my scene: Mettet, Tubbergen, Spa, Assen— any of those. Fast corners really sort out the good guys—places like Abbey Curve at Silverstone, for instance—and that's why Imola certainly was one of my favourites.'

Bruno Spaggiari took his 750 Ducati to second place in the 1973 Imola 200

My Island lines—by John Surtees

The only man to have been world champion on both two and four wheels, John Surtees must today be accounted one of the principal surviving post-war experts on riding the Isle of Man TT Mountain course. With six TT victories and a total of 13 replicas to his credit, Surtees outscores those other legendary TT figures Geoff Duke (five and nine respectively) and Jim Redman (five and 17, including several in the lightweight classes which neither Duke nor Surtees contested). Only Giacomo Agostini, with ten wins (tying with the great Stanley Woods) and 13 replicas, has been more successful amongst retired post-war riders, and Ago's rejection of the Mountain course after the death of his friend Gilberto Parlotti in 1972 was one of the principal reasons for the loss of the TT's world championship status. Who better, therefore, than John Surtees to explain the techniques he had to employ to achieve such mastery of the world's most difficult and demanding road-racing circuit?

Considering the honours he was later to gain there, Surtees' Island début could hardly have been more inauspicious. Plans to ride in the Manx GP of 1952 fell through when, as a Vincent apprentice, he was called upon to assist the works in a series of record attempts at Montlhéry in September of that year. However, the following season John and his father obtained a Manx Norton from Gilbert Smith, and entered for the TT. Imagine his astonishment then when the legendary Joe Craig offered him a brace of Norton factory machines on which to make his Island début. 'To say I was both amazed and overawed would be an understatement,' recalls John. 'Here I was, a young lad of 19, still an apprentice, with a history of some success on short circuits but absolutely no experience of the TT course, being entrusted with two of his pet machines by the most famous man in British racing: I was absolutely terrified at the responsibility.' In the end, though, fate interceded, for Surtees had also agreed to ride a 125 cc EMC for Joe Ehrlich in the Ultra-Lightweight race before the offer of the works

Nortons came along. 'I reasoned that any extra mileage I could get in would be worthwhile,' says John, 'and though Joe Craig was very unhappy about my riding the bike, I had promised Ehrlich and felt I had to see it through. Unfortunately, the front forks collapsed on the long left-hander after Ballaugh Bridge—Ballacrye, I believe it's called—and I ended up on my ear with a broken left wrist. I was so disappointed and upset I took the next boat home; it took nearly a year for Joe Craig to bring himself to speak to me again, he was so angry.'

The next year, though, things went much better. Armed with a pair of production Manx Nortons,

John finished 11th and 16th in his first TTs, gaining replicas in each. This, and his increasing domination of the short-circuit scene, led to a renewed invitation to join the works Norton team for the 1955 season, albeit armed only with 'super-Manxes' after the withdrawal of the factory from the GPs. Fourth in the Junior, he was also well placed in the Senior when he ran out of petrol at the Creg on the last lap and had to push in: even Mr Craig was not above making the odd mistake!

Now began the phase of the Surtees career for which he is most famous—his five-year association with the MV team controlled by the equally

A youthful John Surtees (left) shares a bottle of pop with MV Agusta team-mate John Hartle after winning the 1960 350 cc Ulster GP—his penultimate GP victory before retiring from motorcycle racing in favour of cars

legendary Count Domenico Agusta. MV-mounted, John Surtees won his first TT in the 1956 Senior, after being excluded in the Junior when he yet again ran out of petrol on the last lap and had to borrow a milk-bottle-full from a spectator on the Mountain to get home. 'About the worst thing that ever happened to me in the Island, apart from the EMC incident, was running out of fuel twice,' says John ruefully. 'I only ever fell off one other time, when I came round Sarah's Cottage in practice to find a cow loose in the road and wrote off my race bike against her. I was unhurt, the cow pretty much so, but the MV was a basket case. In fact, I never fell off in a race over there, and just as well too.'

Instead, Surtees won most of them; fourth and second behind the Gileras in 1957, he achieved the double-double for the first time ever in the two succeeding years, winning the Junior and Senior races in each. It might have been a remarkable hat

Surtees pushes off at the start of the 1956 Junior TT on the 350 MV Agusta. Unfortunately he retired

trick of double wins but for a series of machine problems in the 1960 Junior, leaving him content to struggle home second behind his good friend and MV team-mate John Hartle. At the end of that year, Surtees moved on to the world of Formula 1 car racing and success on four wheels.

Riding the TT circuit, however, is like speaking a foreign language: once you learn it, you never really forget how to speak it, however many years may pass without doing so. A measure of Surtees' true ability on the Isle of Man came in the inaugural TT Cavalcade in Millennium Year 1979 when, after a 19-year absence from the Island, he lapped at over 96 mph *from a standing start* on a 500 MV, without, moreover, having ridden a racing bike in public for almost that long.

What sort of approach enabled him to perform such amazing feats on the Mountain circuit? 'Well, when I first went there I was regarded as pretty much a short-circuit specialist, and such riders weren't supposed to be able to ride the Island well. There was quite a distinct division in my day between GP riders and short-circuit competitors,

and there was a certain mystique conferred upon the art of riding the TT circuit by people who pretended it was impossible to do well there unless you'd served your apprenticeship at the GPs. Riding at Brands Hatch and Crystal Palace and Silverstone was considered a quite inadequate upbringing for the rigours of the TT, which required specialist skills, or so I was told.

'In fact, this was poppycock, as people like John Hartle and myself subsequently proved. The important thing about the Isle of Man is its length: there's nothing to stop you riding it like a short circuit, but if you do you won't win—just wear yourself and the bike out. But that's not to say that a short-circuit rider can't change his approach and use his skill and ability to attack the Island in the correct fashion. For the most vital ingredient in racing at the TT is rhythm—getting into an established rhythm and sticking to it. This is totally lacking in short-circuit racing, where at least half the time you're engaged in "spoiling"—trying to obstruct the man behind, spoil his overtaking line, outbrake him into corners, and so on. That's why short-circuit races are often won at much slower speeds than if you'd been riding round on your own, whereas on the Island, with the staggered

Tiddlers away! The start of the 1962 Isle of Man 50 cc TT. No. 4 is Ichino's works Suzuki, no. 3 none other than Derek Minter and his eight-speed CR110 Honda production racer

starting intervals, and the length of the circuit, you're engaged in a much purer form of racing—it's just you against the clock. The length is also important in that at the TT there are long sections of road where if you make even a small mistake, you can still be paying for it five miles later, in terms of an extra 200 revs you haven't attained, and so on. You must think much further ahead than on a shorter track.'

So the Isle of Man does need a different approach; did Surtees have any difficulty in adapting his riding style to suit the circuit's demands? 'People like John Hartle and myself tended to bring a kind of short-circuit-type aggressiveness to the Island in terms of attacking some of the corners, more than perhaps the previous generation of riders like Geoff Duke had done. Of course, we were partly also helped by tyre

developments: the rubber war between Avon and Dunlop was just beginning to hot up, which enabled us to scratch perhaps a little more consistently, rather than just make the occasional big effort. I've always contended it's much better to make a 98 per cent effort for the whole race, rather than ride at 101 per cent for short bits and if you and the bike survive that, then stroke it at 95 per cent for others. I think Mike Hailwood proved this particularly when he made his comeback in 1978 and won the race on a bike that was far from being the fastest in the field: he was a master at settling into a rhythm and then keeping it up the whole way through the race. He hadn't ridden on the modern four-stroke multis, which have so much power to spare and are so unfussy with it: you can afford to make a mistake on them, lose a bit of speed, then just squirt it to catch up to where you were before. Do the same thing on a Manx Norton—or even the MV or Mike's Ducati—and you've lost 700 revs that can take you literally miles to build up to again. A little error that might lose you a couple of seconds with a modern Honda or Kawasaki would have

Fred Stevens aviates the 500 Hannah Paton on Bray Hill in the 1967 Senior TT. He finished fifth

been paid for in tens of seconds on a Norton or Matchless, and even on the MV. For above all, the Mountain course is an ultra-high-speed circuit, and it was vital to keep that momentum going once you'd achieved it.'

How did John Surtees learn the circuit in the first place? 'Simply by driving round and round in a car—not on a road bike, because there were too many distractions and anyway it was important not to get into the subconscious mentality of having to keep on the left-hand side of the white line if you were riding a bike. Doing it in the car was different enough, and anyway I quite often preferred someone else to drive while I just looked around at everything, picked out a tree here, a cottage there, a change in the colour of the road or the shape of the kerb—all little landmarks that I could identify and would help me know where I was. It was like making a film, really: gradually you'd be cutting and splicing whole sections together in your mind till there was a complete 37¾-mile-long production. Then each year when I went back it was a question of using the first few laps of practice to speed the film up, till by the fourth or fifth lap it was running at full speed. I can tell you, I buzzed down Bray Hill

The great Bob McIntyre rounds Quarter Bridge on his works 250 cc Honda four, en route to an incredible 99.58 mph lap in the 1961 Lightweight TT before retiring

many hundred times more in my mind than I ever did in real life!'

And how was it in real life? 'Well, you always knew the bike was going to leap around a fair bit going down Bray Hill, so it was sometimes more than a little difficult to aim for that ominous-looking manhole cover about two feet out from the kerb on the right of the road: you were supposed to pass between it and the kerb. But the technique of riding bumps was often a major factor in doing well on the Island—and still is, I'm sure. I never liked to be riding with the power off in a bumpy section—I always kept it wound on, but in a higher gear than might otherwise have been the case, to stop the

The unmistakable style of Renzo Pasolini on the 350 Benelli four at the exit from Braddan Bridge

engine being overstressed as the rear wheel hopped about. Keeping the power on helps keep the bike more stable, and ensures a better chance of the rear wheel staying in contact with the ground while the front end does all the leaping—a steering damper is an essential asset on the Island! The best possible way to get a wobble at the bottom of Bray is to whistle down the hill and then start easing it in the dip: far better to ease it halfway down and then accelerate into the dip to get a drive straight through and out.'

Did he try to keep it as far over to the right as possible after that to reduce the risk of aviating on 'Ago's Leap'? 'I've never really subscribed to that school of thought. I always used to go straight down the middle of the road, because I reckoned that if I was going to get into trouble I wanted to give myself as much room as possible to get out of it. It *was* rather hairy if you went too far over to the left at the point where Les [Graham—Surtees' predecessor in the MV team] had the start of his accident, though. My technique was always to approach such a point *already* riding on the

footrests—the last thing I would do is stay sitting in the seat until I'd been bumped up in the air by the jump. There are lots of places like these on the Isle of Man, and you have to put all your weight on the footpegs and let the bike do the jumping around under you. This particularly applied with the MV, probably because being a higher-revving machine it was less stable over bumps, whereas a single-cylinder plodding along tended to dampen itself. Another reason probably was the height of the crankshaft on the multi—being a wide four-cylinder engine, the MV's motor sat high in the frame for increased ground clearance, and the higher centre of gravity made it a handful over the bumps.'

Next comes Quarter Bridge—scene of many a gentle slide-off and early retirement. 'I have a philosophy about corners like Quarter Bridge: you can only lose time on them, not gain any. It's never been a place to scratch round, and I always adopted a very orthodox, conservative line. The important thing at places like that is to get your braking right into the corner—from quite a high speed, remember—then get a good, early drive out of it. There was no roundabout there in those days, like there is now, but the road still fell away on the exit, and there was always a fair sprinkling of petrol on the road from full tanks—no one-way valves in

171

breather pipes then, remember. I should think quite a few people fell off on their own fuel there. So you had to be very careful, and always tending to be a fairly early corner-taker myself, I was particularly careful on the exit not to wind it up too hard.

'Talking of full tanks reminds me that in those days we used to carry the most incredible fuel loads—I remember that for the eight-lap race one year I was carting around 9½ gallons of petrol on the MV: it was a right pig to ride. Quite honestly, it would have been much better to have stopped more often—it was ludicrous. Even the pannier tanks on some of the singles made them very difficult to control—we had some misguided ideas then, I'm afraid!

'Another important factor about places like Quarter Bridge you have to bear in mind when you're racing there is that it's one of the parts of the course which are most heavily travelled by ordinary road traffic. Consequently the surface is always a bit slippier, no matter how well they sweep it, because the oil and dirt gets down into the tarmac. Same thing in Ramsey, especially going up out of the town into Cruickshanks, where people living in the houses on the right park their cars outside at night. Did you ever look at the floor of your garage after you've taken the car out in the morning? Well, you have to peel off for a very tricky corner on that same sort of surface, and this is just one of the many different little factors that all come together to make

Two contrasting methods of taking the famous jump at Ballaugh Bridge. Left, the approved method displayed by Geoff Duke, riding the Rennsport BMW in the twilight of his illustrious Island career in 1958. Below, Hugh Anderson demonstrates a front-wheel landing aboard the works Suzuki 125 twin in the 1965 TT. Behind, Mike Duff's Yamaha is about to overtake the Kiwi en route to third place in the race. Anderson was fifth

the TT such a unique and real challenge for the rider.'

Braddan Bridge is another place at which many a good rider has bitten the dust—including even Mike the Bike himself on his 250 Yamaha in his comeback year. Did it pose any special problems? 'Not really, though there's a deceptive climb up out of it so you have to exit the second part with a good drive on, especially since there you're starting the really high-speed part of the circuit. When I rode in the Cavalcade in 1979 I arrived at the next part though, and discovered I was completely lost! What used to be Snugborough had completely disappeared, so that makes the entry into Union Mills even quicker than before.

'Union Mills really sorts people out, and it's a classic instance of where if you make even a slight mistake going through you pay for it all the way up the long drag up the hill afterwards, and even further on. So you have to do it right and I freely admit I used to take it short-circuit style, physically wrestling the bike through and lifting it over from one side to another: it always paid off in terms of greater exit velocity.

'At the top of the big climb out of Union Mills is the corner I consider to be one of the most difficult ones ever to get right on the TT course—Glen Vine. It always gives you the feeling it'll bite back— certainly not a place to take liberties with! But it is typical of the Island, in that while on the short circuits races are won and lost on usually the slower kind of turn, over on the Isle of Man it's the fast ones that really sort people out. At Glen Vine I always took very strict control of myself and the bike, especially since it always seemed to catch whatever sun was going, and in those days when they used big granite chippings and tar the road surface would often be breaking up on a hot day. Then the

Ian Tomkinson's BSA three at the entry to Union Mills in the rain-lashed inaugural TT Formula 1 race in the Island in 1977

bike would get very light going in, at the point at which you peeled off, but if you left it too late you'd be scratching off that wall on the exit in the most almighty fashion; there was also a very worrying telegraph pole bang in the line of fire on the way out. But if you did it all right, and went through absolutely on the limit, not only was it one of the most satisfying things on earth, but you also got a good run at the hill up into Crosby and down past the Highlander.'

Did Surtees feel the Highlander to be the fastest part of the circuit, rather than the drop from the Creg to Brandish as would appear to be the case nowadays? 'They were both equally fast in my day,' recalls John, 'but the difference was that then the Brandish section was extremely bumpy. On the other hand, you were almost home then, so perhaps subconsciously it felt a bit quicker, while at the Highlander you were just starting out on another lap, and there were all the attendant worries of whether you'd make it over the Mountain again, and so on. They were both very quick sections.

'Greeba Castle was like Glen Vine—a real teaser which, however, strangely never had any warmth to it. You had to handle it in a very clinical fashion, choosing your braking and gearchanging points very precisely—no easy matter after travelling for so long at such high speed. Appledene, soon after, is another corner which you could really make time up on other people if you did it right: I used to do the whole section in third on the MVs on a five-speed box, and it would be like playing a musical instrument in more ways than one—I often wondered what it must have been like to hear the sound of those four pipes rising and falling through the trees.

'Greeba Bridge is a nothing sort of corner, quite straightforward, then the run to Ballacraine was

Women riders have been few and far between in the Isle of Man, but fastest of the few by some way so far is German lady Margret Lingen, seen here at Sulby Bridge on her way to a Finishers Award in the 1984 Formula 2 race on her Ducati

quite simple too, though you had to watch the last long right-hander before the short straight into the pub. I treated Ballacraine just like Quarter Bridge, with the entry and exit the most important parts, braking from high speed and getting a good early drive up the hill to Ballaspur. I never used to scratch round the apex—what's the point of putting in a 101 per cent effort if there's a stone wall facing you? Lots of people did, though—which usually meant them having to push themselves off the bank and losing all their steam up the hill. Daft.'

The Glen Helen section is often regarded as being one of the most tricky on the entire Mountain circuit; did John agree? 'Yes, and for that reason I always treated it with great respect. The best way was to drive through it as if you were in a 1000 km race, rather than try to make up time. If you did start scratching, you would not only lose time but also run the risk of hurting yourself very badly, if not terminally: a lot of good riders have been killed in that short section. The controlled rhythm I referred to earlier was vital here, and you always felt fairly happy you'd got to the pub at Glen Helen OK. The strange thing is that the whole section from Ballacraine to there consists virtually entirely of

The cheerful Czech, Franta Stastny, rounds Ginger Hall on the works dohc Jawa twin in the 1961 Junior TT. He finished fifth

double corners, requiring a series of most unconventional lines. Often you'd have to go into a corner on what appeared to be the wrong side of the road simply to be correctly placed for its partner. I think that's where a lot of people have come unstuck—taking conventional lines when they've stopped concentrating, and then finding themselves all off line for the second corner.

'Getting up the hill away from the pub was always a bit of a struggle; it's very bumpy still and all off-camber, and there are slippery patches under the trees even when it hasn't rained for a while. I always stuck to the middle of the road, then peeled off late for Sarah's; just after going round that right-hander was where I hit the cow in practice for the 1957 Senior—they'd just taken her calf away from her or something and she'd kicked down the fence. Count Agusta wouldn't believe me at first when I told him I'd written off my race bike against a cow: he thought it was some kind of crazy English excuse as a way of covering up a mistake! Magni knew, though.

'The next couple of corners are important for a good top speed on the extremely bumpy straight afterwards—Creg Willey's. Thereafter followed one of the most important sections on the circuit, where you could really make up time on other people provided you didn't concentrate too much on the feet as getting the inches right: it required a very precise, controlled type of riding to get the best out of the circuit. There are some parts of the Island where you can ride with a really cavalier approach, laying it over on the footrests, but not here. This is an important part of the course.'

Why so? 'Well, it was all a question of momentum again—if you could get through the wiggly bits absolutely on the limit, you'd be saving seconds and seconds on the straight parts. Take the 11th Milestone, for instance: I could do it all in fourth gear on the MV, starting over on the left, then letting the bike drift over to the right so I could just clip the next left-hander, driving hard all the way. At Handley's, I used to come up the left side of the road, then just flick it one way then another to get round the stone wall—I'm amazed to hear present-day riders actually make an S-bend out of it, because they have to lose time in doing so. In our day you'd just roll it off the stop ever so slightly in top, but it was almost a straight line.

'But the next one—my, well that's a real teaser, isn't it: Barregaroo. Took me quite a while to work up to doing both top and bottom flat out, especially on the 500 MV. If you did the top flat then the bottom was awfully quick. Many people would ease off at the top before accelerating down the hill, which made it not so bad. I gave myself a mental pat on the back the first time I did the whole section against the stop. Everything bottoms with an almighty crunch at the bottom of Barregaroo—worse than at Bray Hill—so you had to be certain you didn't break your shocks or stick the rear tyre up through the mudguard. I never could do the top part flat on the first MV with the built-up frame—it was a real beast to ride—and it wasn't just Bob Mac, whom I always regarded as the very top of the pile amongst TT riders, but also the Gilera which had proven superiority in the 1957 Jubilee races. Next year we got a new frame organized that was streets better, but by then Gilera had retired, of course. Pity.

'You really had to wrestle the bike back into line after crunching through the bottom of Barregaroo—the front end would flap around like nobody's business. It was the same thing going into the 13th—it really got a wiggle on at the right-hander. I got a right old tank-slapper there in the 1979 parade, thought to myself: "Oh, dear, what's this?", but then I remembered: "Yes, it used to do that!"

'I always liked rushing through the streets of Kirkmichael—that was fun, going as fast as you could through a little village with all the people

'The last straight into Schoolhouse Corner was always very bumpy.' Surtees demonstrates just how bumpy on the 350 MV in the 1960 Junior TT, when he finished second to team-mate Hartle after mechanical trouble

looking out of their windows at you. After riding so long in open country it made quite a big change—you said to yourself: "Ah, I'm going somewhere." But you had to be very careful of the wind between the houses, especially with the full streamlining we used before it was banned for 1958—the bike could often get away from you in bad conditions. In fact, the Isle of Man is a full-fairing circuit because it's so fast, provided you knew what you were doing when you designed the streamlining: Guzzi and Gilera certainly did, because their bikes were quite safe. Ours weren't! We suffered from being aeronautical engineers [Agusta were, and still are, the largest helicopter manufacturers in Europe], so we applied aircraft technology to motorcycles and got it all wrong. The others had their own little wind tunnels, started without preconceived notions, and got it right; our bikes used to take off into the wind, just like airplanes! In the end it was probably because of MV that the FIM banned full streamlining—now I see it's creeping back again, but this time I'm sure they know what they're up to.'

Was Kirkmichael the worst place on the circuit for wind—how about up on the Mountain? 'No, it wasn't there, because it was so open the wind

didn't take you by surprise. The worst place by far was the Sulby Straight, especially the last part: the wind gusts in off the sea through the gaps in the hedge. On the Mountain you were generally quite sheltered, as well. But Kirkmichael still required a careful approach to avoid hitting a kerb on your way through. Next was Rhencullen—a real teaser too, but I used to love it. I treated it as a short-circuit corner—clip all the sides all the way through in top gear. You had to lift the bike up smartish after the house though, I remember, because there's quite a fair jump immediately after. Then the next bit was very fast, except I never could quite do Alpine Cottage flat out on the 500 MV; the 350 was no

Surtees rounds Parliament Square, Ramsey, on the 500 MV Agusta in the 1956 Senior race—his first TT victory

problem—chin on tank all the way through—but the big four was a different cup of tea. In the end I got up to the stage of just easing it slightly and scrubbing off a little speed on the entry to be able to crack it wide open for the exit. With the MV's high centre of gravity it was sometimes difficult to get it back on line if you went into a corner late, so my natural short-circuit style of going in early really suited the bike more than perhaps the Manx Nortons. Full tanks only made it worse, so you had to go into the corner early, even if it meant using up more road—wasn't a slide really, more a controlled high-speed drift which tyre developments were beginning to permit.'

Ballaugh Bridge is one of the most spectacular places on the Mountain circuit for spectators, even if universally disliked by riders; how did John Surtees feel about it? 'I remember Joe Craig saying to me once: "All the time you're flying you're not going anywhere." He was quite right, of course, but it was inevitable you'd aviate if you were going at any speed. It's very easy to go in too quickly, especially after all those miles at high speed; look how many riders arrive at the crest of the bridge with both brakes hard on, the front of the bike diving, the back sitting up—it's inevitable they'll land on the front wheel. I used to finish all my braking just before actually getting on the bridge, then just at the point of take-off I'd get back on the gas and aim for a flat or slightly nose-up landing, using second gear on all bikes. I'd also make sure that when I landed I'd be facing in the direction I wanted to go—I didn't want to be guiding it at all but just using every bit of power I had to get out of there as quickly as possible.

'The next bit is where I fell off on the EMC my first time over—you have to get set up for Ballacrye about half a mile beforehand, but when you go through flat out over the little jump and the engine goes "wheee!", just for a moment it's very satisfying—a safe jump, that. But the Quarrys—ah, they were a bit physical, but I used to love them even more. Always reminded me of riding round Aberdare Park or somewhere like that, only a bit quicker, flicking it around over the bumps, one side then another. It was always very dark in there, even on a sunny day, and the light transition used to upset a lot of riders. I would never use curved-lens goggles, because I believed they gave me distorted vision, yet look at the photos and you'll see most riders in those days used lenses with a slight curvature at the edge. I always used a very thin glass lens—an old Octopus goggle, actually—and fairly small because I reckoned that they helped me to focus better on the high-speed stuff, and didn't cause so many problems going from light into shade.'

Was Sulby Straight as bumpy as it is today? 'At least! Especially the first part as far as the crossroads; coming out of the Quarrys you'd always drop the bike into top earlier than usual—say 10,300 instead of 10,500 rpm. I did tend to pick one side of the road or the other as being more comfortable, but it varied from day to day depending on the wind. Usually I went up the right-hand side before the church hall, then crossed over to the left—nearly hit a dog there one year, I remember. We used to have a signal station in the fields on the left after the crossroads, and that was usually the only one I ever bothered with apart from once when I used another at Ramsey Hairpin: that was enough to let me know where I was in the race. But the wind rather than the bumps was the main thing you had to watch out for on the full streamliners. . . .

'Sulby Bridge was quite easy and conventional—I used to turn the power on quite early, because if the rear wheel stepped out, well, then the bridge parapet on the left would stop it going too far—it was an added safety factor, really. The kerbs could be very handy in the wet, because you could bring them in as an added factor to stop the wheels slipping too far away from you on the exit from a corner—use all the road, get the power on early, and just clip the kerb if you had to. Quite useful.

'Then next you used to tip your hat to Mr Telegraph Pole at Kerrowmoar! I never believed in painting things on walls or using markers—I preferred to concentrate on getting an overall picture; if you were too busy looking for your marker, you'd probably miss the pool of water lying in the road. But Kerrowmoar is a blind corner, and you have to be dead right going in, to avoid falling down the adverse camber on the exit, as well as be upright for the little jump after that, so the GPO pole on the right was a definite marker. Very satisfying little bit, that.'

The section from Sulby to Ramsey is often felt by many riders to be the most difficult to learn—so many corners look the same, especially round the Milntown area, that it is easy to become confused and find yourself in the wrong gear, off line, headed for a kerb that is not supposed to be there. Certainly, it took me longer to learn that part of the course than any other. How did John Surtees feel about it?

'Well, it does all look the same rather, and I can

Few TT victories have been as well-deserved or as well-received as Peter Williams' long-awaited win in the 1973 Formula 750 race on the monocoque John Player Norton

understand why it might seem awkward, but to be truthful I didn't find it so difficult, probably because I decided it was one of the most important parts of the whole circuit and had to be thoroughly sorted out. It's so consistently fast that you need to know precisely where you are—but the racing line is also extremely narrow: it's one of the parts of the circuit where if you went round in a car you wouldn't be able to lap it as fast as on a bike, because even on a single-track vehicle you're clipping first one side then the other, from one kerb to another. I did it mostly in fourth gear on the MVs, and always reckoned it to be one of *the* sections I could pick up time on.

'The last straight into Schoolhouse Corner was

*The greatest TT exponent of all time? The late Mike
Hailwood at Ramsey Hairpin on the fabulous 250 cc
Honda six, during his ride to victory at an average
speed of over 100 mph in 1966*

always very bumpy too—I just used to put a little
more pressure on the footrests to let the bike do the
leaping around.' John must have been very fit to
have wrestled the MVs round the Mountain circuit;
did he do any special training for racing on two
wheels? 'No, but I was originally quite fit simply
through doing a lot of riding on different bikes, as
well as a lot of walking. One thing I got so upset
with MV about was I came from doing 76 races a
year down to only 15 or so, and they kept on
squeezing down even from that, and I didn't like it.
That was one of the several reasons I eventually
packed up and went car racing—I just wasn't doing
enough racing.

'Ramsey is all a bit like Quarter Bridge—it's a
well-used piece of road that you can easily come to
grief on if you're not careful. I treated it with great
respect and never used any extremes. One corner I
loved though—Stella Maris; it was a real sorter,

another place where if you were going to make up
time this was where to do it. I used to go through
flat out in third on the MV, using every bit of road.
But the hairpin was another place you could lose
time on, rather than make any up—I tried every
conceivable line round there, and ended just doing
the orthodox shortest way round. But I did make
sure that I completed all my braking well before
peeling off into it, so that I would have the power
already on as I approached the apex. That way, I'd
be sure of a good drive up the hill, which was a bit of
a struggle otherwise, especially on a single; the gear
you had to pull for the TT circuit, being so fast,
didn't help either.

'All this business about setting the carburation up
just right for the Mountain simply wasn't so—it was
places like Ramsey Hairpin you had to have it fine-
tuned for. If you could get the thing sharp enough
and lean enough, it should really steam out of tight
corners like that, especially on a Norton, which
really goes when it's just about burning. But if you
were a jet or two too high—forget it! You'd really
learn the meaning of megaphonitis too—that's why
the 500 MV was such a delight out of corners like

that; the 350 was a little sick, but the big bike just breezed away out of them.

'I hated slow corners, whether I was racing a car or a bike: I just had to make the best job possible of them. But arriving at Waterworks was like a breath of fresh air—two nice challenging corners, the bike would really be singing again and you'd be recapturing your rhythm after that lousy hairpin— great! After that, the road suddenly narrowed quite considerably and became more of a mountain track—that's when you knew you were really leaving civilization and heading off into the wilderness. . . !

'Often when you look at the Gooseneck it seems to be a much slower corner than it really is—you can do it quite fast, which is important for the struggle up the hill to Guthrie's. That's an important bit as well, since it dictates your speed over the Mountain Mile, though actually it's the left-hander immediately after which is really crucial—you must at all costs keep it wound on and use every bit of the road to ensure you get the best possible launch up the Mountain. That was a real teaser, that one.

'Then suddenly you find yourself all alone in the middle of nowhere—you're on the Mountain. It's an eerie sensation—the bike sounds completely different; you feel like you're on the surface of the moon. You let it find its own way up the Mile while you relax a little—time to do a general evaluation of the situation: you've had your signal in Sulby, so you'll have known what you had to do over the Mountain. If you're in a good position, you'll let the bike have a bit of a rest—it's earned it after all that Ramsey section, so you might change up a couple of hundred revs lower, and so forth. Have a general look round and make sure nothing's hanging off or about to collapse; it's a good time to catch up on the bike's health and review your race plan.'

Did John find the Mountain section difficult? 'Not at all, because you can see a long way in front of you, and most of the corners are wide open, short-circuit style, like Black Hut, or Windy Corner. Of course, you had to learn it very carefully all the same, because the chance of bad weather was much greater here, so if it was misty you had to know exactly where you were. But on a clear day there were really only two tricky bits: the Verandah was one, because the racing line through the four right-handers was so narrow and, before they eventually resurfaced it, it was extremely bumpy. But the king of the Mountain is the 32nd Milestone: it's one of the most crucial parts of the course, because if you really get it right you can gain an

extra 400 revs down to Windy Corner, and that's a lot of extra speed. I liked the three left-handers, but treated them with a lot of respect: even if you were a fraction off line at the speeds you were travelling at you'd be wrong for the next corner and could never hope to get it back in time. So it was essential to concentrate 100 per cent and get it right—but it paid off handsomely.

'The same thing is true of Kate's Cottage— another very important bit which if you got right would give you a higher top speed down to the Creg than if you just pussy-footed through. You had to bank into Kate's, but then lift it up because you knew very well that the bumps would cause the bike to leap so far over to the right. The Creg was quite straightforward, and I'm glad to say I never actually went straight on there under braking, though you sometimes wondered if you'd get round. It was like coming back to civilization, with all the people there watching and hanging out waving at you—you could usually tell how well you

'Arriving at Waterworks was a breath of fresh air!' Surtees in the 1959 Junior race which he won

John Surtees

John Blanchard climbs the Mountain on the four-cylinder Seeley-framed Munch-URS. Blanchard was lying fourth in this 1967 Senior TT when the chain broke

were doing simply by their actions. You know, it's a funny thing but even though I'd be super-concentrating, I'd always be aware of the people, especially the ones up on the hillsides on the Mountain section, overlooking Windy Corner and the like.

'Going down to Brandish was extremely fast even then, though it was also very bumpy. The problem was with the high banks you used to get a false sense of your own speed, and sometimes you'd wonder if you were going to get round. Just took a bit of judgement, that's all. Hillberry was fine on the approach—come down close to the wall in fourth and clip the right-hand kerb—but then you'd get a real wiggle on going up the hill to Cronk-ny-Mona because it was so bumpy; if you've ever listened to those old records you can hear the engines rising and falling as the bikes squirm around! On the Manx I generally preferred to do Hillberry in third, then change up to top for the Cronk, because otherwise you tended to stagger up the hill a bit and run off the powerband. It was a toss-up, really.

'When you got to Signpost you'd know you had to start looking out for melting tar again on a hot day—it seemed to catch the sun more than elsewhere. The next bit was always very bumpy (can't think of a more inappropriate name than Bedstead, unless they're talking about a hospital bed!), and you were always riding on the rests, getting through as best you could. I never used to use footrest rubbers, by the way. Our boots were much thicker then, so we didn't get blisters, and frankly the old singles especially leaked oil so much I was afraid of getting it on the rubbers and having my feet slip off.'

Governor's Bridge must be the most photographed section of the TT course; any special problems about getting round? 'Well, the one thing you were most concerned about was not falling off and making a big fool of yourself in front of everyone on the slowest part of the circuit. The technique was quite different for the MV and the Norton. On the multi, you'd come down through the gears, running along the wall on the left, then at the last minute give it a little blip, drop down into the corner, open up a little to get round the dip, then away—quite simple, really. On the single it was much trickier though, because you had mega-phonitis to contend with. However, if you had the carburation really set up well, you could clutch it just as you turned into the drop round the corner, then trickle round on the pilot jet before opening up again and slipping the clutch to come out of the dip. Sounds complicated, but it came good with practice.'

Did John ever have a problem with the adverse camber on the exit from Governor's, as you rejoin the Glencrutchery Road? 'At first, yes, but once you knew it was there you'd let the bike use all the road as you wound it on coming out of the dip. There

'Please do not feed the birds!' The hazards of low-flying seagulls at the Creg in the 1965 Junior TT. Alan Dugdale (no. 34) and Dan Shorey (no. 33), each mounted on a Manx Norton, both won bronze replicas

wasn't a deep gutter there, so if it did step out the kerb would be a stopper and you could accelerate as hard as you liked.'

So off down the Glencrutchery Road to Bray Hill and another lap. But before the lap we had just taken together would have come the question of getting under way in the first place, at the start; how did Surtees do this? 'I was always quite well known for my starting style, because I used to sit side-saddle on the bike until it was well under way, then cross my leg over and at once change up into second. I didn't run and bump in the normal way, but would take about three steps then sit on the bike, relying on it to start first time. On the MVs, being unit-construction jobs, you had to be careful not to overtax the clutch. I always thought other riders

'Yer Maun', the great TT ace Joey Dunlop, slips his RS750R works Honda round Governor's Bridge, just half a mile from victory in the 1984 Formula 1 TT

wasted a lot of crucial time getting on the bike, instead of getting away as fast as possible.'

Any special Island memories not specifically connected with the circuit? 'I remember all the riders used to go to a chap called Griffiths, who was a masseur—he lived somewhere behind the grandstand. He really put us into shape, especially after a hard race when you had to be fit for the next one. MVs stayed at the old Majestic the first time I went there with them, then they moved over to the Douglas Bay because of the garages, and that was very nice and convenient. Everybody had their own places—just like nowadays, I expect; you always knew where to find the trade at their digs, and so on.'

Worst race on the Island? 'Well, from the point of view of comfort it was certainly the 1959 Senior, when the weather was absolutely awful. I was so cold and wet after winning the race I had to thaw

out for hours after. But the most frightening time in the Isle of Man was undoubtedly the time that Joe Craig gave me control of a pair of works Nortons—I was really terrified with the responsibility. Then afterwards I remember when I'd broken my wrist on the EMC and was coming back on the boat, I never heard Les Graham's name mentioned—you knew he'd had a terrible accident.'

Greatest disappointment? 'I was very unhappy about losing out to Bob Mac and the Gileras in 1957—but I was realistic about it; he was faster than me at that time round the Island, and the Gilera was a better bike. Bob had this very neat style which was well-suited to the Isle of Men—I'd certainly say he was my most respected rival over there in the years I was racing in the TT.' Greatest satisfaction? 'Well, any time you set a lap record and can say to yourself: "I went round that amazing circuit faster than anyone else on a similar-size bike!', you're bound to feel a great sense of achievement. But if I'm honest I must say that winning my first TT on the MV in 1956 was the highlight of my Island career. That was the moment I truly felt I'd mastered the greatest and most difficult circuit in the world.'

Index

Other motorcycle titles from Osprey

Moto Guzzi Singles
Mick Walker
0 85045 712 2

Moto Guzzi Twins
Mick Walker
0 85045 650 9

MV Agusta
Mick Walker
0 85045 711 4

Norton Singles
Roy Bacon
0 85045 485 9

Norton Twins
Roy Bacon
0 85045 423 9

Royal Enfield – The Postwar Models
Roy Bacon
0 85045 459 X

Spanish Post-war Road and Racing Motorcycles
Mick Walker
0 85045 705 X

Suzuki Two-Strokes
Roy Bacon
0 85045 588 X

Triumph Singles
Roy Bacon
0 85045 566 9

Triumph Twins & Triples
Roy Bacon
0 85045 700 9

Velocette Flat Twins
Roy Bacon
0 85045 632 0

Villiers Singles & Twins
Roy Bacon
0 85045 486 7

Vincent Vee Twins
Roy Harper
0 85045 435 2

Yamaha Dirtbikes
Colin MacKellar
0 85045 660 6

Yamaha Two-Stroke Twins
Colin MacKellar
0 85045 582 0

Continued overleaf

Osprey Colour Series

Cult of the Harley-Davidson
Gerald Foster
0 85045 463 8

Harley-Davidson – the cult lives on
Gerald Foster
0 85045 577 4

Italian Motorcycles
Tim Parker
0 85045 576 6

Japanese 100hp/ 11 sec./150 mph Motorcycles
Tim Parker
0 85045 647 9

Road Racers Revealed
Alan Cathcart
0 85045 762 9

Restoration Series

BSA Twin Restoration
Roy Bacon
0 85045 699 X

Norton Twin Restoration
Roy Bacon
0 85045 708 4

Triumph Twin Restoration
Roy Bacon
0 85045 635 5

General

British Motorcycles of the 1930s
Roy Bacon
0 85045 657 6

**The Art & Science of Motor Cycle Road Racing
2nd Edition**
Peter Clifford
0 905138 35 X

Ducati Motorcycles
Alan Cathcart
0 85045 510 3

Honda Gold Wing
Peter Rae
0 85045 567 7

Motorcycle Chassis Design: the theory and practice
Tony Foale and Vic Willoughby
0 85045 560 X

Motorcycle Road Racing in the Fifties
Andrew McKinnon
0 85045 405 0

Superbiking
Blackett Ditchburn
0 85045 487 5

Write for a free catalogue of motorcycle books to:
The Sales Manager,
Osprey Publishing Limited,
27A Floral Street,
London WC2E 9DP